Ending Isolation

"For virtually the entire history of the prison, incarcerated people and their allies have sought to end solitary confinement, a punishment as desperately flawed as the institution that spawned it. These compelling reflections by people who have been entrapped within the tortures of solitary, and by those who bring them lifelines from the outside, should rekindle our abolitionist impulses at an especially critical moment in our history."

—Angela Y. Davis

"Prison journalists Christopher Blackwell and Kwaneta Harris team up with scholars to make a powerful case for ending the torture used in our prisons: solitary confinement. This oral history, which includes excruciating accounts from many incarcerated people across the country, even shocked me as I read it in the madhouse of Sing Sing. By revealing the real-life horror story of what's happening in the American prison, *Ending Isolation* is an urgent call to do away with solitary confinement."

—John J. Lennon, contributing editor at *Esquire* and author of *The Tragedy of True Crime*

"Every day, hundreds of thousands of people are tortured in prisons and jails funded by U.S. taxpayers. *Ending Isolation* is a comprehensive accounting of the physical, psychological, and societal costs of solitary confinement — and an urgent call for change."

—Jessica Schulberg, senior reporter at *HuffPost*

"It's one thing to be aware, as most people are, of the existence of solitary confinement. But reading this book is a revelation, if a disturbing one. In the continuing debate over the legitimacy and efficacy of solitary confinement, *Ending Isolation* will be a powerful brief for its abolition."

—Jeffrey Toobin, Legal Analyst and author of *The Pardon*

"The use and abuse of solitary confinement has grown over recent decades in many countries, most significantly in the United States. The recognition that prolonged or indefinite isolation, no matter its purpose, inflicts mental pain and suffering amounting to torture is, finally, providing impulse to advocacy and mobilization to outlaw this cruel practice. An indispensable tool to campaigns for abolition everywhere."

—Juan E. Mendez, Professor of Human Rights in Residence, Washington College of Law at American University, and Former UN Special Rapporteur on Torture (2010–16)

"Solitary confinement is torture. This innovative book, told across too many prison walls, demonstrates why it must end—and, by confronting solitary through solidarity, *Ending Isolation* begins to show us how."

—Dan Berger, author of *Stayed on Freedom: The Long Journey of Black Power Through One Family's Journey*

"Solitary confinement is one of the most pressing humanitarian crises of our time. By combining powerful firsthand accounts of solitary confinement with compelling evidence of its devastating harms, Blackwell and Zalesne have created both a highly readable primer on solitary and an urgent call to finally end this torturous practice."

—Jean Casella, Director, Solitary Watch

"A searing indictment of solitary confinement, blending personal testimony, legal insight, and medical expertise to expose its devastating human toll. Urgent and unflinching, it dismantles harmful myths and calls for humane alternatives to this system of state-sanctioned torture."

—Jessica Sandoval, National Director of the Unlock the Box Campaign

"Blackwell and Zalesne mount a heartbreakingly compelling case against the use of solitary confinement. They paint a vivid portrait of its terrible effects on physical, mental, and emotional health and demand that we find alternatives to this torturous practice. This book combines Blackwell's hard-won knowledge from within prison walls and Zalesne's legal expertise, and it highlights many other voices of those most affected by this appalling—and appallingly common—penal practice. Truly an eye-opening read, even for those who think they already know what solitary confinement is and does.'

—Carol S. Steiker, Professor, Harvard Law School

"A critical book to read to understand the harms and torture that occurs daily in American prisons when people are placed in solitary confinement. This book uniquely combines the authors' personal experience with expert medical and legal knowledge."

—Jules Lobel, Bessie McKee Professor of Law, University of Pittsburgh Law School

"I know firsthand the psychological devastation of being locked in a cell for 23 hours a day. *Ending Isolation* brings the truth to light with piercing clarity—this is not rehabilitation, it's state-sponsored psychological torture. What makes this book indispensable is its fusion of lived experience, legal scholarship, and medical expertise. At a time when political leaders are doubling down on fear-based punishment and supermax prisons are expanding globally, this book is more than a warning—it's a moral call to action. It arms the reader with the knowledge—and the moral clarity—needed to dismantle one of the most brutal tools in the American penal system. We cannot claim to value justice while legislating cruelty."

—Johnny Perez, Director, US Prisons Program, National Religious Campaign Against Torture

"Chris Blackwell is a gifted writer who gives voice to those silenced and brutalized by the justice system. In this honest, unflinching book, Chris and his co-authors expose the cruelty and futility of solitary confinement. A searing indictment and urgent call to action."

—Udi Ofer, John L. Weinberg Visiting Professor and Lecturer in Public and International Affairs, Princeton School of Public and International Affairs

Ending Isolation

The Case Against Solitary Confinement

Christopher William Blackwell
and Deborah Zalesne

With Kwaneta Harris and Terry Kupers

First published 2025 by Pluto Press
New Wing, Somerset House, Strand, London WC2R 1LA
and Pluto Press, Inc.
1930 Village Center Circle, 3-834, Las Vegas, NV 89134

www.plutobooks.com

British Library Cataloguing in Publication Data
A catalogue record for this book is available from the British Library

ISBN 978 0 7 453 5127 8 Paperback
ISBN 978 0 7453 5129 2 PDF
ISBN 978 0 7453 5128 5 EPUB

Typeset by Stanford DTP Services, Northampton, England

Simultaneously printed in the United Kingdom and United States of America

EU GPSR Authorised Representative
LOGOS EUROPE, 9 rue Nicolas Poussin, 17000, LA ROCHELLE, France
Email: Contact@logoseurope.eu

This book is dedicated to the millions of people who have endured and continue to endure the tortures of solitary confinement, and to all those who have fought tirelessly to end this barbaric practice. Most of all, it is dedicated to the countless lives lost to suicide in those cold, lonely concrete cells.

Contents

Preliminary statement

This book draws on a number of previously published works written by Christopher Blackwell, Deborah Zalesne, Terry Kupers, Kwaneta Harris, and other contributors, with permission:

Christopher Blackwell, "Chaos and Noise: One Man's Harrowing Stint in Solitary Confinement," *Narratively*, March 27, 2024. www.narratively.com/p/chaos-noise-one-mans-harrowing-stint-in-the-hole?utm_campaign=post&utm_medium=web

Christopher Blackwell, "End Solitary in All its Forms," *The Progressive Magazine*, December 28, 2021, https://progressive.org/op-eds/end-solitary-all-forms-blackwell-211228/

Christopher Blackwell, "Just a Kid," *Compassion Prison Project*, February 27, 2021, https://compassionprisonproject.org/just-a-kid/

Christopher Blackwell, "Quarantined in Solitary is Still Solitary," *The Prison Journalism Project*, May 4, 2021, https://prisonjournalismproject.org/2021/05/04/quarantined-in-solitary-is-still-solitary/

Christopher Blackwell and Kevin Light-Roth, "The Unceasing Noise of Solitary Confinement," *The Progressive Magazine*, July 28, 2023.

Christopher Blackwell, Aaron Edward Olson, Antoine Davis, Raymond Williams, and Jonathan Kirkpatrick, "In the Hole," *Jewish Currents*, April 20, 2023, https://jewishcurrents.org/in-the-hole

Christopher Blackwell and Jessica Sandoval, "Seeing the Light." *Inquest*, December 2, 2021, https://inquest.org/seeing-the-light/

Christopher Blackwell and Sarah Sax, "Decarceration is the Best Way Prisons Can Adapt to Climate Change," *Prism*, July 25, 2024.

Chris Blackwell and Rachael Seevers, "Abolish All Forms of Solitary Confinement in Washington State," *The Seattle Times*, October 6, 2021, www.seattletimes.com/opinion/abolish-all-forms-of-solitary-confinement-in-washington-state/

Christopher Blackwell and Deborah Zalesne, "Eric Adams' Thoughts on Solitary Confinement are Dangerous and Cruel," *The Appeal*, February 7, 2024, https://theappeal.org/eric-adams-new-york-solitary-confinement/

Christopher Blackwell and Nina Zweig, "Prisoners Say New Jersey's Alternative to Solitary Confinement is Pretty Much the Same," *HuffPost*, October 7, 2023, www.huffpost.com/entry/new-jersey-solitary-confinement investigation_n_651578bee4b09c7605f9527d

Kwaneta Harris, "The Hell Inside Hell: Solitary Confinement in Texas Hides the Sexual Abuse of Women and Girls," *Scalawag*, May 30, 2024, https://scalawagmagazine.org/2024/05/hell-inside-hell-texas-solitary-confinement-sexual-abuse/

Kwaneta Harris, "'I wasn't Sentenced to be Cooked': Heat Desperation in a Texas Prison," *Prism Reports*, July 12, 2023, https://prismreports.org/2023/07/12/heat-desperation-texas-prison/

Kwaneta Harris, "In Solitary Confinement, Banned Books Are a Lifeline," *The Emancipator*, October 2, 2023, www.theemancipator.org/articles/in-solitary-confinement-banned-books-are-a-lifeline

Kwaneta Harris, "It Never Warms Up': Surviving Extreme Cold in Texas Prisons," *Prism Reports,* April 1, 2024, https://prismreports.org/2024/04/01/it-never-warms-up-extreme-cold-texas-prisons/

Kwaneta Harris and Leigh Goodmark, "Summer Heat is Killing Incarcerated People – It's Cruel and Unusual Punishment," *Truthout*, September 12, 2023.

Lanae Tipton, "Voices from Solitary: The Toll Isolation Takes," *Solitary Watch*, February 21, 2025, https://solitarywatch.org/2025/02/21/voices-from-solitary-the-toll-isolation-takes/

Lanae Tipton and Xandan Gulley, "Cooked in Custody." *Prism Reports*, September 11, 2024, https://prismreports.org/2024/09/11/cooked-in-custody/

Kwaneta Harris *with* Deborah Zalesne, "At My Texas Prison, Solitary Confinement All But Guarantees Sexual Exploitation by Guards," *The Marshall Project*, March 10, 2025, https://www.themarshallproject.org/2025/03/10/solitary-confinement-guards-sexual-abuse-texas

Kevin Light-Roth, "When You've Been in the Hole Long Enough, Even Your Dreams Take Place in a Cell," *The Small Bow*, January 28, 2025, https://thesmallbow.substack.com/p/recovery-from-solitary-is-an-illusion

Prologue: Chris's Story*

"Let's go, you know the drill!" a guard yells.

I'm sitting in a tiny concrete cell as two guards begin the intake process of placing me in the hole, in solitary confinement. I know they will take everything in my possession, but I'm desperate to keep my phone book and photos of loved ones.

I remove my socks and shoes. My naked feet come into contact with the cold and filthy concrete floor, bits of dirt and grime and other prisoners' bodily fluids sticking to my skin.

Though I have no choice but to comply, I hate myself for it. I strip all the way down. Once I'm fully naked, the guards look me up and down, and it takes all the strength I have to hold my head high, but I do. All I have left is my pride.

One of the guards looks at me and says, "Run your hands through your hair and shake it out. Now bend your ears so I can look behind them. Open your mouth. Run your finger through your gum lines. Now lift your arms, now your nuts. Turn around and bend over, spread 'em and cough. OK, let me see the bottoms of your feet. Get dressed." The guard barking at me is emotionless in his commands.

Through the slot, the guard throws a worn-out orange jumpsuit and a roll of pink underclothes into my cell. I get dressed as quickly as I can, brimming with frustration and loathing; it feels as if all the work I've done to transform myself into someone positive might be erased. No one will tell me why I've been brought into solitary. I was simply cuffed and taken without explanation.

My life of confinement started at age 12. I remember sitting in the police car that first time, handcuffed and afraid, knowing I was in a lot

---

* A version of this story was first published as Christopher Blackwell, "Chaos and Noise: One Man's Harrowing Stint in Solitary Confinement," *Narratively*, March 27, 2024,https://www.narratively.com/p/chaos-noise-one-mans-harrowing-stint-in-the-hole?utm_campaign=post&utm_medium=web

of trouble. I had just been caught in a stolen car after taking the police on a high-speed chase that ended in a very bad accident. The car was totaled but somehow, thankfully, no one got hurt. I was sentenced to 52 weeks in the juvenile system, which seemed like a lifetime.

While in the juvenile prison, I refused to follow rules and be controlled by authority figures – I rebelled, constantly. This led to my first solitary confinement at age 12, an experience that solidified my distrust for authority figures forever and drove me into a deep hate for "the system." They warehoused me until my sentence came to an end, then released me right back into the environment from whence I came: an overpoliced community consumed by poverty. I started smoking weed and drinking whenever I could afford it, which led to my friends and me stealing to keep up with our new habits.

In my neighborhood, nobody talked to or trusted the police, and from a very young age this was imprinted on me. By age 15, I started to give up on my education. I'd get frustrated and act out whenever I fell behind in school, going into class clown mode, making fun of the teacher and anyone else in my vicinity. I was eventually expelled from every school in Tacoma, Washington, and the surrounding areas. I was then placed in special education classes taught by overworked teachers who were only there to focus on our behavior, not our education. When these classes didn't work out, my only option was alternative schools, which were even worse. Students were actually given smoke breaks at these schools, even though we weren't old enough to buy cigarettes. A third of the girls in my class were pregnant, and it was clear that the teachers didn't care about what we did.

By this time, I had morphed into a full-time criminal. I decided I was done with school and committed myself to a life of crime, drug dealing mostly. Before long I was selling drugs and committing other petty crimes while running the streets of Tacoma. This was in the early 1990s when crime rates were at their highest here – they were some of the highest in the nation. There were even new narratives going around the country to describe the kids in communities like mine. They were calling us super predators.

The money came fast, and for the first time I felt like I was in control. I was following the lead of the only successful people I knew in my neighborhood – drug dealers. My role models were guys who had nice clothes, big gold necklaces, and fancy cars. They always seemed happy and everybody on the block respected and loved them. At least that was how it looked from a distance. What I didn't realize is that this type of life never lasts long, and once you get caught up in the system, you lose everything and remain part of it forever. By age 18, I'd been locked up more than 20 times and had nine (non-violent) felonies.

While the crimes remained more or less the same, the institutions I was sent to began to change. They were nothing like the "summer camp" I had gone to when I was 12 years old. The problem with that was that the tougher the institution, the more I had to harden who I was. Only one thing was respected in these institutions – how well one could fight. If you were tough, then you were good. If you were not, well then life was not all that great. Hardening myself to remain safe and alive in tough prison settings taught me not to express feelings other than anger and not to trust anyone with my vulnerabilities or secrets. The prison experience exacerbates some of the worst of male traits and makes men feel very isolated, even in a crowded facility.

Then, one night, when I was 22, I committed an act I would never be able to repair. I took a young man's life during a drug-related robbery gone wrong. Not only would I never be able to repair it, I would never be able to forget the pain and harm I caused.

After I got to prison, I struggled to accept my situation. I had just been given a 45-year sentence – my life was over. I got involved with prison politics, fought when the opportunity presented itself, and used drugs to mask the pain I was feeling. I refused to address why I was in prison or the harm I'd caused. I just shoved everything deep down and worked to have a position within the community where I would most likely spend the rest of my life.

Many more trips to solitary confinement followed in the next few years. If someone picks a fight, you have to react! If you don't, then you're seen as weak and become a target. Nothing is worse than becoming a target in prison. I refused to comply with what I felt was a constant abuse of power, and guards refused to allow me to rebel without punishment for my actions. This back and forth never facilitated a single thought that I should change my behavior, it only continued to push me to distrust the system even more, further distancing me from feeling as if I could ever be a part of society.

When I took my last trip to solitary confinement (aside from medical isolation during COVID-19), I was in my mid-30s. By then, I was no stranger to this place. This time, I faced the draconian experience simply because prison administrators had been fed false information by a prison informant. I spent almost a month in that cold concrete room before I was returned back to the prison mainline without even the slightest understanding of what was even said to put me there in the first place.

And so here I sit today, 22 years into a 45-year sentence in a Washington State prison. Forty-five years is an awfully long time to be away from family, but unlike the young man whose life I took, I still wake up in the morning, still have my family and my family still has me, albeit locked away in a cage.

I have spent half of my life incarcerated. I have no one to blame but myself. However, I also know that I should have received support in my early years. The trauma that kids endure through their interactions with solitary, institutions, and authority lasts a lifetime. I have so much trauma around my experiences with solitary, I still have a hard time to this day expressing what I went through while in there. I sometimes wonder if my mind has been wiped; I can barely remember most of the days I spent in solitary as a youth. I know that sounds like a line from a movie, but it is a reality and reflects the harm traumatic experiences can cause.

Until I received an education in prison, I never had an effective way to express my feelings around solitary. Now 44 years old, I know the damage those trips to solitary confinement caused. I have spent over a decade rehabilitating myself and processing the traumas I've caused and suffered. I know none of those trips to solitary were for my own good, but simply an easy way for guards to control me – oppression through fear.

The idea of solitary confinement has never sat well with me. I struggle to see the benefit it has for the people who are forced to experience it, or for the communities that will receive the vast majority of those same people after they leave its gripping hold. The only benefit

I see is that it offers a tool for prison officials to utilize when someone becomes an annoyance. Rather than proactively dealing with the person's behavior, prison guards hide them away.

What I have learned over the years is that people can change, if given the opportunity. Not only have I seen this transformation in myself, but I see it every day with the young men I mentor in prison. No one wants to be condemned to a life of pain, loneliness, and misery. Given the chance, almost anyone will opt out of such a life and move into a much more productive and healthy one. And as a society, that is what we should be striving for. If we continue to treat people like monsters, that is exactly what they will become.

Through my experience with solitary confinement, I feel qualified to share my thoughts and feelings about it and to propose changes to the current structure of how our prison system uses solitary. When I first got a chance to talk with my mom after being thrown in "the hole" when I was 35, she told me to write about what I was experiencing and that writing about it would help me deal with my feelings and maintain my sanity. So that is what I did. I wanted to keep it authentic and raw. Some of the story may paint people in prison in a bad light, but I can only share what I heard and what I saw and how I felt throughout the whole process – including my interaction with and observation of the "corrections officers," whom I'll call "guards."

I find comfort and inspiration from the words of Wilbert Rideau, who did his time on death row in Angola State Prison in Louisiana and spent many years in solitary confinement before he was allowed in the prison's general population. Rideau spent close to 40 years in prison before he was paroled. Personally, I found his story to be one of triumph, as he could have so easily given in to the system that surrounded him. Most would have caved or grown bitter. Yet, he did not.

Rideau took the negativity that encircled him and spent his time helping the many that crossed his path. However, he did not forget the horrible environment that he was forced to live in for so many years. In his memoir, "In the Place of Justice," he wrote:

> *I've been transported from a drab and colorless realm: a world almost totally devoid of love or beauty; a world in which our basic impulse*

to trust – that virtue by which we know ourselves and connect to others – makes treachery nearly inevitable; a world where decade-long friendships are betrayed overnight for an imagined chance at freedom or for the faintest hope of bettering one's conditions of confinement; a world where chaos and depravity are the norm and normalcy is the rarest feature of daily life; a world where softness has all but vanished in the hardscrabble struggle to survive; a world where brightness atrophies year by year as friends and family either die or just get on with their own lives, leaving you increasingly alone. To suffer deprivation on such a scale is a terrible punishment; to see its effects reflected in the lifeless or ferocious eyes of so many around you is worse, terrifyingly worse. I understand that prison is where society sends offenders to be punished for their crimes, but does any civilization really intend to create infernos that stamp out the humanity of those it sends there? I will never believe that about the ordinary men and women in whose name this is done.[1]

A note to the reader:

Throughout this book, you'll find first-person reflections and personal stories set apart in text boxes. These sections represent the voice and experiences of Chris Blackwell speaking directly. This format helps distinguish his unique voice from the broader context which is jointly written.

1
Introduction[1]

Too often, solitary confinement is forgotten or swept under the rug. You can read statistics and legal arguments about it, but they never fully capture the toll it takes on the people who endure it every day. To fully understand something, we must immerse ourselves in it – hear the sounds, smell the smells, and absorb the environment as it truly is. What is going on in our prisons is *wrong*, plain and simple. Many developed countries have abandoned the use of solitary confinement, yet it remains entrenched in the American prison system, despite overwhelming evidence of the harm it causes to the mind, body, and soul. Nothing that is taking place in solitary confinement helps to correct disruptive, misguided, or violent behavior. Period.

Information surrounding what goes on inside prisons has been extremely limited, by design. Those in power go to great lengths to keep the general public in the dark about what happens, especially inside solitary confinement, where the conditions are brutal and sometimes blatantly unlawful. Until recently, incarcerated people had limited ways to communicate with the outside world. But now, with new technology, and the advent of tablets (available in most prisons across the country) that allow incarcerated people to message people on the outside who are on their contact list, it has become easier for incarcerated people to tell their stories. This, of course, is only if correctional authorities implement better communication in good faith, which is not always the case.

As said so clearly by the advocacy group Unlock the Box in an email to its supporters:

> Once you hear the horror stories of abuse and see the statistics on the damage it causes, it's hard to continue ignoring the problem.

> The more people know – the more they care. Research shows that, regardless of political affiliation, the more a person knows about solitary confinement, the more likely they are to support severely limiting its use.

We hope this book, and the many stories within its pages, help shed light on this pressing national emergency.

Charles Dickens, who witnessed solitary confinement in the US when he toured Eastern State Penitentiary in Philadelphia in 1842, understood solitary this way:

> I believe that very few men are capable of estimating the immense amount of torture and agony which this dreadful punishment, prolonged for years, inflicts upon the sufferers; and in guessing at it myself, and in reasoning from what I have seen written upon their faces, and what to my certain knowledge they feel within, I am only the more convinced that there is a depth of terrible endurance which none but the sufferers themselves can fathom, and which no man has a right to inflict upon his fellow creatures.[2]

Most of the time, individuals who end up in solitary confinement are people who suffer from mental health issues, are addicted to drugs, or are simply young and misguided. No one who suffers from such issues changes for the better after being locked in a concrete box with nothing but their own thoughts. The authorities say they need solitary confinement to control violence and maintain order, but there is no research evidence that violence or rule-breaking are reduced with solitary confinement; meanwhile, the human damage is immense and people who are transferred out of solitary back to the general population have less ability to resolve disputes peacefully. Thus, solitary only tends to magnify and exacerbate the problems it is allegedly used to treat. Punishments of isolation and torture only cause negative feelings and behaviors, such as hate and discontent, leaving people to feel as if they don't belong anywhere, that they are less than, and even disposable.

We need to find better ways to rehabilitate, help people process trauma, treat mental illness, and change negative behaviors so that when people are released back into society, as over 90 percent of incarcerated people eventually are, they can function without harming those around them. We need trust-building and rehabilitative programs that address the traumas that send many of us into the system in the first place, and adequate mental health treatment programs. Our efforts should be geared toward developing skills that will help us lead successful lives after incarceration. This happens with the development of one's confidence and self-esteem – building us up, not continuously breaking us down. Locking someone – isolated – in a cold concrete box doesn't make them want to correct their behavior. This is especially true for those under the age of 25, who, science has proven, have underdeveloped brains that lead them to make choices without contemplating the ramifications.

While someone is locked behind a wall or fence, solitary confinement may be a convenient way to control them, but how convenient is it to have a damaged person released from prison, only to cause more damage in our communities? Hurt people *hurt* people. Something we must all remember.

Although many people before us have made the argument for ending the use of solitary confinement, we offer a unique perspective, shaped by both lived experience and professional expertise. Chris is currently incarcerated, approximately halfway through a 45-year sentence. From inside prison, he has established himself as a prominent journalist, educator, and activist. Chris offers firsthand insight into the realities of solitary confinement based on his extensive personal experience. His narratives are supplemented by many stories told by Kwaneta Harris, an incarcerated journalist and essayist who spent over eight years in solitary confinement in a women's prison in Texas. As a law professor and co-founder with Chris of Narrative Change Lab's Writers Development Program for aspiring incarcerated writers, Deborah brings a legal perspective. Terry Kupers, a doctor and one of the world's leading experts on the medical harms of isolation who has testified in key solitary confinement cases across the country, adds medical expertise. Together, we combine personal experience with legal and medical analysis to make a thorough case against solitary confinement.

In the book, we highlight the many conclusive studies that demonstrate that solitary confinement *causes* mental illness and harm in just about every instance. We also detail the cruel nature of prolonged isolation through harrowing stories told to us by dozens of real people, Chris and Kwaneta included, who collectively have over a century of solitary confinement. We journey through the corridors of isolation, describing in vivid detail a world draped in shadows, where minds become tangled in the cobwebs of isolation, and we witness the struggle between resilience and desolation. We hope these first-hand accounts will go a long way in supporting the legal case we build for why extended solitary confinement is always cruel and unusual punishment in violation of the Eighth Amendment of the Constitution and should be *per se* unconstitutional.

All of the incarcerated and formerly incarcerated people who participated in this book have spent portions of their lives in solitary confinement, some long-lasting, some as adolescents, and others as young adults. The process of constructing these short stories left each of the writers in a troubled state, forced to dredge up some of the bleakest moments of their lives – times when feelings of hope, belonging, and love were pushed deep down and walled up, while feelings of depression and loneliness reigned. But they are courageous enough to want to write about it anyway. We have stories to tell that have historically remained locked away from the public – stories that can help people outside understand what actually occurs behind the concrete walls of solitary confinement.

Some of the stories may sound fictional, but we promise you they are not.

2
Buried Alive

Take a moment and try to imagine being placed in a box the size of a small bathroom. You're stuck in this box for at least 90 straight days, and you're allowed to leave this box for an hour once a day. When you are in that box you can't talk to other people because of strategic structural restrictions. On top of that, imagine you have a history of being inflicted with a mild case of claustrophobia.

Confinement in the box is like being buried alive. Picture yourself being placed in a coffin with its lid nailed shut. Your ability to move is restricted by the coffin's walls. The coffin is placed in a hole in the ground, covered with mounds of dirt. There is no escape, even when a hyperventilating sensation starts to consume your very being, demanding that you flee such mind-torturing claustrophobia, and those who put you there give you just enough food and water to keep you alive. The only difference between the box and the coffin is the size of the container; one is a bit smaller than the other.

– John "Divine G" Whitfield (portrayed in the movie *Sing Sing* by Colman Domingo).

Divine G is not the first person to analogize a solitary cell to a coffin. Lacino Hamilton wrote in *Truthout* in 2018:

Risking understatement, I am buried alive inside Michigan's Marquette Maximum Security Prison. I am locked in a windowless cell measuring 10×8 feet, 24 hours per day. For one hour every other day, I am handcuffed, chained around the waist and allowed exercise and a shower in a small cage. I am not allowed to interact with others, or to participate in any educational, vocational, or employ-

ment programs. All meals are delivered to the cell. I have no access to a phone. And while I am permitted two, one-hour non-contact visits per month – always conducted through glass – Marquette is 455 miles away from my hometown of Detroit. Opportunities to visit family and friends are rare.

For all intents and purposes, I am dead to everything but melancholic anxieties and horrible despair. This is torture.

I have existed under these conditions for over seven months with no prospect of release in the near future. The system here is rigid, strict and hopeless solitary confinement. It is not natural or humane to be isolated like this day after day, month after month.[1]

Victor Pate, Co-Director of the #HALTsolitary Campaign and solitary survivor, describes solitary as a dungeon:

I can picture my experience in the "dungeon" as if it were yesterday: dark, damp, lonely and abandoned. I compare my experience in the dungeon with medieval-times prisons. In a cold cell with no windows or sunlight, a small slot in the door, oftentimes located in the darkest recesses of the prison, it almost feels like you're in a coffin. I lost all sense of time. I lost myself completely, sometimes hallucinating and having conversations with myself (something I still do).

In the cold isolation of solitary confinement, the day unfurls like a colorless canvas, devoid of the sun's warmth or the laughter of shared moments. The grinding monotony of idleness, hunger, uncertainty, and madness is the horrifying everyday reality for over 122,000 people[2] in American jails and prisons, including more than 600 people here in Washington State.[3]

When incarcerated people are housed in solitary confinement,[4] they are removed from the general prison population, where people can more or less move freely about the unit for much of the day, and placed in a tiny locked cell, typically the size of a parking space, where they stay for 22–24 hours per day. In many cases, bright lights stay on at all times. There are often no windows. Showers and phone access are limited. Under complete isolation and control, incarcerated people are handcuffed, shackled at the waist, and placed in leg irons every time they leave their cell. Outdoor time is either banned or requires stepping alone into what resembles a dog cage usually no bigger than their cell – that's the "yard." People in solitary have minimal exercise or stimulation and rarely have access to prison programs or activities. The walls of the narrow cell seem to close in with every breath.

A small, grated window high above arm's reach might offer a cruel glimpse of the outside world, often only a view of a prison wall or coils of barbed wire, teasing with only slivers of daylight. The bed, a cold slab of metal, offers little solace. Meals arrive in nondescript trays through a slot on the metal door. They are small, infrequent, and served cold, or lukewarm at best, a tasteless reminder of the world beyond the unforgiving concrete. Cell temperatures are often extremely hot or extremely cold.

Jason Burdett describes his experience in solitary:

> *Solitary Confinement goes by many names; the box, lockup, seg, SHU, Special Management … but the most common term used in penitentiaries across the United States is – the hole.*
>
> *The first time I took a trip to the hole I was 19 years old. The jail commander had caught me with a long chord of tightly wound toilet paper. The Owyhee County Jail allowed inmates to smoke cigarettes in the outdoor recreation area. The contraband I was caught with is called a Wick. I'd palm a lit cigarette while returning from a smoke break then hold the hot ember to one end of the toilet paper until it smoldered. The Wick would slowly burn, allowing all of the inmates living in the dorm with me to sneak into the bathroom for a quick puff between smoke breaks.*
>
> *When I came into the prison system inmates went to the hole for just about anything and everything that security staff didn't like. I went to the hole routinely. I've been to the hole for disobedience, battery,*

positive urine analysis, menacing staff, staff manipulation, group disruption, and investigations more times than I care to count. As I've aged my trips have become less frequent. I was in my 30s when I finally found myself staying clear of lockup for a year or two at a time. I am currently 46 years old. Two weeks ago, I went to the hole for fighting. Not a wise choice and yes, I am a little too old for such immaturity, however, I was fighting with my celly so off to the hole I went.

When I was younger, I'd have conversations through the ventilation system with neighbors. I'd make toilet paper dice and play solitaire, Yahtzee, or 10,000. Now, all I did was shuffle back and forth while I inched my way through one of the two books I got my hands on the second day I was in there. While reading I unfortunately had neighbors who, for hours a day, chose to yell/talk through the vent. Profane glorifications about drugs, violent war stories, gossip, sports commentary ... all the typical prison subject matter. Makes it hard to concentrate or enjoy a book peacefully. If it isn't the many voices in the vent, it's slamming doors, jingling keys, handcuffs, radio traffic, and yelling. Inmates get easily agitated and kick doors. The Hole is a cacophony of stress-inducing noise. The only break is the two hours in a recreation cage.

Segregation hasn't taught me a thing. Retribution is a poor deterrent. A man accepts lockup as part of the prison experience, some are even proud of their record. I toughed out the conditions like a seasoned veteran. It is what it is, although I can't help but think about how I need to exercise patience, tolerance, and learn to swallow my pride. Violence is not a solution and starting from scratch is a fool's game. Hopefully this is the last time I see the hole.

Marc Ramirez describes his solitary cell at Metropolitan Correctional Center (MCC) in New York, where he spent a few months while a claim was being investigated against him:

It was January 1991. I had been in jail less than three weeks and was still learning to adjust. They came to get me in the middle of the night to take me to the hole. They wouldn't let me put on my sneakers, I had to walk in flip-flops.

The hole was the 9-South unit. When I got there I was stripped of everything, searched and given a T-shirt, underwear, and an orange jumpsuit that was way too big, and had frayed cuffs at both arms and both legs. I wasn't given socks but was allowed to trade my flip-flops for well-worn canvas slip-ons. They gave me a bed roll and sent me to a total-separation cell, a one-person cell, where you are sent when they want you to interact with as few other detained people as possible. Total-separation cells are usually reserved for people on suicide watch or in "dry-cell" status. A dry-cell is a cell with no running water because they believe you are on a hunger strike, and they want to observe whether you consume any food or fluids, or they suspect you of having drugs hidden within your body. They wait for you to defecate, then yank you out of the cell to search your feces.

My cell was at the far end of the tier. It had a stainless steel combination toilet/sink, a steel desk with a built-in stool, and a steel slab bolted to the wall with a thin mattress for a bed. It had a steel door with a feed slot, and the window was covered with a steel mesh that allowed in some sunlight, but made it difficult to see out of.

The walls facing the outside were covered with steel plate. Since I was in a corner cell, two of the walls had steel plates. Since it was so cold outside, the steel plate held the cold and made the cell feel like a refrigerator. For at least the first month there I wasn't allowed a change of clothes, even on shower days. Once a week or so, I was allowed to have an orderly wash my clothes. I would strip, turn my clothes over to the orderly, and lay under my blanket until I got my clothes back. That made for some uncomfortable interactions with corrections staff if they came to my cell when my clothes were being washed.

The above accounts of solitary confinement are generally consistent with Chris's own experience.

According to Chris and his friend Kevin Light-Roth:

The noise is ceaseless. You're startled awake throughout the night by the repetitive slam of heavy steel doors and the shrill jangle of guards' keys hanging from their belts, by the sound of their walkie-talkies crackling through the vast empty space, and by the deafening screams and banging from others experiencing a mental breakdown. Once you're awake, the light that never sleeps takes over – the long fluorescent bulb mounted above you burns bright. You cover your head with a blanket trying to evade its encompassing glare. As soon as you drift off, a guard kicks your door and tells you to show yourself, so they know you're alive. When you do sleep, the garbled screams of your neighbors invade your dreams.

During the day, the noise distracts you. You find yourself staring at an open book – reading the same sentence again and again, listening to fists beating discordant rhythms against the hard steel doors.

Incomprehensible announcements squawk from the loudspeakers. Someone's shoes thud on the concrete floor of the cell above yours, as the prisoner paces back and forth. Someone else is finding comfort in kicking their metal sink next door. A steady asthmatic gasp emanates from the ancient, dust-choked ventilation system. Conversations and arguments hollered from one cell to another – the echo bouncing from wall to wall – force their way into your mind and shut down your thoughts. And beneath it all, the bedrock of this cacophony is made of the rants and cries of humans forced to live inside their minds, sliding into a place with no doors, into deep dark holes within themselves.

You drink water to fend off the hunger inflicted by small, cold meals that never satisfy. You could complain, but that only leads to trouble. You mindlessly pace, sometimes counting the steps – one, two, three ... turn, one, two, three ... turn – to expel anxious energy.

You never see a clock. Time is for another world. The window slit at the back of your cell is painted over or out of view, even when you are on the tips of your toes. You crave the sun and its warmth. There is only night and day, and both seem endless.

Your time out of the cold cell could come long before breakfast, long after dinner, or at any point in between. Guards arrive to strip you of your clothes and dignity; after kneeling on the floor, you are tightly cuffed and attached to a dog leash. Two guards grab you tightly as the cuffs cut into your wrists and you are led down the hall to the yard.

But the yard isn't a yard and there is no grass. It's a dog run, narrow with high concrete walls. There is no roof. You will not see trees or other people. Just an abbreviated segment of sky. You are unlikely to see the sun, but you will be exposed to whatever the day's elements happen to be – rain, heat, snow, hail. The space has little to offer aside from a chin-up bar and a payphone bolted to the wall. The phone might work – often, it doesn't. Instead of hearing a loved one's voice when you place the receiver next to your ear you hear the intractable silence of a dead line.

The guards come back to collect you within an hour, maybe. They could be early, depriving you of the mere hour you're due. Or maybe they will be gone for hours, leaving you in the rain, or cold, or heat, while they are attending to some intervening event – a use of force incident where another prisoner was being abused, or a football game on the break room television. You have no way of knowing.

When the guards do return, they walk you, shackled and on a leash, to your concrete box, where nothing has changed. You look around at the thin plastic pad that serves as a mattress, the few sheets of paper on your concrete desk, a couple of tattered books, the obscured window, and the same inescapable light that glares down upon your face. The cell somehow feels smaller and more enclosed and claustrophobic every time you re-enter it. You are in a tomb, a place where you're breathing, yet have ceased to exist in the world.

The next day is exactly the same, over and over, until some distant group of people decides you have had enough.[5]

Lanae Tipton, a 23-year-old woman who has been in solitary confinement in a Texas prison for almost two years, describes the mental stress of solitary this way:

> *A day-to-day routine here in "ad-seg" in simplest terms is stressful. When you are caged up like this at all times, day in and day out, it takes a toll on your mental state. There are hardly any visual changes or distractions in ad-seg and it ultimately leaves you with nothing but your own racing mind and the same four walls that tend to mock you.*
>
> *I just got transferred to a different facility and the ad-seg here is mentally draining, at least in my opinion. It is literally four walls and no movement at all, not even outside your window, to keep your mind from corruption. No recreation at all. There are people who have been over here for five months who say they've only been to rec once or twice. In comparison, at my previous unit there was rec twice a week. Recreation consisted of a small cage the size of an average walk-in closet. Inside the cage there is a table, a pull-up bar for exercising, and a TV that does not work. But at least there was a window with traffic to keep your mind focused on getting out. Over here there are none of those things. You're not allowed to talk on the run* [when you're out of your cell] *because it echoes, and that's really all we have to keep our minds from out of our cells. These four walls started caving in on me on day one!*
>
> *Everyone is angry down here, so of course everyone is arguing constantly, yelling from their cells for hours on end. The atmosphere holds a heavy depressing feel and is potent with bitterness that spreads like wildfire. Officers come to work miserable and we become their easy punching bags because we're stuck behind these doors and can't respond to their mistreatment.*

Such experiences recur again and again in accounts of solitary confinement. For Nathan "Freedom" Gray, who spent more than 370 days in restricted housing units (RHUs) in New Jersey, it was the perpetual noise and lack of sleep that wore him down: "A constant noise that yells in your face, and no matter how hard I try to block it out it has become a part of my psyche. For many in RHU, we must 'half sleep.'"

Matthew J. Murphy, who endured 36 months in solitary confinement, told us:

> *I questioned many things while in solitary – relationships, family, loved ones, society. But most of all my place among them. My relationships with them. Do they matter? Do I matter? Does my life matter? As human beings we are meant to interact with one another. To care for one another. To be compassionate. To learn from one another. That's what makes us human. Our interconnectedness to one another. That's what gives life meaning. As I have grown I've learned that these are essential in life. Otherwise, we wither away. In solitary, I was deprived of these things. These essentials of life. And I withered. I was 18 when I was stripped of humanity.*

Kwaneta Harris spent over eight consecutive years in the Lane Murray solitary confinement unit at the Texas Department of Criminal Justice adult women's prison. She explains how her solitary unit was worse than death row:[6]

> *It is so bad. Nobody talks about women's experiences. I have written on my wall "This Is Not Normal" to remind myself. I asked the warden to transfer me to death row. The men's death row conditions are exactly the same as our solitary, but the women's death row conditions are better. The few women there are allowed to congregate and watch TV. They have access to a private rec yard, air-conditioning, heat, hot meals, and hot showers. Plus, I've seen more deaths here in solitary than the girls on death row have seen. It's horrible here.*

And the monotony of isolation is described by Aaron Olson, who endured 24 months in solitary confinement:

My family doesn't understand when I explain that my memories of my time in solitary are blurred. They have months or years of distinct memories. In solitary, I only had one. Each day was the same, and began with the worst part: waking up. "Nothing" happens each moment of every day. Yet in those moments of nothingness, the absence of life, happiness, and experience gives birth to misery and despair – the torture of knowing that your life is worth nothing, that it holds nothing: no casual conversations with a neighbor or coworker, no hugs from friends and family, no kisses from a spouse. There is nothing left but bare survival.[7]

Kevin Light-Roth explains that "[w]hen you've been in the hole long enough, even your dreams take place in a cell." He describes living through the experience in a dream-like state of confusion and despair:

This will set in after about six months. You put a letter out through the slot in your cell door to mail it, then find the same letter sitting on your desk and realize you only mailed it in a dream. You dream of petty catastrophes – knocking your radio off the desk and breaking it, losing your only pen.

You dream, constantly, of fighting with the guards. Your cell door slides open and a squad of them rushes in to attack you, or you impulsively slip your handcuffs during an escort and punch one, incurring new rule infractions and extending your time in solitary. You wake with your chest cinching down on your lungs, panicking.

As the months of isolation proceed, it becomes increasingly difficult to distinguish dreams from reality. Then reality itself takes on a dream-like texture. You drift between the sad little tasks you've invented to give your day a semblance of purpose. Making your bed and stretching the threadbare wool blanket to a pristine smoothness, tucking and re-tucking the corners. Cleaning the cement floor with a washcloth and soap. Getting the edges of the papers on your desk lined up just so.

> *You forget what you're doing as you're doing it. Your brain's neurons seem to sputter when they should be firing. To focus on anything for longer than a few minutes is impossible. Try to get a letter going, or read, or think along a linear course, and your thoughts turn to ether.*
>
> *Your mind retreats into daydreams and your daydreams grow complex and immersive. They tug you along on a course of their own devising, heeding none of your direction. Invariably they involve conflict with someone, a real person from the life you once had or some imagined antagonist. You pace your cell reciting aloud the clever points you would make to these chimeras, issuing ultimatums to them. The daydreams are in no way pleasant, and altogether unwanted. They enrage you.*[8]

A 2023 report from the watchdog group Solitary Watch and the advocacy coalition Unlock the Box indicates that more than 122,000 people are housed in solitary confinement in the United States on any given day.[9] It is not uncommon for incarcerated people to be forced to endure solitary confinement for many months, years, or even decades at a time. Studies show that most stays start at 30 days and last much longer.[10] Consider Albert Woodfox, who spent 42 grueling years in solitary confinement in Angola Prison before his conviction was overturned, despite the fact that he had an exemplary prison record. (He passed away shortly after his release.)[11] In April of 2023, the Supreme Court turned down a case brought by Dennis Hope, a man held in solitary confinement for 27 years (we'll hear more from Dennis later in this book).[12] That is 27 years with practically no human interaction, and very limited exposure to the light of day. Kwaneta, who started her successful journalism career from within the confines of solitary confinement, endured over eight long years in isolation in Texas because of the high-profile nature of her case. She was likely only released from solitary because of the relentless efforts of Emily Nonko and others advocating on her behalf.

Being left in a concrete box with nothing to do except explore your own mind is dangerous for those who carry significant trauma from the past. There are some dark corners in our minds that we do not have to explore most of the time, but in solitary you have all the time in the world and no part of your mind is off limits. Time becomes a relentless warden. Sleep, a tenuous escape, offers brief respite before the cycle restarts. Every day becomes a silent struggle against the erosion of self.

3

A Brief History of Solitary Confinement in America

> The prisoner was expected to turn his thoughts inward, to meet God, to repent his crimes, and eventually to return to society as a morally cleansed Christian citizen.[1]

In the United States, solitary confinement was introduced at the Maple Street Jail in Philadelphia in the late 1790s and at the Eastern State Penitentiary (or "Cherry Hill") in Philadelphia in 1826, establishing what was called the "Cherry Hill" or Pennsylvania model, where incarcerated persons were confined to their cells and unable to speak or communicate with others.[2] This model was heavily influenced by Quaker philosophy.[3] Quakers at Cherry Hill believed that isolating men in cold concrete cells would give them time to reflect, study, and pray and thus leave their criminal ways behind. At Maple Street Jail, the warden was supposed to visit people in solitary daily to discuss their progress.

The model was adopted by many prisons in other states, but it was quickly abandoned after just a few years. As jails (short-term facilities typically run by local counties and cities) and prisons (long-term facilities typically run by state or federal governments) became more crowded, incarcerated people were forced to share their cells and the warden no longer visited daily. More importantly, prison administrators found that the practice did not reform men but instead made them lose their minds. As Gustave de Beaumont and Alexis de Tocqueville observed in 1833 while visiting the United States from France in order to understand the workings of American democracy: "This experiment, of which such favourable results had been anticipated, proved fatal for the majority of the prisoners. It devours the victim incessantly and unmercifully; it does not reform, it kills. The unfortunate creatures submitted to this experiment wasted away. . . ."[4] The combination of expense and disturbing mental health effects led to a consensus among all states that tried the Cherry Hill model between 1830 and 1880 that the practice was a "failed experiment" that should not be repeated.[5]

United States Supreme Court criticism of solitary confinement traces back to *In Re Medley* in 1890.[6] In *Medley*, the Supreme Court effectively declared solitary confinement to be a failure and an impermissible form of torture. In that case, after James Medley was convicted of murder and sentenced to death, but before his sentencing, Colorado enacted a new law requiring people on death row to spend time in solitary confinement before being executed. The Supreme Court found the new requirement to be "an additional punishment of the most important and painful character" in violation of *ex post facto* laws. Upon examining the practice, the Supreme Court called it "too severe," in part due to the psychological deterioration people suffered:

> [E]xperience demonstrated that there were serious objections to it. A considerable number of the prisoners fell, after even a short confinement, into a semi-fatuous condition, from which it was next to impossible to arouse them, and others became violently insane; others still, committed suicide; while those who stood the ordeal better were not generally reformed, and in most cases did not recover sufficient mental activity to be of any subsequent service to the community.[7]

The diminished use of solitary confinement continued well into the twentieth century,[8] and extreme isolation was not widely utilized in practice again until the 1980s, after an explosion of the prison population that started in the 1970s. In 1972, the incarceration rate was 93 per 100,000 people. The prison expansion that began in 1973 reached its peak in 2009, achieving a seven-fold increase over the intervening years.[9] As new prisons were rapidly built to accommodate higher incarceration rates and longer sentences, most prisons were plagued by extreme overcrowding, creating unsanitary and dangerous conditions, all of which correlate with increased violence and psychiatric breakdown. One response to these problems was the increased use of solitary confinement.

The rapid expansion of the prison population since the 1970s can be explained by a confluence of several social conditions. First, this was the era of the "war on drugs," which resulted in mass criminalization and imprisonment (especially impacting lower-income and more vulnerable people) with mandatory and longer sentencing. Around the same time, in the 1960s and 1970s during the deinstitutionalization movement, mental health facilities started closing in large numbers,[10] but because resources were never transferred to community mental health clinics, adequate psychiatric care became widely unavailable for the majority of those who needed it.[11] Meanwhile, with the emergence of "neoliberalism" in policy discussions, budgets for social welfare safety net programs were incrementally slashed and disadvantaged people found themselves lacking resources to stay afloat.

Along with a "tough-on-crime" mentality that fueled the lengthening of prison sentences more generally, these factors led to the spike in the prison population, including an unprecedented number of people with serious mental illness. When prison crowding exacerbated the violence within prisons, prison authorities turned to solitary confinement as a remedy.[12]

To make matters worse, there was a concurrent shift during the 1970s and the 1980s from a focus on rehabilitation to a focus on managerial control and punishment in prisons.[13] This period saw sharp increases in solitary confinement for administrative reasons involving "efficient warehousing," or keeping order and control over incarcerated people.[14] The reduced emphasis on rehabilitation also increased the violence – having a large number of idle men on a prison yard creates risky conditions – thereby further driving the trend toward the use of solitary confinement.

After solitary confinement reemerged as a dominant disciplinary practice, it soon became more extreme in both duration and intensity than the nineteenth-century practice.[15] Beginning in 1972, prolonged solitary began to proliferate as a disciplinary measure with the construction of the control unit at the United States Penitentiary at Marion in Illinois.[16] But the first supermax prison (an entire architectural structure – either a cell block or an entire prison – dedicated to solitary confinement, for supposedly the "worst of the worst"), took form in 1983 when prison officials locked down the entirety of Marion indefinitely after two prison guards were murdered.[17] Marion instituted a rule requiring incarcerated people to isolate in their cells for 23 hours a day, with no communal yard time for an indefinite period,[18] and the use of solitary confinement as a tool became commonplace after that point.[19] Several years later, the Federal Bureau of Prisons constructed and opened the ADX supermax control unit in Florence, Colorado, which is also entirely dedicated to solitary confinement.

Eventually, in 1989, California built Pelican Bay State Prison, one of the first prison units built solely for individuals in solitary confinement – with no congregate recreation, cafeteria, classrooms, or shops.[20] The prison's notoriously brutal Security Housing Unit (SHU) is made up of windowless cells that are 7.6' × 11.6'. Pelican Bay is the site of the legendary hunger strikes by people in solitary and others, discussed later in Chapter 14: Reform, Advocacy, and Activism by Impacted People and Communities.

The opening of Pelican Bay State Prison was followed by the construction of many additional supermaxes in the 1990s. By 2004, 44 states had super-maximum-security prisons.[21] During the years that followed, solitary confinement became even more widely used and accompanied by longer durations of solitary as well as crueler and more intense practices throughout the United States.[22]

Notably, the expanded use of solitary confinement that started in the 1970s was largely driven by corrections officials rather than legislators. Prison administrators saw solitary confinement as a useful tool to combat overcrowding and violence. Supermax prisons were thought to be "vital to the security of general population prisons, because the facilities segregate dangerous or disruptive inmates who would otherwise threaten the safety of other inmates and guards, and allow highly volatile inmates to be supervised more closely."[23]

However, as explained by Jules Lobel, noted human rights activist, law professor, author, and lead attorney in *Ashker v. Governor of California*,[24] the rise of mass solitary confinement in prisons across the United States was actually tied closely to the need for social control over "turmoil" caused by mass civil rights protests, litigation, and changing societal attitudes toward inequities and racism.[25] According to Lobel, the rationale that fueled both mass incarceration and mass solitary was based on a preventive solution to the possibility of riots or disorder.[26] Lobel noted that the change of Marion's character to a solitary confinement supermax had been planned before the 1983 violence and was in fact a "response to political non-violent disturbances," like protests against guard abuses and mistreatment.[27]

Legally, things shifted during this time as well. In 1978, in *Hutto v. Finney*, the Supreme Court upheld remedial orders placing a maximum limit of 30 days on confinement in solitary and upheld the lower court's findings that conditions in solitary were cruel and unusual punishment in violation of the Eighth Amendment;[28] this is widely considered to be a high point in protections for people incarcerated in solitary confinement. But in the decades that followed, Supreme Court cases started upholding the extreme use of solitary confinement. In 1981, in perhaps a turning point consistent with the explosion of prison populations during that time, the Supreme Court in *Rhodes v. Chapman* refused to find that a state prison violated the Eighth Amendment, noting that "the Constitution does not mandate comfortable prisons."[29] While the case was not about solitary confinement, the Court made it clear that "restrictive, and even harsh" conditions are "part of the penalty that criminal offenders pay for their offenses against society."[30]

Following *Rhodes*, courts became less willing to accept challenges to solitary confinement. By this period, solitary confinement had become so normalized that the Supreme Court was finding shocking conditions to be acceptable forms of punishment as ways of containing and controlling incarcerated people. In cases like *Hewitt v. Helms*[31] in 1983, and later *Sandin v. Conner*[32] in 1995, individuals challenged the procedure by which they were placed in solitary confinement, but the Court consistently found that incarcerated individuals' liberty interests were generally outweighed by institutional interests of prison management. In *Hewitt* the Court articulated the preventive rationale particularly insidiously, explaining that incarcerated individuals were not owed "the trial-type procedural safeguards suggested by the respondent," because they would basically hinder the ability of prison administrators to manage their institution.[33]

Some concurrences and dissents to Supreme Court majorities, however, reflect a strong desire by certain justices to move away from the practice of solitary confinement as a whole.[33] These justices saw solitary confinement not as a practice with a long history of acceptance in the United States, but rather as one that has exploded only in the country's more recent history and must be abated.

Tom (who does not want us to use his real name for fear of retaliation) has been incarcerated in and out of solitary in the Washington State Penitentiary at Walla Walla since the early 1980s. He witnessed first-hand the changes that occurred from the 1980s until today.

> *I first came to prison in April 1981. To give some context, the Department of Corrections didn't exist until July 1981. I was sent to Walla Walla. In 1981, solitary was a building notoriously known as "Big Red" (the building was made with red bricks). It was two stories with two tiers on each. The tiers were 24 cells long and cells were open bars, except for A tier.*
>
> *A tier was different – the first ten cells were isolation cells. They had a wooden facade built over the front. They could only put you there for ten days at a time back then. Those cells were typically kept dark around the clock, completely disorienting the occupants.*
>
> *They had a more nefarious purpose as well. Since they had this facade, even the person in the next cell was completely isolated from anything outside of their own cell. Twice while I was there, prisoners who had a high-profile relationship with the guards committed suicide in isolation cells. The belief of many was that the guards drugged their food and came in and hung them while they were unconscious.*

This belief was confirmed by a friend of mine who had stabbed a guard. They presumably drugged his food one evening but he gave his cake to another guy that night (he wasn't on A tier). Anyway, when they came by to hang him, he was still awake so they aborted. The guy he gave his cake to didn't wake up until the next evening.

Disciplinary seg and ad-seg were mixed. That meant that many of the guys on the tier had TVs. They let guys out for an hour a day, six at a time. Sometimes, seemingly for entertainment, they'd let out guys who were known not to get along at the same time. This resulted in murders, rapes, stabbings, and other incidents of violence.

Every day, they would leave several doors open for shower time, which also resulted in many bad things happening, including vicious fights. The guards typically let these incidents run their course and would only come on the tiers once the combatants were locked in their cells.

The thing that was better back then was that guys didn't have to do ridiculous amounts of time there. Most guys got out in 30–60 days even for such things as fighting guards. For the most part, solitary was used to contain violence and the threat of violence back then. Bed space was limited, so the violation had to be real serious.

Today, there is much greater capacity to send people to solitary and no one would claim that they don't use it. Back in the 1980s, the penitentiary held only 1,400 prisoners and they had fewer than 100 seg beds. Now, they've built these control units at every prison in the state.

When they opened the first IMU [Intensive Management Unit in the Washington DOC] in Washington, Captain Dick Morgan instituted a policy where everyone sent there would be "digitally raped" by a staff member. They called it a "cavity search" and claimed it was to ensure no contraband made it into IMU.

They did this for about 18 months before the courts made them stop. The routine went like this: The incarcerated guy would be in a 6-foot by 9-foot short-term segregation cell. After he was sentenced to IMU, guards would show up at the cell-front with a waiver form. No one ever wanted to consent to what was in the form. After the guy refused to sign, they'd get the fire hose.

They'd spray the guy down with the fire hose until they thought they beat the fight out of him. Then they'd rush in the cell and smash the guy to the floor. They'd put him in restraints and drag him over to the infirmary. Guards would pull the guy's coveralls aside and an abusive prison guard wearing a medical uniform would stick his hand up the guy's ass and root around. Then he'd wipe his hand off on their leg and the guy would be dragged to a van and taken to IMU.

They quit doing this so long ago that even the people in Olympia don't know about it. Now they accomplish the exact same thing just by stuffing a guy in one of those cement tombs and leaving them until he becomes compliant. I might call it: until they've driven him insane.

Today they film incidents, seemingly to verify that they no longer follow the practices of their predecessors. But in truth, they never film what led up to incidents, which are nearly always provoked by the guards. By the time the camera shows up, it looks like the incident was inevitable and totally instigated by the prisoner. But in my experience, this is almost never the case.

Despite the growth in the use of solitary confinement, and the increased severity of the conditions, the origins of Supreme Court jurisprudence in *In Re Medley* serve as an important reminder: the Court has long known that solitary confinement is dangerous and cruel, at least since 1890.

4

Who Gets Sent to the Hole

I wake to the sight of a man staring through my cell window. He tells me that he's my counselor, here to do an initial review on why I'm here.

Maybe I can finally defend myself.

The counselor stops me when I start to ask questions and instead begins to read from the paper in front of him. He sounds like a robot, and I realize this is just another formality.

"Mr. Blackwell, you have been placed in administrative segregation under investigation for suspected gang activity." (Administrative segregation is used for protective custody or when an investigation is pending, as opposed to disciplinary segregation, which is used to punish a prisoner for a rule violation or infraction – but both are forms of solitary confinement and the conditions are generally the same even when solitary confinement is not being used as a punishment.) He looks at me and asks if I understand what that is.

"I do. But why? I'm not a gang member."

"Blackwell, I am surprised too," he looked at me and said, "But it says here to take you to IMU and you are under investigation for STG [security threat group] activity."

When he said this, I was even more confused than before.

They were saying that I was suspected of being involved with an active gang. Here is why I was so shocked: I have never been a part of a gang, nor would I ever be. I have done a whole lot in my life, but never have I wanted to be in a gang. This is true for my time inside of prison and out on the streets. Not to mention, I was 36 years old at the time of this extraction, and I would have looked quite foolish trying to act like a gang member at that point in my life.

The counselor goes on to tell me that he doesn't know any details, that he's only here to inform me of what the paper says. I lose all hope of anything productive coming from this conversation.

"Your next two reviews will be on July 26 and August 23," he says.

I look at him with shock. It's June now.

"I could be held in here till the end of August under investigation, for nothing?"

"That's quite possible. These investigations can move slow, as staff are busy," he says. "Just relax and let the investigation run its course."

I stare at him in shock, wondering why he even came to do a review at all.

At this moment, a million thoughts were running through my head. Since I had been in prison for quite a while by that point, I knew that people in these types of situations can sit in the hole under investigation for a long time. It can range anywhere from 30 to 90 days to be exact. I start to think about all the stuff that will take place during this amount of time. The first thing that comes to mind are all my classes … I was so close to finishing my college degree and, yet, here I am on my way to the hole.

Then the mentor program I was creating came to mind. I thought, "There goes that." My mind became a nightmare of thoughts and worries played out to every negative outcome it could construct.

One might ask, "If you did nothing wrong, then you had nothing to worry about, right?" In the real world that might be true, but this is not the real world; it is prison, and nothing in here is logical. In here, things just happen and sometimes there is no rhyme or reason for them. It just is.

Like all prisoners, I knew it didn't really matter what I did to end up in solitary, only that prison administrators wanted me in the hole. It is their go-to "stick," – weaponized constantly against those in their care.[1]

Contrary to popular belief, solitary confinement is not used sparingly to punish only the most dangerous criminals and protect the general population and guards from violence. Correction officials say that they use solitary confinement to maintain order, and SHU (the accepted acronym used for solitary confinement) cells are claimed to be reserved for "the worst of the worst," such as people affiliated with prison gangs or those who commit "serious disciplinary actions once in prison."[2] In reality, people are often sent to solitary for vague reasons or minor offenses, often with no evidence of wrongdoing (such as during investigations, as in Chris's case), and sometimes even with no allegations of any offense at all (such as with medical isolation, suicide watch, and protective custody).

Women who allege sexual abuse perpetrated by staff are typically consigned to solitary confinement while an investigation proceeds. Or, in states where jobs are mandatory and some people refuse to work because they have medical or psychiatric conditions that are worsened in the workplace, or merely because they do not want to be forced "like a slave" to perform undesirable or dangerous jobs, they are punished with solitary. Then there are "lockdowns" – periods of time that can last for months, when everyone in a cell block or an entire prison must remain in their cells 24 hours a day while staff investigate a violent incident or escape attempt – even though almost all of the incarcerated people have done nothing wrong.

Most every incarcerated person we've spoken to who has been in prison for more than just a short while has served time in solitary at one time or another for a broad range of reasons, sometimes for no discernable reason at all. We're talking about people from prisons around the country, across gender, race, and class spectrums, serving time for white-collar or blue-collar crimes, with a range of sentences.

Prison investigations that land someone in solitary can be triggered by something as simple as one incarcerated person telling prison administrators that another incarcerated person is involved in something or has threatened them, even before the analysis of any evidence. For example, our friend Aaron Olson, also incarcerated in Washington State, spent six months in solitary based on an accusation that was never proven. In fact, no complaint was ever even filed in connection with his alleged actions – the action against him was based on just a rumor:

Being escorted from my cell in cuffs was humiliating. When I opened my cell door, the goon squad recoiled, all eight guards tensing into a slight crouch. "Face the wall, and stand for search!" barked the guard. He leaned on my back with one forearm, his gut pushing against my waistline as he patted my side and legs. I could smell his body odor, a mix of stale tobacco, coffee, and tooth decay that he attempted to cover up with cheap aftershave. This was turning into a spectacle, with 120 men watching from the day room. Even though many of these men have endured similar cell extractions for various reasons, their faces said exactly what I would be thinking if the roles were reversed: What did he do? I was asking myself the same question, racking my memory for anything that made sense. As a prisoner, you are conditioned to believe you've done something wrong, but I could think of nothing. My routine was simple: work, school, exercise, and church. That was it.

The steel door slammed shut, and I entered my new home: a 6-by-8-foot concrete box, with none of my books, clothes, or basic personal items to soften the hard steel and concrete. The drab room, barely bigger than a closet, held a steel bunk on a bare concrete floor. The toilet was a hunk of metal, a hole, with no lid. The cell was musty, with wafts of mildew and urine.

I would wait there in suspense for the next ten days before I received a hearing. Finally, I was ushered into the court by two guards; I wore a bright orange jumpsuit, belly chains, wrist cuffs, and leg irons, and a chain that swept the floor with every step. My attire could not hope to inspire an unbiased verdict. "Do you know why you are here?" asked the hearings officer. "No," I replied. He proceeded to read a report and formal accusation: "Inmate Olson has become fixated on a female staff member, and exhibited predatory behavior."

I was stunned. I scanned the room, seeing eyes of disgust and contempt. I was scum to them, and surely guilty of the accusation. I cleared my throat, and mustered a plea to every person present. "Please, investigate this. This is not true. I would never do this," I said. "That's not what your criminal history suggests," smirked the case manager – the man appointed to advocate for my best interest.

When you've been guilty of something before, it's not hard for people to believe you've done it again. The accusation had come from "Santa," my mental health counselor, who now recommended I be referred for a six-month Intensive Management Unit (IMU) program, which included a facility separation requirement, meaning I had to serve the solitary time at a different prison and could never return to Stafford Creek. (I learned only much later, after I got legal help to investigate the charges, that Santa's animosity toward me appeared rooted in his disagreements with other staff members over how best to treat me; I was a casualty of long-standing office politics.) I had thought he was trying to help me. Instead, he punished me for my past and crippled my hope for the future.

Though Santa's accusation was recorded in a note on my permanent record – meaning I am still dealing with the consequences over a decade later – I received no official infraction, and therefore no option to appeal. No accusation was ever made against me by any female staff member. Yet I was still sentenced to eight months in solitary confinement. So much for mental health treatment. The dark, cold, lonely concrete walls of isolation were my counselor's "prescription." With the judgment decreed, I was escorted back to my solitary cell, where I spent the next 50 days, until being transferred to another facility several hours away for another six months in the hole.[3]

One of the most common reasons a person is sent to solitary confinement is for the violation of a prison rule. This is not as rational as it sounds. Prison rules are pervasive and controlling, including restrictions against possessing contraband (which can include anything from possessing clothing that is not state issued, having too many stamps in your cell, or even possessing Ibuprofen pills after their use date has expired, according to prison rules), against ignoring the orders of a guard (even when those orders themselves would amount to violations, such as demands to engage in intimate contact), or against something as small as simply using profanity. "Tickets," or rule violation reports or disciplinary infraction notices, are written by guards when an incarcerated person breaks a rule. There is a hearing, and in well over 90 percent of all cases the incarcerated person is found guilty of the infraction cited.[4] Because they have little hope of a fair hearing, incarcerated persons hesitate to appeal even when they believe a ticket was unfair.

Chris's own experiences in solitary were almost always for a so-called "behavioral" issue, such as disrespecting prison guards or refusing to snitch, which prison administrators hate and look to make an example from,[5] but very rarely for anything violent.

Reports by the Vera Institute for Justice have found that minor infractions were among the most common reason cited by states for the imposition of solitary confinement.[6] In Illinois, for example, the overwhelming majority of people punished with solitary during a one-year period had been charged with low-level violations such as "not standing for a count and using abusive language."[7] And in Pennsylvania, the so-called "failure to obey an order" can land you in the hole 85 percent of the time.[8]

Orange is the New Black author Piper Kerman, who was incarcerated in a federal prison, reported to the United States Senate Judiciary Committee that she saw many women sent to solitary confinement for at least 30 days for minor infractions – such as moving around a housing unit during a "prisoner count," refusing an order from a corrections officer, and possession of contraband such as small amounts of cash or underwear other than that issued by the prison.[9]

Marissa Potts, incarcerated with Kwaneta in Texas, told us about her close friend who was sent to solitary for going to see another friend in the pill line (where people pick up their medications) – she was told she had no reason to be there and that she was "out of place."

She was then arrested and sent to solitary confinement. Being "out of place" is being anywhere you weren't given permission to be.

In another example, Kwaneta recounts a story about her friend whose father passed away while she was in prison:

> *Loretta's father died recently, and she was discovered in her ex-girlfriend's cell 30 minutes after hearing the news – the Sargent I spoke to said they were just sitting on the bed crying. Because that's against the rules, they put her in solitary. Loretta has a non-violent crime and, with only a year left on her sentence, she would have been eligible to attend her dad's funeral. Now, with this disciplinary, not only is she ineligible, but she won't even have phone access for 60 days.*

Kwaneta also describes one of the tiniest infractions that can send a person to solitary, which at the same time is one of the biggest indignities of being in solitary confinement:

> *Though we spend 23–24 hours of the day with only bright lights, loud noises, and smells of unwashed bodies to accompany the complete isolation, we walk past general population on the rare excursion to the medical building, which involves a strip-search, handcuffs, ankle shackles, and a belly chain. As we're escorted, our peers in general population are ordered to "Catch a wall!" That's prison lingo for demanding everyone turn their backs to us. Per policy, making eye contact or speaking to us is punishable as a disciplinary infraction. Breaking this rule often results in the person joining us in the box, effectively criminalizing all human emotions, concern, contact, and love for other prisoners, especially those in isolation.*[10]

In Texas, like in most other states around the country, the prison rules give corrections officers unfettered discretion to send an incarcerated person to solitary "for health, safety, or security reasons." Categories of people who are sent to solitary in Texas include: "Offenders in Death Row Segregation," "Offenders in Restrictive Housing" (which includes "security detention, pre-hearing detention, and transient status pending the outcome of an Offender Protection Investigation"), and "Offenders with Medical or Mental Health Problems or Developmental Disabilities." Safekeeping characteristics used to determine the need for solitary include "no acceptable cell partners" and "vulnerable offenders." "Offenders" can be deemed vulnerable based on "sexual orientation issues," "a transgender or intersex offender with visible physical characteristics," or "an offender who may be victimized due to age, size, developmental disability, physical weakness, or other similar traits."

Consider these recent events in Kwaneta's life. Kwaneta, to remind you, was in solitary for over eight years. Only two months after being released from solitary and sent to medium-security, she was abruptly sent back to the hole because of a shortage of living space in her unit and "no acceptable cell partner." In Texas, cellmates generally can't be more than ten years apart in age, presumably to protect the younger, potentially more vulnerable person. (Notably, significant weight differences can also be a factor in whether two people can share a cell in Texas prisons.) As Kwaneta is in her 50s, the prison was unable to find a suitable cellmate for her and needed to use both beds in her cell, so they moved her back to solitary. She assumed she would maintain some privileges in solitary since she was not there for any infraction, but she was treated no differently from those who were there for penological reasons. Her video visits with her family were canceled and she was once again shackled every time she left her cell, which was no more than one to two hours per day.

Based on first-hand accounts from incarcerated and formerly incarcerated people who shared their stories for this book, we have compiled a list of other absurd reasons that people have been sent to solitary. These might technically be violations according to state policies being applied according to the letter of the law, but they are all non-violent and very small infractions that should not reasonably result in isolation. Our list of non-violent reasons that people have been sent to solitary speaks for itself:[11]

- Having an extreme hairstyle (such as an afro)
- Female cutting her hair like a boy

- Talking in code (when speaking their indigenous language on the phone)
- Having phone sex
- Sewing a Valentine's gift of boy shorts/tank top
- Painting your face blue (Avatar) for Halloween
- Giving someone a hug because they're on the phone crying
- Rolling your eyes
- Refusing an inappropriate relationship
- Having an inappropriate relationship and getting caught by a jealous or angry coworker
- Being deaf
- Being on the Autism spectrum and not being able to follow guards' orders
- Arguing on the phone
- Using aggressive body language when talking with security
- Drawing your nine-year-old granddaughter pictures of the buildings you eat, sleep, and work in
- Joking with your nieces over the phone that they should pick you up on the way to the Beyonce concert in Houston
- Having another incarcerated person's property (TV, radio, hair clippers, photographs, legal mail, etc. – even if they were left to an indigent person when someone was released)
- Wearing shoes without a property slip because someone gave you their pair after they bought a new pair
- Possessing contraband: e.g., makeup from the outside (CVS, Target, Walmart, Walgreens), candy, too many stamps or envelopes in the cell, or an extra orange
- Stealing discarded food that guards threw away from their lunch
- Insulting the Cowboys football team after a guard was pissed because he lost betting on the Cowboys
- Refusing to tell a guard who is in an intimate relationship with other guards
- Disturbing the peace in the chapel
- Looking like you might be high
- Asking when you can take a shower

- Getting over $10 worth of food from another incarcerated person
- Using bad language toward a guard
- Talking with your hands, which is deemed aggressive behavior
- Talking back to prison guards
- Getting into an argument with another incarcerated person
- Making pruno ("hooch" or prison wine)
- Not removing a hat quickly enough after entering the chow hall
- Stepping over a "yellow" line which is out of bounds
- Engaging in horseplay
- Preaching, which is often defined as inciting a riot
- "Reckless eyeballing," which is a term down south that means being caught glancing at a female staff's butt
- Banging one's head against a wall
- Praying in a group of three
- Sewing belt loops onto state-issued pants
- Posting on Facebook
- Cheering too loudly for the Patriots during the Superbowl
- Writing an article in the *Prison Legal News*
- Failing to make the bed
- "Unauthorized selling of souls" (whatever that means)
- Leaving chow hall with a hamburger

A typical catch-22 faced by incarcerated people is explained by Aaron Olson:

> *It is not uncommon to receive a directive, which is a demand by a staff member, only to receive a contrary directive from a different staff member while carrying out the first directive. Example: A guard tells you, "Go take this bucket of water and dump it in the sink." On the way, another guard sees you and says, "Set that bucket down, we need that water to mop the floor." Whether you set the bucket down, or dump it in the sink, you can be sent to solitary for refusing a directive.*

Another ploy that is commonly used is the "staff assault." A source, who doesn't want his name used for fear of retaliation, explains that this might sound like a legitimate reason to send a person to solitary, but it can easily fall under the category of a minor infraction that violates only the letter of the law:

The one thing that comes to mind when I'm thinking of common bum beefs that land guys in IMU are staff assaults. Sounds bad, huh? We've got to protect our staff, right? But that is overlooking the very nature of a typical staff assault.

One of the intimidation tactics they teach guards is to ask for a person's ID card. This typically means they intend to write the person an infraction. I know people who lost their release date over a petty infraction. So the guy starts to plead not to be written up. The abusive guard revels in this. Finally, the prisoner gets frustrated and throws their ID card at the guard's feet. Staff assault.

Unbelievable, right? Yet it happens all the time.

In addition to the minor "infractions" discussed above, there are many other common justifications for solitary that do not involve bad behavior or disobedience or allegations of any offense at all, such as for medical isolation, suicide watch, protective custody, and dealing with mental health and drug issues. Reasons given for protective custody include because they are "children in need of 'protection,' are gay or transgender, are Muslim, have unpopular political beliefs, have been identified by others as gang members, or report rape or abuse by prison officials."[12]

Stacy Berry spent most of his years of incarceration in solitary confinement simply because he is gay. He explains what led to his first consignment there:

My celly was a seasoned veteran. She was a tall dark-skinned trans girl named Kora. She taught me the ropes in our little time together. She seemed to enjoy the jail. I was depressed and not very recep-

tive to leaving my cell. Kora fixed my ponytail and forced me to go outside to watch the guys play basketball. I was curious. So we got cute, and we walked the yard. We stopped and got ice-cream pops and I felt like things might be alright. It was my first day in Lancaster State Prison in Lancaster, California. Walking the yard with Kora, was quite the experience. She knew all the guys and the guys knew her and she was more than happy to show off the new girl on the yard. "Her name is Stacy. She ain't like me. She got class." I still giggle at our interactions. She walked me around and showed me off like a new doll. The guys were in love. All 1,000 of them.

I was terrified but loved all the attention at the same time. That night groceries and love letters flooded in. Me and Kora ate good that night, and she said I had some decisions to make. "Stacy you can't be a hoe, they will throw your ass in the hole. You need to find a man. You can move into his room and he will take care of you. I'm getting out in less than a week!"

Kora made everything better! I was at ease when she was around. The guys were essentially afraid of her. She knew all their secrets. With all the fanfare of a new gay person on the yard, it was common knowledge the officers would likely throw the gay person in the hole. They would let you know it's for your protection. We had many names for it throughout my multiple times incarcerated. We called it the hole. Some places called it administrative segregation. I have been to another jail that called it a sensitive needs yard. For most of my time incarcerated, I called it home.

I have been through my stints in prison in multiple places separated from the "GP." General population was where the "normal" prisoners went. For the guards, anything that disrupted their day-to-day schedule would end you up in the hole. The little educated gay boy that all the guys liked was a problem. I was destined for the hole.

On the first day you get to the prison they ask you a few questions. "Do you have sex, or have you ever had sex with the same sex?"

When I answered yes, I had no idea what the next few weeks and then years would be. Having a "homosexual chrono" ensures that you will be separated and at most facilities isolated. There are a few other kinds of people who they separate in the same fashion, most notably dropouts (guys who are no longer associated with their gang – e.g., snitches) and child molesters (the cho-mo).

Kora's departure ultimately led me to the hole. I was transferred shortly after she left and after several guys refused to be in a cell with me. I wondered what had I done wrong, as I was essentially being penalized for my sexuality. Well, they said it was for my protection. I wondered who wanted to hurt me. The only alternative I was given was the hole. I didn't know any better, and I thought "Well, maybe it's safer here."

My hole cell was a dreary and dark place. I can still remember the musty smell of the room and the leaky toilet. Days became weeks and weeks in the hole became months. I showered two times a week and I had an opportunity to walk in this little area where I could sometimes see the sunlight. Seems like it was always cloudy – I only really remember the clouds. The prison alternative to the hole is a transfer. "We're going to get you out of here," an officer proclaimed. One thing about prison is that you always have the idea that the next prison would be better than the one you're at. But that's never the reality.

This was also the case with Amber Kim, a trans woman housed in solitary confinement in a male prison, "for her own safety:"

Words become hard when one only speaks once or twice a week. Life in solitary is a form of slow starvation. Care, concern, and kindness are rarer than rain in the desert. It has been almost a year since the last time I've had a hug. The only contact I have is the rough imposition of being handcuffed before leaving my cell, and a firm hand grasping my upper arm while being escorted to and from the shower or "Yard" (the yard being a smallish concrete box with a phone and a window covered in a grid of steel bars).

While at yard I have caught moths on a few occasions. Felt the gentle panic of the poor creature while I carry it to the window and lose it to the wider world through bars it failed to navigate on its own – each of us confused in our own way by artificial lights that never, ever, turn off.

Prior to living in the hole, I was housed in a woman's facility. I'd been there for over three years, without a single write-up for breaking the rules, when I made the mistake of believing that the acceptance I had experienced as a trans woman meant I would always be treated the same as the other women there.

One woman told me she loved me and that she wanted to explore a relationship with me, and I, fool that I am, said yes. Love is against the rules in prison. When we were caught being intimate together, she received a stern talking to, but I was exiled back to a men's facility. I had previously spent 14 years in men's prisons, and while there are good people there, more than half of the men in prison are so steeped in a culture of violence, homophobia, and addiction that I simply can't live like that anymore. The hypersexual verbal abuse that is simply the water I lived in in the men's prisons, and the violence I was subjected to because of my trans status, is not something I can go back to, now that I have experienced actual safety in a woman's facility.

So, I made a choice. I decided to live in solitary confinement while I argue with prison administrators about sending me back to a woman's facility. I've been here for nearly a year so far and I know I am, psychologically speaking, not OK.

If an incarcerated person is deemed to be suicidal, they will be taken to a solitary room and stripped of everything, even clothes and bedding, while being watched by a camera in their cell 24 hours a day. Similarly, if an incarcerated person tells staff they do not feel safe on a prison mainline (e.g., in cases of transgender people or informants), they are often taken to be rehoused in a solitary unit until other arrangements can be made. Solitary is also a common way to deal with incarcerated people who suffer severe mental health issues and is frequently used as a means of separating dangerous psychiatric patients from the general population, even if they face no criminal charges. Rather than receiving treatment, they are typically sedated with medication and placed in solitary.

Kwaneta observed how solitary was used as a way of dealing with the mental health issues suffered by her neighbor Ray:

> *In the five months since I've left solitary confinement, I noticed Ray. She lives a few doors down. A 31-year-old young woman who everyone says resembles me. Same coloring, light eyes, similar build, and quiet demeanor. I would soon learn we're similar in other ways, too. Ray has joined my collection of surrogate kids in prison. Every time the guards respond to our fellow neighbors with excessive force, including body slamming, punching, slapping, choking, or, the verbal threats and insults, Ray always freaks out. She begins shaking, crying, and rocking. Then, if there's room, she goes to solitary confinement for a few days and returns.*
>
> *I don't ask anyone's conviction. It's not my business. A few days ago, while we were sitting at the table, someone mentioned that the face tattoo on her arm resembles me. Ray replied, That's my mother. She passed. I looked closer and was struck by her youth. I said, "She looks young. Was she ill?" "No," Ray replied. "She was killed in 2013 by my pregnant sister's boyfriend because my sister didn't answer his call." The boyfriend, Amos Wells, went to her mother's home and executed her 20-year-old pregnant sister, her mother, her 10-year-old brother, and her 17-year-old sister. Another teenage brother wasn't home because he had permission to go swimming. Ray was in prison for theft at the time. She learned of her family's death sitting in the prison dayroom watching TV and seeing her grand-*

> *mother's home on the news. Staff were coming to notify her but she already knew.*
>
> *Fast forward to 2024. Whenever Ray witnesses an argument with the majority male staff it triggers panic attacks. They send her to solitary when she really just wants to be here with us and feel safe. Reading the trial of Amos Wells left me with whatever word is stronger than furious. But, witnessing the way the prison system exacerbates Ray's harm with solitary makes me understand why she's worsening.*

Immigration and Customs Enforcement (ICE) is also using solitary in great numbers in its immigration detention centers. In a recent Solitary Watch fact sheet, "Solitary Confinement in Immigration Detention," Francisco Rodriguez reports:

> Solitary confinement is utilized daily on migrants at Immigration and Customs Enforcement detention centers across the country, often violating international human rights standards and even the US government's own policies. The practice is used as a method of control and punishment and is frequently applied arbitrarily. This not only enables physical abuse and racial discrimination against detainees, but also causes or worsens mental health damage, often leading to lifelong trauma or even suicide.[13]

Solitary Watch also makes the troubling observation that "the number of migrants held in solitary is likely to grow under the new Trump administration, which has pledged to both greatly expand the use of immigration detention and further lower standards for detention conditions."

Another form of solitary confinement occurs on death rows around the country. Most "rows" are inside supermax solitary confinement units. There is no "penological objective" to keeping incarcerated people on death row in solitary confinement until they are executed. Most death row inmates are focused on fighting their appeals and do not want trouble.

During the COVID-19 pandemic, Solitary Watch reported (based on a study by Unlock the Box) that the use of solitary confinement had increased by 500 percent.[14] More or less the entire prison population experienced solitary confinement.

Chris reported in 2021:

The outbreak at my prison that we learned about on Christmas Day of 2020 happened so fast. One minute, we were eating our Christmas meal in the chow hall, and the next minute we were on full lockdown. Prisoners were being hauled off by the dozens, and we didn't know where they were being taken. All we could do was wait to see if we would hear our numbers called and be told we had a positive COVID-19 test result to see if we would be extracted from our tiny concrete boxes and relocated ... somewhere, but where?

It was nerve-racking and exhausting, not knowing if and when our numbers would come up or what would happen to us if they did. Each guard had a different answer when we asked where we would be taken. Most of them knew little more than we did. They had a list of people to round up, and that's what they were doing.

It didn't take long before the rumor was confirmed: sick prisoners were being housed in solitary confinement "for their own protection." Guards repeated this over and over. They said, "We understand what you're feeling and dealing with. Just know we're not trying to punish you. We only want everyone to be safe and healthy." I couldn't help but think, "When is the last time you spent two weeks in solitary confinement? How do you know what it's like?" Just because someone works in solitary, doesn't mean they know what it's like to live on the other side of that door.

"It's for your own good." Anyone who's lived through an abusive relationship will recognize this sentiment. When I was young and my dad beat me for simple things, like not getting ready to leave

the house as quickly as he wanted me to, he would say, "Son, this is for your own good. You need to learn a lesson so you know how to behave."

When it was my turn to be relocated to solitary for 15 days, it felt like that childhood abuse all over again. They put me there not because I tested positive but because I was one of 13 people left on my unit of 170 who had remained free of the virus, and they had run out of room to quarantine sick people elsewhere.

Over and over, the Washington State Department of Corrections (DOC) had refused to follow the simple protocols that would have prevented this outbreak: providing alcohol-based hand sanitizer and adequate masks; ceasing the transfer of prisoners from prison to prison; holding guards accountable for refusing to follow mask mandates and social distancing rules; waiting for sick prisoners to receive test results before returning them to the unit.

Now, all of a sudden, I was meant to believe they had my best interest at heart when they threw me in solitary?

When solitary became quarantine quarters, many prisoners were forced to live two to a cell, forcing one of them to sleep on the floor next to the toilet – meaning that neither had privacy to use the restroom. On my second morning in solitary, one guard told us, "Stop crying about what you are and are not getting. You guys are only here for 14 days. Just suck it up."

The guards knew we weren't in solitary because we had broken rules, and they promised that we would have more privileges than those in solitary are normally granted: It would be like life in our regular unit, just in a different area of the prison. But once we were locked behind that thick steel door, we were in solitary, and we were treated as such.[15]

Tom, who has been incarcerated for almost four decades, has been repeatedly sent to solitary at the whim of other incarcerated people, who either made false claims about him or simply requested it from the administration:

I've probably spent a cumulative total of about a year in seg, over five different prisons. The longest was four months. The reasons:

The first time, in 1981, was legit. When I got to prison, I was led to believe everyone kept a shank to defend themselves. Nobody told me people just had access to one and you never keep it in your cell.

Next, they sent me to a place where this informant was, a man who got a bunch of my friends thrown in the hole at Walla Walla. He was some kind of drug dealer there but he knew as soon as folks heard what I had to say about him, nobody would pay him, so he went to the prison administration and told them I was the drug kingpin. They threw me in the hole on his word.

The next time, a gang guy bashed me in the head with a claw hammer and ran off with some of my stuff. The cops heard about it, not from me, and threw him and a couple of his friends in the hole. When they were supposed to get out, I was waiting near the doorway they'd have come through for several days. One of their friends was concerned that things might not go well for their friend and he got the prison administration to throw me in the hole so they could let his friends out, which they did.

Next, I was making inlaid Scrabble boards in the hobby shop. One of their informants offered to buy one in exchange for tobacco, which was illegal. I declined his offer. A couple months later, I had all the inlay work done on eight of the Scrabble boards. The informant told his handlers in the prison administration that I was distributing tobacco throughout the facility. They threw me in the hole for investigation. When I was found not guilty, I made the mistake of sending a kite [a message] to the hobby shop supervisor, telling him I'd be back soon. Well, the guy had already stolen my Scrabble boards, so he got them to transfer me instead of just letting me out of the hole.

Next, I wrote a letter to my brother complaining about how my counselor kept blocking me from getting a job. The mail room opened the letter on the way out and instead of sending it to someone who might view it objectively, they sent it directly to my counselor, who threw me in the hole for threatening them. I was found not guilty.

Next, I was accused of being in close proximity to a staff member who had COVID. He got five days off with pay. But I got ten days in the hole in spite of producing multiple negative covid tests.

And, finally, I did eventually catch Covid and did three weeks of quarantine. Two months later, they gave me a PCR test in preparation for a surgery. It came up positive. The infirmary staff told me this test can continue to show positive for up to nine months. They sent me back to my cell but soon they sent the guards to throw me in the hole, in spite of my providing multiple negative rapid tests.

A common use of solitary by prison administration is to handle *perceived* threats and to curb suspected gang affiliation. Dolores Canales, founder of California Families Against Solitary Confinement and a formerly incarcerated person who spent years in solitary confinement, was a leader in community support for the hunger strikers at Pelican Bay (discussed further in Chapter 14: Reform, Advocacy, and Activism by Impacted People and the Community). She reports:

In 2001, I was 42 years old. I was potentially facing 25 years to life because of the three strikes law. My son Johnny had been in solitary at Pelican Bay for almost six years at that point. When I was in the hole it was a nine-month-maximum sentence. I knew I'd get out. For my son it's indefinite – because he's validated as a "gang associate" and that's how it works in California. Every six years they revalidate him. The only evidence they used the first time was his name. They found it written in a note that somebody else had in their cell. People hear this and they don't want to believe it – that in California someone can be put in solitary confinement indefinitely for some-

thing so small – not even close to violent. That they're put there just for associating – which all of us who have loved ones in there know is unconstitutional. The lawyers know it. Johnny didn't even write the note, but his name was in it, and that's enough for them.

Prior to the settlement of the *Ashker v. Governor of California* class action lawsuit after the hunger strikes in 2015, suspected gang members and those labeled as gang-affiliated or vocalizing their political beliefs were automatically housed in solitary confinement at Pelican Bay's supermax facility, even if they hadn't committed any actual disciplinary infraction.[16] The concern was not so much punishment as preventing gang killings in prisons and attacks on staff members. Thus, since the use of solitary was largely for preemptive reasons, gang members were housed there indefinitely, sometimes for decades at a time, and often for the remainder of their lives.

Brant Daniel was incarcerated at Pelican Bay SHU from 2000–2015. Brant describes his arrival there:

Upon arriving at Pelican Bay and seeing the long hallways I thought "wow, where the hell am I?!" CDCR [California Department of Corrections] used "gang validation" [legally designating someone as a member of a gang thereby justifying consigning them to solitary confinement] to put me in the SHU forever. Life term in the SHU. It only takes three points by their gang unit, such as knowing someone in Pelican Bay SHU who's already validated. This can happen if someone rats, saying I'm running this prison, or rats and makes up stories. It can be anything, like me talking to someone of the same race or borrowing a book, or sharing a coffee with him, and then one rat to say, "oh yeah, they friends." CDCR just believes those stories and then you go to SHU for life. They used five points on me to label me as a gang associate and that was enough. So back to Pelican Bay SHU I went, but this time for life.

Most residents of the Pelican Bay SHU were alleged gang members or affiliates. But as Dolores and Brant note, the allegations were based on very thin, or often even falsified, evidence. In a typical scenario, guards transferred an incarcerated person they suspected of gang involvement to the SHU; he would protest "I'm not affiliated with any gang!"; and they would say "Too late for that, the only way you can get out of SHU is to 'de-brief.'" De-briefing is a procedure where the incarcerated person who denies gang involvement has to give guards the names of three other incarcerated people who are in a gang and have committed illegal acts, with details about those acts. This of course is "snitching," which in a high-security prison can get a person killed. Incarcerated people called the process "Snitch, Parole, or Die." The only three choices a person consigned to SHU had were to "de-brief," thus "snitching out" three other incarcerated persons; parole or reach the end of a sentence and be released; or die, which is the fate of very many people consigned to solitary confinement.[17]

PRISON JOURNALISM

In reality, guards often use solitary as a tool to control or target incarcerated people. This often happens to prison journalists, who must navigate risky waters daily. Their struggle to document life behind bars and share vital information with the public is regularly met with retaliation. Commonly, the threat of solitary can be used to curb legitimate journalism in order to maintain the shroud of secrecy around what goes on behind prison walls.

Many prison writers have told us about cases of guards using the threat of solitary in an attempt to prevent prison journalism that holds prisons accountable for human rights violations. For example, our friend Aaron Olson was targeted because of an article he was writing about conditions in his prison:

> *There are so many instances of going to solitary confinement for simply breathing, but the most recent threat came in the form of retaliation for my journalism. Those who control what happens deep within the prison industrial complex, also want to control the public narrative. When that narrative is challenged with the truth and supported facts and sources, from a prisoner's publication, it*

enrages many prison workers who have dedicated their lives to the daily dehumanization and abuse of over 2 million women, men, and children.

One morning during my day off from a mandatory work program, I ventured into the unit foyer to check the institutional kiosk for any messages. After I was finished, I noticed the Unit Sergeant standing in his office doorway, and I remembered that I needed to ask him about getting a pair of new state-issued shoes. I approached, and asked. His reply? "Step into my office so that I can get your name and DOC number." A name and number he already knew, based off of his follow-up.

"So," he said, "you like to write?"

"It's no secret," I responded nervously. "Everybody knows that I publish articles and I run a podcast."

He narrowed his gaze, and squinted his eyes, pursing his lips. "I think your writing is misguided, and a hustle!" he said, opening his eyes wide, in an attempt at a mic-drop moment.

"I simply report what happens within prison. I tell the truth and report the facts." I continued.

"Look!" he snapped. "I don't want to be answering questions from my superiors about what I allow in my unit! Now, we both know that you aren't squeaky clean!"

I looked at him dumbfounded, and replied, "Sir, I follow the rules, and I live like a square." He looked down at the boot socks I was wearing, a pair I typically wore on work days. "We both know that those aren't state-issued socks! Plus, you're not wearing your ID. See, I can get you for anything! Are we clear!?"

The implication was that he could make my life hell if he chose to, and if I gave him reason. Including a trip to the hole.

"I'll get rid of these socks," I said as I exited his office.

"I know you will!" Were his last words.

Jeremy Busby, incarcerated in solitary confinement in Texas, has also spent prolonged time in solitary for reasons he believes are connected to his reporting. He explains that after he started the viral hashtag #AllEyesOnTDCJ and started reporting about COVID-19-related issues on social media, including the number of incarcerated people who died from the virus, Texas prison officials responded by writing him a disciplinary case and tossing him in solitary confinement for 22 months. He explains:

Texas prison is a brutal place to serve time. Most of the world knows this by watching how frequently executions are carried out. What the majority of the world doesn't know is that the Texas execution chamber is not limited to the room that condemned prisoners are killed. Conversely, the state's prison system operates a massive – mostly hidden, but equally as deadly – extension of its main execution chamber, that it calls restricted housing, a fancy name for solitary confinement. On a daily basis, thousands of prisoners are subjected to a deadly three-ingredient cocktail of severe isolation, extreme deplorable living conditions, and inadequate mental and physical health care that results in cold-blooded state-sanctioned murder!

Personally, I have been subjected to some severe retaliatory measures by Texas prison officials for my willingness to work with the media and expose the unchecked brutalities and inhumanities inside this agency. They have tossed me into long-term indefinite solitary confinement, transferred me to four different prisons in the past four months, destroyed all my personal property at least twice, and restricted me from using the tablet/phone until a few days ago.

Indeed, any violation of Texas's ban on creating a social media account, even one run by someone on the outside on behalf of an incarcerated person, can result in placement in solitary confinement, loss of parole eligibility, or a fine, in a clear attempt to suppress free speech. Kwaneta's eight years in solitary were under the justification that her case was "high profile," which is notably not one of the official reasons stated in the policy for holding someone in Security Detention. Based on comments Kwaneta received from various corrections officers over the years, we believe the real reasons were linked to her journalism.

Solitary can be used to suppress another type of speech as well – it is not uncommon for solitary to be used as retaliation for filing complaints. For example, Tomiekia Johnson tells about a time she faced retaliation after reporting sexual abuse:

> *Black women constantly have to prove with hard evidence that we've been abused, and for people who are abused in prison, it's twice as difficult to get justice.*
>
> *After Dublin Federal Women's Prison in California was dubbed "rape club" and ultimately shuttered, 96 rape, sodomy, and other sex crime charges were filed against the Central California Women's Facility (CCWF). When I stood firm on business and apprised a lieutenant in the Investigative Services Unit about a biological male inmate who was stalking and assaulting me, I was detained under the false guise of "protective custody." I later learned that the guard who detained me was actually building other false charges against me, including: filing a false claim, obstruction of justice, and, if that didn't stick, harassing another. I was looking at 120 days in solitary and a Rules Violation – Victim to Perp in eight days.*
>
> *Eight days in ad-seg felt like months because my 14-year-old daughter never knew where I was. In those eight days, I was only allowed one day of outdoor recreation for just two hours and two showers. Every time I was escorted in ad-seg, I was re-shackled. I had no Bible, no radio, no support. To add insult to injury, when*

> *I was discharged, staff locked me in a shower for three hours while they raided my cell and stole all my evidence.*

We have found that the people who survive a term in solitary and come out relatively intact are those who do not blame themselves for the torture they had to endure in the hole. They do not sink into low self-esteem, and they study hard to understand the roots of their misfortune in unfair social arrangements (such as racism, as we will see in Chapter 9: Racism). The common denominator among formerly incarcerated folks who maintain their pride and work hard to make sure other youngsters are not condemned to the same fate they had to endure, is that they understand the torture that is solitary as part and parcel of the unjust and inequitable social arrangements that we all struggle to transform. That's one of the beauties of prison journalism. Men and women who have been targeted and tortured by the system have an opportunity to explain what went wrong, and bring to the project their undefeated self-esteem and a profound social analysis that expands the public's understanding of the evil of mass incarceration.

5

Cruel and Unusual Punishment: Stories of Torture

After an altercation with some guards, I was taken and placed in the isolation cell, after the guards roughed me up, of course. Once in the isolation cell, I was stripped of all my clothing. The isolation cell does not even have a mattress; it has a one-inch-thick rubber pad. The door to the recreation yard was opened to allow the winter air in. After this was done, the guards placed a fan in front of the door, turned it on high and pointed it right at the isolation cell I was in. You have no clue how cold those next few hours were ... I had to earn my humanity back, clothing, and eventually a regular cell with a mattress.

– Steven Nall (survived five years in solitary confinement)

Solitary confinement, by its very nature, regardless of the conditions in specific cases, is already torture. But to make matters worse, isolation from the outside world creates an environment in which guards can more easily abuse their power and commit additional torture. There are essentially no witnesses, and so there is little accountability for the use of excessive force. People in solitary face immense barriers to reporting abuse.

We have spoken to dozens of people across the country who have been housed in solitary confinement. Many of them describe extreme physical abuse, oppressive living conditions in extreme heat or cold, complete and long-term deprivation of exercise and sunlight, and the withholding of food, water, medicine, mattresses, toilet paper, tampons, and other necessities. The stories in this chapter are but a few examples of the ways guards can inflict torture on their charges. These stories may sound extreme, but they are relatively common.

Violent relationships between incarcerated people and staff, often involving excessive force, beatings, or other violent altercations, have become normalized in most prisons. Standards published by the American Correctional Association and the National Commission on Correctional Health Care[1] prohibit the use of force for the purpose of punishment. According to these standards, the use of force can legitimately be initiated only after less severe interventions, including robust attempts at de-escalation, have been attempted and failed, and only enough force is to be used to restore order. In spite of very clear standards, corrections officers resort to the use of force in many situations where it is no longer needed to restore order or prevent harm, and then the use of force becomes a punishment in itself. For example, an incarcerated person is subdued by guards, and even after he is lying face down on the ground with his arms constrained by handcuffs behind his back, guards continue to pummel and kick him. Excessive use of force is abusive, very often qualifying in federal courts as a violation of the Eighth Amendment's prohibition of cruel and unusual punishment.

When guards use force on incarcerated people, they typically begin by spraying them in their cells with immobilizing gas or "pepper spray." While instructions from manufacturers of immobilizing gas include spraying a small amount of gas and then waiting for several minutes to assess the effect, guards quite often, contrary to these instructions, spray an incarcerated person with multiple bursts of spray and then leave them for many minutes or even hours to suffer, struggling to breathe. In fact, in many cases, they "empty the can," meaning they use the whole can of spray on the person, something guards brag about.

Then, when there is the perceived need to place a recalcitrant person in mechanical restraints, a "cell extraction" is called. The gruesome procedure involves five or six guards in riot gear with helmets and gas masks first spraying the cell with immobilizing gas and then barging in on the incarcerated person in force, each guard assigned to grab a limb and force the incarcerated person to the ground. Injuries from such excessive use of force are frequent and can be quite severe. If it's a guard who gets injured in the scuffle, the incarcerated person is likely to be charged with an assault.

Jarvis Jay Masters was housed in solitary confinement at San Quentin's Adjustment Center from 1985-2007, longer than almost any other prisoner in history, because his case involved a San Quentin guard. Sentenced to death in 1990, Jarvis transferred out of San Quentin with nearly 600 others when its condemned housing unit on East Block was dissolved in 2024. Jarvis recounts one such cell extraction:

> *Not long after I'd been relocated, the evening chow cart came rolling down the tier. The guards started with the end cell and moved toward the front. They unlocked each cell's food port and gave the prisoner whatever portion of food he wanted from the cart. Today was Mexican food, my favorite.*
>
> *When the cart was just a few cells away from mine, I saw a hand lunge out of an open port and fling a cup of urine and feces into the faces of the two guards serving the food. It took a few seconds before I could believe my eyes and nose. The guards stood there with faces dripping, their serving spatulas still in their hands. Then a maniacal laugh broke the silence.*
>
> *About an hour later I heard what sounded like an army of guards preparing to enter the tier: there were lots of keys jingling and guards' shields clanking and the huge plastic emergency gurney rattling as it was taken off the wall.*
>
> *Then a dozen guards marched past my cell dressed in full armored gear, with helmets and batons, and riot shields held tightly to their chests. The Unit Sergeant had a Taser and a stun gun, and several other guards carried block guns, which shoot a high-velocity wooden block that can severely disable a person.*

They gathered in front of my neighbor Walter's cell. When I stood close to my cell bars, I could just see down the tier to where they were. The Unit Sergeant had opened the food port, then shouted the order for Walter to step to his cell door immediately to be handcuffed.

"Are you going to cuff up?" he demanded.

Walter's response was quick. "Yes, sir! I don't want any problems. I am fully cooperating. I'm not resisting."

"That's not fast enough," said the sergeant. He stepped aside to give the gunmen a clear shot into the port of Walter's cell. The gun blasts sounded like shotguns. Pow! Pow! Then the electric cell door came open, and the guards rushed inside. The whole tier heard the beating and Walter's screams. I could smell his flesh burning from the Taser device.

They went on beating Walter until the screams stopped and their kicks and punches sounded like thuds on a corpse.[2]

This cell extraction clearly involved excessive use of force, as the violent beating happened well after the incident in question, when there was no need to subdue the incarcerated person or maintain order and no reason for the brutal beating other than punishment.

Beyond "cell extractions," incarcerated people can be bound in a "restraint chair" or on a bed, with straps securing their limbs and their head. The American Correctional Association and the National Commission on Correctional Health Care have published standards for the restraint chair and other forms of "four-point restraint," for example, on a bed or platform, and require that this gruesome technique be used only after less restrictive measures have been tried, not as punishment, and for the shortest time necessary to restore order.[3] In many states, this kind of restraint is limited to two or four hours. But in practice in too many locales, people are left strapped in restraint chairs or in four-point restraints on a bed for days at a time, often with inattention to their bathroom needs. Gail Brashear, who endured solitary confinement on and off for years, explains:

> *I had been in segregation for some time and things between staff and me were pretty hostile. It was like a game of tit-for-tat. For example, they would deny me toilet paper and I would react by covering my windows with paper bags, blocking their view into my cell.*
>
> *One day things escalated in a way I was unprepared for. I can't remember what the guards had done to upset me but I had just finished covering my windows when I heard comments from staff that they were calling in the Quick Response Team. This usually meant that a group of male staff were putting on riot gear to come into my cell, tackle me, and put me in a padded room.*
>
> *However, on this day, it wasn't a padded room they took me to. Once they had tackled me to the floor, six men lifted me up and placed me onto a gurney. This was by no means a normal gurney that you would envision at a hospital. There were heavy straps all around it to secure my body down. They had straps on each of my arms and legs and one across the top of my chest. I can still remember the pressure of them all being secured so tight. I was trying to keep myself calm so that I wouldn't hyperventilate, which would've made the situation so much worse.*
>
> *I had no idea what was in store for me and was terrified that they had plans of moving me to another prison out of state or to a mental institution for long-term evaluation as a form of punishment. Oh, how wrong I was.*
>
> *They rolled me back into the dark cell and slammed the door shut behind me. I waited there for an hour before they came and rolled me back out. Instead of releasing me from the bed as I had expected, one of the guards asked me to pick a limb that they could untie for 45 seconds, allowing the blood to recirculate. I picked my left leg. They untied it and I was allowed to move and shake it around for*

less than a minute before they tied it up again and wheeled me back into the cell.

This went on for the rest of the day. Every hour they would wheel me out and let me pick a different body part to move around, then wheel me back into the cold room. I can remember the ache in my body from not being able to move. It was all-consuming. The way my hands and arms would go numb from lack of circulation.

Throughout this whole process, no one ever talked to me except for when they asked me to pick a limb. It wasn't until many hours later someone finally told me that they would release me off the bed, but before that I had to sign a bunch of paperwork acknowledging that if I acted out again I was getting strapped back to the gurney. In hindsight I recognize this was a way for them to control me, but at the time it just felt so inhumane and I believe that if there had just been simple communication between the officers and me, there would've been no need for any of this.

Staff are notorious for brutally assaulting the people they guard. According to the aforementioned standards, a person restrained in a chair or on a gurney must be closely monitored and never left in a cell alone, and there is a strict time limit to the restraint (two or four hours in most corrections departments). Thus, what was done to Gail Brashear constitutes excessive force and violates all standards.

Augustus E. Cooper was in solitary confinement for over two years when he was just 17 years old. He was in a "Strip Cell Program," where every morning guards removed the person's limited possessions from the cell, often including even the toilet paper. He describes the force used against him after he got angry at a guard for withholding toilet paper when he needed it:

When it came time for my daily hour of recreation, I went through the process of preparing to come out of my cell. This required that I first put my hands through the cuff port to have my hands cuffed. Then a long leash was attached to my handcuffs. I was then instructed to walk to the back of my cell and kneel on my bed with my legs crossed and my head against the wall. At this time a belly chain was wrapped around my stomach and my hands were secured to the belly chain. Leg shackles were then applied; then a chain that went from the shackles to the belly chain was added. After all of this, a long leash was attached to a key ring hook on the chain near my feet. This was called the "Leather-Tether Program." The purpose was to give the escorting staff complete control over the prisoner's movement, and, if the prisoner was to make any threatening movement, the staff could then yank on the leash which would effectively pull the prisoner's feet out from under them and face plant them.

I have seen kids walk away missing teeth, missing parts of their tongues or lips, and broken/smashed noses. Not a pretty sight.

Just after we stepped out of the cell I heard the guard say, "Cooper stop moving," and before I could even ask a question about what he was talking about, I felt my legs being pulled out from under me. The fast and furious fall to the floor began. "Fuck" is all I remember having time to think before I met the ground with a solid impact. At this point, the guard proceeded to pounce on top of my chained and shackled body and apply a quick strike to a pressure point under my chin while continuing to repeat, "Quit resisting." As if such an action were even possible given my current situation.

In addition to excessive force, there are other ways that guards can inflict torture on their charges. Like Augustus, other people across the country who have spent substantial time in solitary often describe the withholding of essential items. Lanae Tipton, who has been in solitary for almost two years and counting at the time of writing, describes various such occasions during her time in solitary:

Last week they skipped my neighbor Lisa for chow because she had a book sitting on her window. It is not unusual to get skipped for meals for various reasons. We are told chow is a privilege. One day an officer did chow in silence – no announcement or chow call. He just walked quietly down the runway and skipped anyone and everyone who wasn't at their doors. This same officer had a past issue with a friend of mine and every time that particular officer works she spits in the food, rearranges it, or goes as far as dropping it then picking it up and handing it to this prisoner. I've even heard a different officer actually admit that when someone pisses her off she puts roaches in their food down here. I have yet to see that happen.

The officers can turn off our power or water any time they see fit. They do this if an officer decides we spoke to them wrong or if we demand our human rights such as asking for feminine products, toiletries, and bedding for the mattress to sleep with. All because they can. When you're treated like a dog in a cage inside of a cage it makes the rage burn more fierce.

Another time, I had just started my cycle and was transferred with a fresh tampon in, but I kept asking in advance for the proper products to avoid an overflow. I was ignored and I went a whole twelve-hour shift forced to sit in my own blood, holding the gown I came in with between my legs.

And Jeremiah Bourgeois, who survived seven and a half years in isolation, describes being denied most of his meals for three full weeks:

"Mainline," the officer's voice boomed, signaling prisoners to stand at their door if they wanted to be fed. I had just finished brushing my teeth and went to the yellow line that indicated exactly where to stand. The two officers delivered the trays one by one, with one officer pushing the cart and the other opening the slots to pass the food through. I could smell the eggs as the cart moved closer. After the officer handed the guy on the right side of my cell his tray, they bypassed my cell, handed the guy on the left side of my cell his tray, and then continued down the tier.

They never looked in my direction. They never said a word.

Lunch arrived four hours later, and again I was skipped.

As I lay in bed throughout the afternoon all I could do was hope that the officers on the next shift were not in cahoots with this crew. Then I'd be able to eat dinner. I nodded off at some point and awoke when a different voice boomed, "Mainline." I jumped out of bed, rushed to the yellow line, and waited. The guy on the right side of me got his tray, then the officers stopped in front of my cell. When one of them opened the slot on my door to pass me the tray, I felt so relieved. My relief turned to rage when he shoved the tray so forcefully that the food flew all over the floor. The slot then quickly closed and the two continued passing out meals as if nothing out of the ordinary had occurred.

I ate that spaghetti right off the floor, and scraped the apple sauce off the wall with my hand, licking it off my fingers. Of course, I waited until my tormentors left the tier lest they get to enjoy bearing witness to the spectacle. When they returned to pick up my tray, I handed it to them as if nothing out of the ordinary had occurred. My face showed no emotion. I said not one word.

This day replayed itself 21 times. No breakfast, no lunch. Dinner eaten off the wall and the floor. For 21 days I was never let out of that cell. No shower. No telephone. There was nothing I could do about it.

In supermax isolation units, there is very little opportunity for incarcerated people and staff to talk and get to know each other and certainly very little in the way of counseling or mentoring. Rather, meting out punishment becomes the main way that staff relate to incarcerated people, and the ostensible misbehavior of incarcerated people is the trigger and rationale for these measures.

Just a few decades ago, incarcerated people at every level of security spent most of their waking hours out of their cells and in public spaces at work or on the yard or in a dayroom, interacting with staff. When incarcerated people are out of their cells and participate in recreation and rehabilitative programs, guards and incarcerated people engage in informal ways as they pass each other on the yard or sit with each other across a desk. There can even be friendly banter, the guard chiding the young incarcerated person for getting into another fight, both appreciating the underlying message: "I'm sad you're in trouble again, I want you to succeed." According to research, where guards are consistently friendly and respectful, there is greater peace and the environment is much more conducive to rehabilitation.[4]

In contrast, relationships between the incarcerated people and staff in solitary confinement today are very fraught. The environment fosters anger and resentment, and when incarcerated people break rules, guards respond with attempts to subdue and punish them. Incarcerated people are prone to anger toward guards because the conditions are so unbearable and because the guards so often resort to "use of force" against them. Limited interactions between guards and incarcerated people, combined with guards' singular focus on punishment, leads to additional friction between staff and incarcerated people in solitary confinement settings. Guards are quick to write a disciplinary ticket and send an incarcerated person to solitary confinement. The solitary conditions tend to exacerbate the anger even further.

When resentment builds, it can eventually surface in a sudden attack on a guard or a group melee. Staff who once walked the halls and yards freely in the company of incarcerated people and chatted with their wards become afraid to be in a room with incarcerated people from solitary confinement who are not in shackles or in a cage-like cubicle. Staff who are inclined to focus almost exclusively on punishment become even less inclined to get to know the incarcerated people and to talk with them in a way that isn't aggressive.

Once an incarcerated person has been placed in long-term solitary confinement, what further punishments are available to custody staff to punish and control them? One widespread practice is lengthening their time in solitary. An incarcerated person might enter solitary confinement with a three-month solitary sentence and then, because he erupted in anger at a guard who was taunting him, he might be given six additional months of solitary, and then six months more, and so on. It is not unheard of to encounter an incarcerated person in a supermax unit who has spent the prior 40 years in solitary confinement.

In addition to targeted abuse of an incarcerated person based on specific misconduct, another type of torture relates to the general living conditions in the unit. This can come in the form of extreme heat or freezing conditions or unsanitary conditions. Willie Russell, the lead plaintiff in a class action lawsuit about horrid conditions on death row in Mississippi's notorious Unit 32 Supermax Security Unit at the Mississippi State Penitentiary at Parchman, spent two years subjected to the following shocking and vile conditions. These are described in the testimony of Dr. Terry Kupers:

> *Willie Russell describes his experience being housed in Cell 225 for two years, one of four "punishment" cells on death row with plexiglass doors (covering the standard door). I have seen this kind of double door in super-maximum-security units in other states. Once one is locked inside such a cell, the temperature and humidity begin to rise within minutes because the plexiglass (or Lexan, an indestructible form of plastic) retains the heat and humidity within the cell. The temperature rises rapidly, and life in the cell becomes unbearable. In the summer heat at Parchman, this one aspect of the punishment cells would make them entirely unacceptable by any standard of human decency or of health and mental health minimum standards.*
>
> *But in addition to this cruel and entirely excessive and punitive measure that clearly serves no legitimate penological objective, Mr. Russell reports that his cell is always filthy, the rain pours in through the walls onto his bed, the toilet floods the cell with backflow from other prisoners' toilets, there are bugs everywhere, the cell is filled with mosquitoes at night, he cannot sleep at night because the lights are on 24 hours per day, he is not permitted to have a fan, he is not permitted television or radio and there are no activities, and he is even more isolated than other prisoners on death row because*

> *the Lexan shield on his door makes it impossible for him to talk to anyone. For two years, he was permitted no mattress, no pillow and no sheets, and had only a blanket and the concrete for a bed. This kind of punitive deprivation and degradation is barbaric, and shocking to human sensibilities. It is the kind of cruel and unusual punishment that is well known to cause intense anxiety and rage, psychiatric breakdown, and in a large proportion of cases, suicide.*[5]

With very little accountability, the unchecked power of guards can transform an already inhumane practice into a breeding ground for unspeakable cruelty. No person should be forced to endure such abusive conditions, regardless of their crime or their behavior once in prison.

6
The Physical and Psychological Harms of Solitary

I used to think there was a timeline for when people lost their minds in solitary confinement. Six months, two years, maybe five. I was wrong. The descent into madness doesn't follow a schedule.

Even now, back in medium-security, I wake up some mornings thinking I'm still in that cell. I understand those videos of dogs who've been caged so long they won't leave even when the door is open. How do you retrain your mind to embrace "freedom" when it's been conditioned for isolation? How do you learn to trust your own sanity when you've watched so many minds shatter around you?

The walls of solitary confinement may no longer surround my body but they still cast shadows in my mind.

– Kwaneta Harris

Before John Powers went to prison, he had no history of mental illness. But after 25 years of solitary confinement, twelve of which in extreme isolation in a federal supermax prison in Florence, Colorado,[1] he amputated his own testicle and scrotum, bit off two fingers, and drilled a hole in his skull.[2] His severe post-traumatic stress disorder (PTSD) and compulsion for self-harm come as no surprise to experts who understand the psychological trauma associated with solitary confinement.

Prolonged solitary confinement is torture. It causes devastating psychological, emotional, and physical harm to those who endure it, and, because it can cause psychotic behavior, it ultimately decreases the safety of others as well. The many harms of solitary confinement include severe anxiety, panic, and sleep problems (the most universally reported symptoms in solitary), depression, mood swings, memory problems, inexplicable anger, withdrawal, paranoia, psychosis, severe loneliness, trouble concentrating, and, all too frequently, suicide and self-harm. Not all of these symptoms occur in every individual in solitary confinement, but almost everyone in solitary experiences some of these symptoms and disabilities, even individuals who were relatively stable from a mental health perspective when they first entered solitary. If there is a pre-existing serious mental illness, solitary exacerbates it (see Chapter 7: Mental Illness and Solitary Confinement). In addition to taking a substantial psychological and physical toll on the people who experience it, solitary confinement also affects the families of incarcerated people and prison staff.

Remember how Divine G described solitary confinement as being "buried alive" in a "coffin with its lid nailed shut"? Here's how he describes the psychological harms that he experienced from the "mind-torturing claustrophobia":

> *Even before I experienced this punishment, I knew that humans are communal beings, and when we are stripped of the ability to interact with other human beings, it causes mental, physical, psychological, emotional, and even spiritual harm. Like so many others, I thought this was just an overexaggerated theory created by an overzealous scientist trying to make a name for himself by making up medical conditions. But, after two weeks into the 90-day disciplinary sentence, I started to realize that this was much more than a half-cocked behavioral science concept that applied to only weak and overly sensitive people.*
>
> *I started experiencing unexplained fear, panic attacks, sensations of impending doom, anger, rage, and acute stress. For no apparent reason, it would suddenly feel like I couldn't breathe, my heart would start pounding in my chest, and a dizzy-like sensation along with cold sweats would come over me. I would have to lay down while sucking in huge lung-filled breaths to get these sensations*

under control. When these symptoms flared up, I couldn't concentrate, or do anything other than lay still until the ordeal faded. I even started routinely talking to myself as a coping tactic to relieve depression and extreme loneliness. What shocked me the most is that the more I was forced to stay in that box, the more irritated and stressed out I became, and the feeling started growing into what can be fairly described as despair. I thought that with time, the more I became acclimated to the situation, it would get better, but that clearly wasn't the case. I am certain these feelings were linked to the box because I never had them before being placed in SHU, and don't recall experiencing them after I got out of solitary confinement.

Although I never returned to the box, many of my friends were not so lucky. Not a small number of individuals "hung up" (AKA committed suicide) because they couldn't deal with the punishment. Indeed, I know of numerous instances where prisoners took their lives because they simply did not have the mental, physical, and psychological fortitude to cope with such cruel punishment.

Isolation and lack of human connection is dehumanizing and can be emotionally crippling. In fact, it is designed to break a human being. Solitary confinement can begin to affect brain activity within days,[3] sometimes even in people without pre-existing mental illnesses. Research suggests that the effects of isolation on the brain may be irreversible.[4] One 2019 study of incarcerated people over a period of nearly two decades found that incarcerated people who spent any amount of time in solitary were nearly 80 percent more likely to die by suicide during their first year out of prison than formerly incarcerated people who didn't.[5]

Many people in solitary confinement report that they no longer read in their isolation cell. One might imagine that reading and writing are virtually the only meaningful pursuits they have available in their cells, but these individuals explain that they cannot remember what they read just three pages earlier due to solitary's impact on their memory and concentration, so they give up.

Recall Tom, who recounted his decades in and out of solitary at Walla Walla in Chapter 3: A Brief History of Solitary Confinement in America. The last two times Tom was at IMU, he couldn't eat at all. He explains: "I am nearing the end of a long sentence and being sent backward through the system made me physically ill. Literally. Both times, I did not have a bite the entire time. Two hours after I got out, my stomach settled and my appetite returned."

Even people who go to solitary without prior mental health problems can develop a specific psychiatric syndrome[6] that results from prolonged isolation. Dr. Stuart Grassian, who first identified the syndrome, notes:

> It is characterized by a progressive inability to tolerate ordinary things, such as the sound of plumbing; hallucinations and illusions; severe panic attacks; difficulties with thinking, concentration, and memory; obsessive, sometimes harmful, thoughts that won't go away; paranoia; problems with impulse control; and delirium.[7]

Even short periods of isolation can cause severe mental health problems,[8] including depression, aggression, psychotic decompensation, and suicidal thoughts and behaviors.

Micaela E. Romero, Neural Systems and Behavior Researcher at the University of Washington, investigates the neurobiological and behavioral impacts of social isolation. Her work bridges neuroscience and social justice, asking what it means for a society to subject humans to conditions that are known to cause stress-related health deterioration, behavioral disruption, and even death. She told us that in Washington State, "incarcerated individuals are subjected to conditions that may be considered too harmful even for many lab animals. In practice, the conditions incarcerated individuals face receive less ethical scrutiny than those for lab mice." Using highly social animal models, such as the bumblebee, she is able to mimic solitary confinement conditions used in the Washington State Department of Corrections to study the long-lasting impacts of isolation. She has found that isolation housing greatly increases mortality as compared to small group housing. She notes that "there's no evidence that solitary confinement makes communities safer, even after hundreds of years of use, but there is overwhelming evidence that it causes harm and premature death."

The harms of solitary confinement are wide-ranging, affecting nearly every aspect of a person's being. In the subsections that follow, we examine these effects in detail, beginning with the profound psychological consequences, such as fear, paranoia, and mounting anger, before turning to the emotional toll of loneliness and post-traumatic stress. We then explore the devastating risks of suicide and self-harm, the physical deterioration that often accompanies prolonged isolation, and the broader social harms that extend beyond the individual to families and entire communities.

FEAR AND PARANOIA

Fear and paranoia are common effects of prolonged solitary confinement. Frank De Palma spent 22 years in solitary confinement at Nevada State Prison. When he first went to prison as a teen he got into a lot of fights. Guards viewed him as a tough guy and threw him in "the hole," where he would remain for over two decades. There he experienced quite a lot of anxiety and panic:

> *It was getting harder to get enthused about rec – just an outdoor version of the cell. But I had to try. And so I pushed myself out to the small enclosure and stared up at the sky. And then, one day, something terrifying happened. I was just starting my chin-ups when the walls of the enclosure seemed to be moving, closing in on me, like I was being crushed. I felt like my heart would explode from my chest. Was I having a heart attack? The space was getting smaller, and I banged on the door. "Help! Get me out of here!" Fortunately, one of the more decent guards was on duty that day, and he unlocked the door quickly. But before he could cuff me, I took off, tearing down the hall as he chased after me, shouting for me to stop. But he needn't have worried. I wasn't going anywhere. The only thing I wanted was to get back into my cell. It was only after I was locked*

back inside that my body calmed down and my breathing returned to normal.

I'd never had a panic attack in my life, and I never really understood what it even meant. But now I do. It was indescribable. I was terrified to go out again and decided to skip rec, at least for the time being. But I still wanted to shower, and although I was nervous about it I decided to take a chance. But no sooner had I begun the walk to the shower than it started up again – the walls in the hall were moving, closing in on me. It felt like the air itself was crushing me. I raced back to my cell.

At first, the guards thought I was being difficult, just trying to give them a hard time. But once they realized I was having panic attacks, they started messing with my head, threatening to pull me out, so they could have a little fun. "Hey, let's bring De Palma out," they would taunt, causing me to quiver in fear.[9]

Jonathan Kirkpatrick, who endured 18 months in solitary confinement, similarly highlights feelings of paranoia that remained even after he was released from solitary:

After leaving solitary, I returned back to the prison where I'd previously been attacked. I was in my cell alone, but the darkness made me feel as if others were there. I felt surrounded by enemies. I stayed up late at night feeling panic and trying to process the day. As I sat up each night, looking out my window, desperation and paranoia settled over me like a cloud that wouldn't blow away. Every look, word, or gesture in my direction could be a threat. Sometimes I didn't understand what people were saying. I'd fill in the blanks using context clues, and I was often wrong. I could sense that something was wrong with me, but I didn't know how to fix it.[10]

In everyday life, we all have momentary paranoid thoughts, which we silently correct with reality testing. But if one is alone in a solitary confinement cell, there is no opportunity to test our thoughts and feelings against reality in this way. For example, the isolated incarcerated person may hear guards joking and cussing loudly down the tier and have the momentary thought that they are talking about him, and believe they are about to come to his cell and attack him. He has no way to test what might be a baseless idea, so the fear stays with him and he interprets subsequent events in line with his belief that guards are going to burst in on him. Of course, the incarcerated person's fear may not be paranoid at all, it may be "protective awareness," as in Jonathan's case. After all, assault by guards is a common occurrence in prison.

MOUNTING ANGER

One of the most widely reported symptoms of solitary confinement is mounting anger, when the anger does not correlate with any particular events and when the individual may not even know why they are so angry.

Take Malcolm, Chris's neighbor in solitary. For days, he was incessantly banging his head against his cell door, swearing and yelling, seemingly at no one in particular. Since the banging didn't get Malcolm the attention he was looking for, he eventually added another element: water. He intentionally clogged his toilet and flooded his cell with toilet water. Toilet water flooded through the unit and creeped under the door of neighboring cells.

Malcolm's erratic and often explosive behavior spurred the involvement of guards, who suited up in riot gear and sprayed him with immobilizing gas. They applied shock shields to Malcolm's tiny, 130-pound body and covered his skin with pepper spray.

It is probably true that Malcolm wanted attention; he desperately wanted to communicate with another human, and his angry outbursts might have actually been an attempt to have human contact. But in solitary confinement, staff dismiss the behavior of people like Malcolm as attention-seeking instead of recognizing the way extreme isolation drives it. The mounting anger and lack of control are driven more by the environment itself than by any proclivities on the part of the people confined.

The treatment meted out to Malcolm is another illustration of the spiraling negation of human sensibilities in solitary and of the deterioration of human interaction and decency. After all, guards are vulnerable to the stresses of solitary confinement too, often becoming more monstrous than they had been prior to working there. Too often, the result is callousness and abuse of incarcerated people as well as high rates of burn-out, alcoholism, domestic violence, and suicide on the part of guards working in solitary confinement units.[11]

LONELINESS

Many severe effects of solitary are less visible. The Surgeon General of the United States has said that the nation is facing an "epidemic of loneliness and isolation" and has called the problem a "public health crisis." According to the surgeon general's study, loneliness can have the same negative health effects as smoking 15 cigarettes a day.[12]

Common sense dictates that this epidemic must be exacerbated by prolonged mandated isolation. Chris's good friend, BJ, spent six of his ten-year prison sentence in solitary confinement. When asked how he was able to cope, the look in his eyes said that it had not been an easy task and that he felt that he had barely survived. He said that there had come a point where he had been so lonely in solitary that he started to write himself letters. This is the reality of many people in the hole, especially when they have no one on the outside – they are forced to take drastic measures just to retain some form of their sanity and normality.

According to Raymond Williams, an incarcerated journalist who was serving a life without parole sentence under a "three strikes" law until his sentence was overturned:

> *Nothing compares to the chronic isolation and loneliness felt by the millions of prisoners enduring long stints in solitary confinement ... [D]uring my year of solitary confinement when I was 17 years old, I was so lonely that I resorted to dialing random phone numbers, hoping that someone would answer my collect call and be a friend*

> *or write me letters. I was that desperate for connection. I remember the sinking feeling when the mail cart would pass my cell, for weeks and months at a time, without a letter for me. The squeak of the wheels passing reminded me that I did not matter to a single person outside that concrete box, challenging me to care about myself enough to go on living.*[13]

Of course, many incarcerated people have family, friends, and support networks from their life before incarceration. But the system doesn't make it easy to maintain those bonds. The average American incarcerated person is hundreds of miles away from their home – an average of 500 miles for those in federal prison[14] – making visits from family or friends difficult. Many prisons also charge exorbitant fees for phone and computer communication, with policies that many people find hard to navigate.

To deal with such loneliness, people in solitary might seek to make connections with guards. But they often discover that guards are not interested in relating to them beyond passing a food tray through the slot in the door and taking them in shackles to medical appointments, making them feel even more isolated than they had previously. Kwaneta explains:

> *When you're locked in a concrete cage the size of a parking space for 23 to 24 hours daily, you're desperate for anything that represents the outside: a leaf, blade of grass, dandelion. All of the above have been smuggled into solitary confinement by incarcerated janitors from general population working to clean the isolation building. As much as that helps, it doesn't stimulate social needs. We really miss conversing with another human being about the outside. Our only real hope at learning about what's going on outside comes from the guards – but I know guards who worked in solitary confinement with me for eight and a half years and never said anything to me that entire time other than "name and number" and only during count time and mail delivery.*

I was lucky because I had a radio. Personal televisions aren't allowed for any folks in Texas prisons. Usually, I listened to NPR but when that signal went out, I would listen to AM right-wing talk radio just to hear different human voices. I was often overheard talking aloud, pretending I was actually participating in their conversation. Like me, my neighbors craved a conversation about normal things – current events that didn't involve prison. Nothing controversial, just the type of small talk you would use if you were stuck for a few minutes in an elevator with someone. We have loved ones on the outside and over 80 percent of us are mothers. But time and time again, I watched women fail at attempting to engage in small talk with staff.

During mealtimes and medication distribution, I've heard my neighbors ask things like: "How much is gas out there? A loaf of bread? A gallon of milk? Is it going to rain anytime soon?" Usually, their questions were met with silence – not even eye contact through the mesh viewing area when they talk. Other guards would say, "If you really wanted to know you should've stayed free." Some male guards, and it's ALWAYS males, assume the questions are an invitation to establish an inappropriate relationship. This causes women to end up in relationships that they didn't even know they were in until they're asked to "sho me a lil something," the price for engaging in small talk. Nothing is free in women's prisons concerning staff. Even conversation is transactional. The women guards are more likely to reply if their male colleagues aren't around. They fear being labeled as "inmate friendly." Unfortunately, the overwhelming majority of staff are male.

We are just desperate to communicate with outsiders and it's not only security staff who take advantage. We also get weekly religious volunteers who come to our cell doors to pray with us. Once, a developmentally challenged young woman yelled to me during this "prayer session": Mama Detroit!!! He ain't s'pose to be askin me my bra size, right?!!! Another time, against my advice, my neighbor asked the self-described Christian Nationalist preacher to pray with her because her mother committed suicide. He sneered: No! Your mother is in hell and if you don't repent from sexual deviancy, you'll join her.

During the pandemic, many folks' desperation reached a fever pitch as we implored staff to tell us what was going on out there. We didn't have phone access, only five minutes every three to four months, if staffing was sufficient. It often wasn't. The silence was deafening. Initially, staff dismissed our concerns. It was a terrifying time for everyone but at least those on the outside could talk with one another to ease fears.

POST-TRAUMATIC STRESS DISORDER

Post-traumatic stress disorder (PTSD) is a psychiatric condition that can occur in people who experience a severe trauma such as witnessing a murder, the personal experience of rape, or some other loss or painful experience. PTSD is quite prevalent among individuals subjected to solitary confinement – the changes in brain morphology that are caused by solitary confinement are equivalent to changes in brain morphology that accompany PTSD,[15] and quite often individuals who have been in solitary confinement experience symptoms and disabilities later on that are consistent with PTSD.[16]

The disorder consists of intrusive symptoms (flashbacks, nightmares, re-living the experience, persistent intrusive thoughts or images related to the trauma), hyper-arousal symptoms (startle reaction, insomnia, hypervigilance), and constrictive symptoms (emotional numbing, isolation, fear of leaving one's room or cell, or participating in activities or relationships reminiscent of the trauma). There are also likely signs of dissociation, feeling unreal, feeling like an outsider viewing one's own life events, or experiencing pervasive feelings of unreality. The intrusive and constrictive symptoms alternate over time until they either resolve, at which point there is no PTSD to diagnose, or evolve as a chronic pattern of symptoms, which can include emotional numbing, depression, constricted life, low self-esteem, insomnia, nightmares, flashbacks, re-living, and panic.

Juan C. Hernandez, who endured 24 months in solitary confinement, describes the PTSD he suffered from doing his time in the hole:

> *The saddest, loneliest and most desperate time in my entire life was when I was doing a yearlong program in Walla Walla State Penitentiary's IMU South, which in short is the hole. Not only was I subjected to extreme segregation with virtually no positive stimulation, but my personal life was also falling apart. The bond with my family was non-existent and the three-year relationship with the mother of my child came crashing down in a blaze of destruction and pain. I felt totally alone in this world, unless you count the three times per day an officer would open the hatch on my cell door and hand me my food tray, carefully through, as if they were feeding a beast at the zoo.*
>
> *When I was younger, I believed that if you spoke to yourself you must be crazy, but with more years and wisdom I now see that it is not a stage of insanity but more of a way to deal with extreme conditions. To this day I'll catch myself speaking to no one but me. I'll laugh a little, although it is a sad laugh mixed with a slice of pity and a nasty scar I am forced to walk around with. It is also a pathetic badge of honor, some would say, to a time in my life where I suffered greatly in seclusion.*
>
> *PTSD is not just something that happens to soldiers, but to anyone that is forced to take on an experience that is not meant for a human to experience. I know this because I walk around with the trauma every day. If you don't believe me, just wait around and listen to the sound of my voice.*

Multiple traumas have a different, more severe effect than a single trauma, and the resulting condition is termed "complex PTSD."[17] The healing process that begins after a single trauma is most likely to succeed if a safe environment and sensitive help are available. On the other hand, if the trauma is repeated (e.g., repeated child abuse or domestic violence, or traumas that occur in captivity such as custodial sexual abuse), the repetitive nature of the traumas multiplies the emotional damage and precludes real healing. A more complicated post-traumatic clinical picture often results in more severe and lasting symptoms and disability.

When sexual and physical abuse as well as long periods in solitary confinement occur at the hands of state employees and an official state agency, it further complicates the picture and exacerbates the damaging effects of the trauma. This is because the abusers were employees of the state and should as such have a duty to protect and care. When one is betrayed and abused by people in positions of official authority who are supposed to be caring for them (for example, prison staff), the betrayal and abuse tends to cause lasting distrust of others in positions of authority. This is "betrayal trauma," and it terribly impedes educational pursuits, where trust in the teacher and administrators is an important propellant of achievement. It also constrains employment possibilities because the sense of overwhelming betrayal by persons in authority interferes with the ability to accept supervision and fit into a work environment. The resultant post-traumatic symptoms or PTSD are much more severe, long-lasting and difficult to treat.[18]

There is significant research linking prior traumas to subsequent problems with substance abuse.[19] The most compelling explanation in case reports as well as in the clinical literature is that previously traumatized individuals utilize illicit drugs and alcohol to "self-medicate" or numb the trauma-related emotional pain and the continuing symptoms that were brought on by the trauma(s). But then the substance abuse itself becomes a serious problem and contributes to worsening disabilities that are comorbid with PTSD and other post-traumatic emotional problems. Many incarcerated people struggle with substance abuse, and there is reason for concern that their eventual recovery is much more difficult than it would be were they to be treated with respect and allowed to partake in social activities and rehabilitation programs.

SUICIDE AND SELF-HARM

Solitary confinement also comes with an extraordinarily high risk of suicide and self-harm. Looking at the various states for which we have figures for prison suicide rates, it becomes clear that 50 percent of prison suicides occur among the approximately five percent of the prison population consigned to some form of solitary confinement.[20] And that figure does not include the much larger number of suicide attempts that did not lead to death or the acts of often serious self-harm that may not be entirely suicidal in intent.

Kwaneta has witnessed more than her share of suicides in solitary confinement:

> *January 23, 2023, 3:40 pm. New girl in Cell 42 hanging from her light! They cut her down just in the nick of time – it's two medical people, seven guards, one Captain. Young white girl – they just handcuffed her and walked her out. The kids in here are yelling, "Y'all don't never gas white girls!" They just brought the girl in here from population.*

> *January 25, 2023. Another suicide attempt, Cell 9, A side. They deployed the entire can of tear gas. New guards always overdo it. That's three in this wing in one week.*

> *A while ago, one of my surrogate kids in here took her life. Her mother wrote me asking questions that I wouldn't want to know the true answers of if I was her. I don't know if I should cause her more pain? She doesn't need to have that on her heart and mind. Who wants to know their kid suffered? I'm wrestling with whether to tell her the truth. I would never want to know these things if it was my daughter. But, who am I to deny her the truth? It is complicated.*

Lacino Hamilton, who was wrongly incarcerated for 26 years (including eleven years in solitary confinement) before being exonerated, describes the extreme behavior he witnessed while in solitary confinement:

Many of the men here with me descend into the horror of self-mutilation, some eating parts of their own bodies.

In solitary, one can hear the madness coming from the throats of men who cannot take it anymore, frustrated souls from behind the bars of each cell, rasping rackets from the walls, the hollow vibrations from sink and toilet combined into one. Our iron beds are bolted to the floor. Lights are never turned off. These things take on frightening significance. They result in loss of appetite, insomnia, irritability, emotional withdrawal, depression, paranoid ideation and easily provoked anger, which may escalate into "acting out."[21]

Many of the men here with me smear themselves with feces. They mumble and scream incoherently all day and night. They descend into the horror of self-mutilation, some eating parts of their own bodies. My first couple of weeks in solitary an older white gentleman in a wheelchair who repeated over and over again how bored he was hanged and killed himself, on a dare. The frequency in which these acts of despair and hopelessness occur should attract administrative as well as clinical concern, but rarely do. The guy in the cell next to me and a guy around the corner both recently attempted suicide.

Not all people locked down in solitary confinement react precisely in these manners. In some, the trauma and harms are less conspicuous. In others, dejection and utter despondence set in earlier, or later. But none are unaffected. Not anyone. Not me. The challenges of writing under the tensions and hostilities created by social and sensory deprivation cannot just be shrugged off. To encourage myself, I repeat out loud the words of Viktor E. Frankl: "Life holds meaning under any conditions – even the most miserable ones." I try to believe this.[22]

Sean Ryan, who has spent 26 of his nearly 50 years in solitary confinement, offers a poem about suicide from his cell in New York Department of Corrections and Community Supervision (DOCCS).

Amari

A lover of Books
Inquisitive and smart
Amari Selton
Had Great Heart

He spent years in a cell
Going Through Hell
Human dignity Abused
Isolated and Confused

Trapped in the Labyrinth
Of his own mind
Psychosis and lucidity
Became Intertwined

Quack Psychologist
Jailhouse Apologist
Psychotropic Dichotomy
Chemical Lobotomy

He's Far Away Now
Thousand yard stare
I keep looking
But Nobody's There

Soul Exhausted
Bereft of Hope
Unable to Cope
He Made a Rope

Attempts to Resuscitate
Echo In The Night
Stressful Sounds
Release finally Found

Of His Name
Only Memories Remain
Sorrowful Mother's Pain
Lamentable Refrain

Marissa Potts, still serving her time in solitary confinement and herself a survivor of multiple suicide attempts, describes an all-too-common type of self-harm she sees in her women's solitary unit:

> *You see these women as they reach for their water with all these scars wrapped around their arms and you think "My God, what made you mutilate yourself like this?" The answer is simple though. Time, unresolved issues, and last but not least isolation. Those three combined can be deadly. Literally.*

At age 26, after making two escape attempts from the Texas Department of Criminal Justice, Dennis Hope was consigned to solitary confinement. He spent nearly three decades there – 27 years. Near the end of this period, Dr. Kupers spoke with him on camera during an interview with Rana Natour, Correspondent for Al-Jazeera's *Fault Lines.*[23] It is impressive how Dennis has remained sane and articulate about the torture he was forced to endure, but he admits he has his moments:

> *I'm hearing voices and seeing things that aren't there ... There's a part of you that's gone. And there's always the fear you'd lose your mind. There are things that I'd do, to like ... make sure I'm in touch with reality. And sometimes I would, um ... bite my forearm, and just to see how far I'd go. It let me know that I'm alive, that I could feel pain ... There are times I think about killing myself. What would it be like?*

According to Dr. Kupers:

> I've thoroughly investigated the cases of quite a few individuals who repeatedly harm themselves while in solitary confinement

> – including cutting their arm, mutilating their body, swallowing harmful objects, and even cutting off bodily parts – who all reported the same pattern: each time they cut themselves or cut off a body part, they are treated medically and sent to a Suicide Observation cell, where they are monitored and counseled for a few days, then they are sent back to their solitary confinement cell with little or no follow-up by mental health staff. Some report "recycling," i.e., going from solitary cell to Observation and back to solitary where they harm themself again, and back to Observation, and onward. I have investigated over three dozen successful suicides in solitary confinement settings and, in just about every case, the clinical chart reflects a cyclical process wherein the incarcerated person repetitively attempted suicide or engaged in self-injurious behavior while in solitary, was transiently transferred to the infirmary or a crisis-stabilization unit, and then was sent back to solitary confinement where he eventually killed himself.[24]
>
> In every lawsuit launched on behalf of the incarcerated people who repeatedly recycle between Observation and solitary cell multiple times, where I've served as psychiatric expert witness, I always find clinical notes in the medical record indicating that the individual is not suffering from any mental illness other than ASPD (antisocial personality disorder), and is merely manipulating or malingering, or is simply being deceptive. In almost all such cases, I conclude that this is an incorrect diagnosis, and instead, the individual is in great distress. Instead of responding to the distress, staff too often rationalize ignoring the individual's needs by falsely alleging manipulation or malingering. Returning the individual to a solitary confinement cell is a very foolhardy treatment plan (actually, there is usually no treatment plan on the chart covering the period subsequent to Suicide Observation).[25]

Individuals who have repeatedly attempted suicide or harmed themselves in a solitary confinement cell must not be sent back to solitary after a brief period in Observation. Rather, a mental health treatment plan must be developed with them, including incrementally diminished monitoring as they evidence lower risk, and they must be transferred out of solitary confinement and into a treatment setting, perhaps a step-down unit.

The strongest root "cause" of prison self-harm and suicide is solitary confinement itself. In that light, self-harm in solitary is iatrogenic[26] – sending an incarcerated person known to be at very high risk of suicide or self-harm to a place that we know is correlated very strongly with self-harming and suicidal behavior can hardly be called anything else. Nonetheless, mental health staff typically perform a pre-segregation evaluation and approve the individual's return to solitary confinement.

Samantha Wohlford's story illustrates this harmful cycle. She bravely recounts how being in solitary caused her to want to take her own life, which then caused her to be sent right back to solitary shortly after being released from Suicide Observation:

> *I've been placed in Solitary confinement on three separate occasions. I'm writing this from solitary right now, actually …*
>
> *The solitude weighs very heavily on me. During my first time in solitary, I started having thoughts of suicide almost immediately, and just when I felt like I couldn't take another day, I got told to pack up and was given a bed in population.*
>
> *I spent a single day in population. I was an emotional mess. I sat on my floor and cut my wrists. I got on the phone and cried to my family and almost started feeling better when a correction officer came and made me go to medical. I was cleaned and then bandaged even though I was no longer bleeding. Then I was taken back to solitary confinement "for my own protection."*
>
> *I was stripped and searched. I had to spend days completely naked with an officer sitting there watching my every move. This did not help my emotional state at all. Being forced to sit in a cold empty room completely naked with nothing to do but think didn't feel productive*

or healthy. I spiraled further into my break with reality and started sleeping constantly. I wouldn't eat. It was the same meals every time: a bologna sandwich or a peanut butter and jelly sandwich. I was finally taken off constant supervision and put in a holding cage to wait for a bed to open. I found a shard of glass the size of my palm. I called for a ranking officer and showed her. I remembered how long it took me to get my hygiene and paper supplies the last time – nine solid days where I couldn't brush my teeth, bathe, comb my hair, or even cover myself with a sheet. She asked me for the glass and I told her I would trade for it: "I want hygiene items, a pen, some paper, and a bed roll. You could try to come take it by force but by the time you get in here I will swallow it." At the time I was serious. But I know without a doubt I never would have gotten so low in my depression outside of solitary confinement. I never would have attempted suicide.

From January 1 to September 5, 2024, there were 43 documented suicides in the Texas Department of Criminal Justice (TDCJ). Lanae Tipton, who's been in solitary there for almost two years, witnessed two of them. Her friend Brooklyn, who was known to be suicidal and had a history of self-harming while in solitary, was #14:

I snatched my headphones off as my neighbor screamed my name. Frantically, she told me my friend Brooklyn hung herself. In that same moment, I noticed the usually inactive hallway of solitary confinement swarming with officers. I hoped it was just a mistake, but it wasn't, it was the second suicide I've witnessed in a six-month span.

A week prior to Brooklyn's suicide, she was stripped of all personal property: books, activities, commissary-purchased food and appliances, along with her tablet and materials for paper correspondence. This disciplinary punishment greatly inhibited her positive distractions and family connections that would ordinarily center her mind while in isolation.

Sitting in her then-bare cell, Brooklyn, a charismatic beauty, was distraught. As we spoke from the threshold of our locked doors, she confided to me that her mother acted as an anchor in her struggles with mental health. Not being able to contact her mother shook Brooklyn to the core.

After the suicide, Brooklyn's fuming and heartbroken mother testified in court: "If my baby could have called me, it wouldn't have happened, she'd still be here." With their tight-knit bond, her mother had diffused many similar situations for Brooklyn's struggles in the past.

A few days before Brooklyn's devastating death, an officer saw fresh incisions on her inner wrist. Being aware of Brooklyn's extensive history of self-harm, the guard escorted Brooklyn to be consulted by the counterproductive mental health staff. Asked the simple question "Are you suicidal?" Brooklyn had answered "No" and was returned minutes later with a packet of antibacterial ointment for her deep cuts.

Like many others incarcerated at TDCJ, Brooklyn dreaded the inhumane punishment that came with admitting suicidal thoughts. Anyone who vocalizes self-harm or shows signs of it are taken to crisis management, a building known better as the ice house, and placed in a hollow cell, forced to sleep on the floor and monitored every 15 minutes, all while butt naked. Temperatures are set to a chilly 65°F year-round, hence the nickname, and you are only allowed a stiff and thin blanket depending on the severity of the suicide attempt made, some even forced for days without one. Plus, the only food option is sandwiches. This, plus psychotropic medication, is the extent of TDCJ's mental health provisions.

The officer working that fateful night was unfamiliar with Brooklyn's high-risk behavior and didn't think twice about the door to her cell being covered up. When I called to check on her, Brooklyn responded glumly that she needed to vent and would write me some mail. After speaking for a short time, nothing seemed amiss, but this was our last conversation before I put my headphones on to listen to music and wait for her mail.

By the time the officer became interested in the obstructed view into Brooklyn's cell, it was already too late. I stood at my door with tears streaming down my face, listening to the panicked commotion of staff attempting resuscitation measures, murmuring silent prayers as EMS rolled her draped body past my cell on a stretcher. My heart crumbled when I noticed my friend's pale blue hand peeking out of the covering.[27]

PHYSICAL HARMS

The physical effects of isolation can manifest in a variety of ways. Jonathan Kirkpatrick describes the physical ailments he suffered immediately upon his release from solitary:

The high levels of stress began to take a toll; soon my body began to fail. Two weeks after leaving solitary, I had suddenly developed an extreme case of shingles, blanketing most of my body, and causing so much pain I had to be sedated with morphine. I began to lose weight at an alarming rate, ten pounds every few weeks. Prison health officials called it wasting disease. My muscle mass diminished and I came down with pneumonia, which seemed to fill my lungs with molasses. As each day passed and I became weaker, I felt more like the end was coming.

The doctors told me that I would be okay. They didn't even keep me in the infirmary. I didn't believe them. I was scared and tired and lonely. They tried to explain how stress could have a physical effect on the body. I followed the conversation but didn't really understand at first. But when you can't do anything else, sometimes the only thing left is self-reflection. I came to understand that I was killing myself – the hate I had spent so much time feeding on in solitary was now eating me from the inside out.[28]

Withholding water, food, or medicine necessary for survival can contribute to the deterioration of the body. For example, Kwaneta has been repeatedly denied medical attention, which has caused several of her health conditions to severely worsen, including cardiovascular issues and a Posterior Vitreous Detachment diagnosis for her eye.

SOCIAL HARMS

In addition to the anxiety, insomnia, paranoia, mental breakdowns, and so forth, another factor that makes solitary so unbearable is the sheer deprivation and boredom of being caged for long periods of time alone in a cell with hardly anything to do. Time in prison could be, to some extent, an opportunity to further one's education, develop social skills and social relationships, or learn vocational skills. But instead, solitary confinement forces isolation and idleness, to the detriment of all the social skills, work skills, and intellectual capacities that are supposedly part of the "rehabilitation" that prisons include in their mission statements and that prison staff have a duty to foster. Kwaneta describes some of the obstacles prison staff put in the way of incarcerated persons' self-education and rehabilitation:

> *After I read a graphic novel titled,* Amazons, Abolitionists, and Activists: A Graphic History of Women's Fight for Their Rights *by Mikki Kendall and A. D'Amico, I knew I would violate prison rules.*
>
> *This prison promotes an anti-reading environment. "Traffic and Trade" is the disciplinary infraction issued for sharing personal property such as books, magazines, or shampoo with other incarcerated people. But I wanted these mostly young women to see what we've accomplished throughout history – to know that being a woman isn't a curse. It left me inspired and wondering: what will my contribution be? Many women in solitary with me have been locked up since childhood.*

The complex dance begins. As a team, my neighbors stick mirrors ut windows to watch for guards.

I secure the book in a sock attached to several connecting shoestrings and dangle it out my window. Waiting for the signal, I swing the heavy sock five cells to my right. It reaches a first-floor window where it's grabbed and passed from outstretched hand to outstretched hand until it reaches its intended recipient. Days pass as the book makes the rounds to all 228 people in solitary.

Then: a message. The book has been confiscated.

A tall Black woman guard sashays up the stairs wearing a smirk and fanning my book. I stand at my cell door turning my ID over and over in my hand, waiting for her to collect it for my disciplinary. She flips through the pages and asks, "Dis yours?"

"Yes," I say.

"Yes what?" she snarls.

"Yes Ma'am," I answer to the woman who is the same age as my son. I just want her to write the disciplinary order and leave me alone. Instead, she tells me that because of its "radical content," the book could promote a riot.

Anger floods me but I remain silent. This guard is known for antagonizing people. She wants an argument, but only the youth argue with the guards. She says she is giving me a warning and waits for an apology from me, her weight shifted to one leg.

Instead, I say, "Write me up," as I take the three steps to my bed.

The dorm is listening. At 51, whether I like it or not, I am a role model. Security staff usually describe me as an "old school – no problem inmate." I have to demonstrate the value of education. To show, by my actions, that there are times you must stand unapologetically for the right to know. Consequences be damned.

A new neighbor arrives and asks me through our shared vent, "Excuse me, I don't know how long Imma be down here for refusing to work. Can I borrow a book?"

"Sure," I answer. "Go to your window."[29]

HARMS TO FAMILIES AND COMMUNITIES

Then there's the harm those sent to solitary pass on to their family members.[30] This damage isn't so easily quantified, but family members suffer dearly in their struggle to support loved ones – incarcerated or formerly incarcerated – who are or have been in the throes of solitary.

Many incarcerated people in solitary confinement have children, who are negatively affected in many ways by this situation.[31] The isolation and powerlessness of those in the hole are passed on to those they love on the outside, who have no way of contacting them, let alone monitoring the state of their safety and health. And isolation follows the person even after they leave prison. As one expert has put it,[32] solitary confinement forces those who have been there "to live in a world without people. And they adapt to it." Loved ones are also made to deal with the lingering impacts that stay with those who leave the hole. Like any other debilitating illness, life with someone who suffered in solitary carries its own human and medical burdens, which the state does next to nothing to help alleviate.

Kwaneta's daughter Summer Knight, who is now 17, endured an entire childhood with her mother in prison, and in solitary during Summer's most crucial teenage years:

I used to think my mother was literally living inside a hole. I was four months old when my mother went to prison in Texas. Because we live in Michigan, my first visit I remember was when I was 5 years old. My second visit I was 8 years old. Right after my second visit my mom was sent to solitary confinement for almost nine years. Nobody explained to me what solitary meant and that it meant she couldn't call me. Before she went to solitary we talked on the phone all the time and that's how I was getting to know her. But when she went to solitary, they didn't allow her to use the phones.

It was a hard time. My sister's father died in 2019 and mom couldn't even call. Then my father passed away in 2022. I felt alone and isolated. Being a teenager was hard without my mom or dad. When I needed my mom the most I had to write her a letter. I knew other people in jail that had access to phones. I thought she just didn't want to call. This forced me to figure out answers on my own without having my mother to talk to. I still hold resentment that she couldn't be there when I needed her the most.

Kwaneta explains that before she went to solitary, she and Summer talked every day using the expensive phone on the wall in the prison dayroom. In solitary, there were no phones:

Solitary shreds family relationships. We only had one five-minute phone call every 3–4 months after midnight, when Summer was already asleep. It was like that for seven years! Sometimes because of staff shortages, the calls would only be twice a year! Texas just got tablets in 2022 but solitary didn't get the phone access with everyone else. Sometimes, I only got two phone calls in a year and my mom had only five minutes to update me. She sounded like an auctioneer.

I didn't want my family to visit because visits were behind a plexiglass window. But, worse, there was an increased risk of visits being canceled at the last second. If staffing is insufficient, they cancel visits. In my case, my kids would take time off work, pay for airfare, hotel, and car rental costs, just to be turned away when they got here. I wouldn't risk letting them down like that.

In another illustrative case, Liza Daniel shares her experience of marriage to her husband Brant who is in solitary. They have been married for 16 years:

> *Life as the wife of a lifer in solitary confinement is like no other. Our first eight years together were primarily correspondence with the occasional visit behind glass. In spite of this we managed to grow very close and are each other's best friends. I have spent the entire time I've been with him fighting for his legal and human rights. It's very hard to stand by and watch him be forced to live this way, while being expected to treat it as normal. Not being able to hug and hold your loved one is anything but normal.*
>
> *When he got the tablet phone it was a real game changer and now we can spend almost all day, every day in each other's company, 15 minutes at a time cuz that's how long the calls last. I can witness the awful food he can't stomach and the ridiculous cherry-picking of rules that adds to his constant state of uncertainty and diminishes his health.*
>
> *I just want him to come home so he can sleep in a real bed and I can cook him real food. I only ever wanted for us to have an ordinary life. He never deserved the kind of punishment that seems to get worse as the years slip by.*

In 2023, *Medical News Today* marshaled research on the overall health effects of time spent in the hole, and the litany of ailments run the gamut from psychological to physiological.[33] The harm, in other words, has a way of reaching a person's whole self. And in keeping with similar conclusions by human rights experts and international treaty bodies, an article in the Journal of the American Academy of Psychiatry and the Law[34] reported that "isolation can be as distressing as physical torture."

7
Mental Illness and Solitary Confinement

I will always remember my first day working in the solitary confinement unit on Rikers Island. As the chief took me on a tour of the punitive unit, my stomach tightened at the sight of the rows of cell doors, each with a small window. She told me that the mental health department played a big role in there. Pointing to the steel doors, she said, "If they had no mental health issues before they entered solitary, they do now." Truer words were never spoken.

– Mary Buser (former Assistant Mental Health Chief
in the Central Punitive Segregation Unit on
Rikers Island for seven months)

More people with serious mental illness are housed in America's jails and prisons than in its psychiatric hospitals.[1] The largest psychiatric facilities in the US include Los Angeles County Jail, Rikers Island Jail in New York, and Cook County Jail in Illinois. Despite the laws against housing people with certain mental illnesses in solitary confinement that we will discuss in Chapter 13: The Legal Boundaries of Solitude, statistics show that they are massively overrepresented in solitary,[2] whether they're sent there for disciplinary reasons (because people with serious mental illness often find it difficult to adhere to prison rules), for the safety of others (because serious mental illness can cause violent behavior), or for their own safety (which can occur when someone is on suicide watch or at risk of harming themselves, or because individuals with serious mental illness are disproportionately victimized behind bars).[3] Reports show that at least half of the people currently in solitary have a serious mental illness, compared to about 25 percent of the general prison population.[4] A recent study at Florida State University found that incarcerated people with mental illness, especially bipolar disorder, severe depression, and schizophrenia, were up to 170 percent more likely to be placed in solitary for extended periods.[5]

In her role as assistant mental health chief in the solitary unit at Rikers, Mary Buser witnessed the torture of solitary day in and day out, and the effects that isolation had on the mental health of the people she treated. She observes:

> *The occupants of these cells were being punished for some type of jailhouse infraction. Solitary, we were told, was a necessary tool in maintaining the safety of the jail. But despite the assuring rhetoric, I quickly discovered that solitary confinement was a grueling punishment. Confinement to a concrete cell for 23 hours a day – for weeks, months, and in some cases, years – induces extreme suffering – depression, despair, insomnia, hallucinations, and suicidal impulses. My early attempts at therapy were useless. Isolation becomes agonizing, and there are no well-intended words to ease it.*
>
> *Our primary tool was medication – anti-depressants, anti-psychotics, mountains of sleeping pills – anything we could think of. Virtually everyone was on medication. And as we doled out these meds, I remember asking myself: What kind of punishment is this that people need to be medicated to endure it? But we did our jobs, and any misgivings I had were assuaged by the fact that I worked side-by-side with professionals – nurses, psychologists, board-certified doctors. Surrounded by such respectability, it had to be okay.*
>
> *Despite our best efforts, the meds only went so far. When they could no longer hold a human psyche together, we were called to cell doors to face frantic scenes of people covered in blood, smeared in feces, makeshift nooses, and agonized, shell-shocked faces begging for relief. And in fact, the mental health department had the authority to issue a reprieve, but only if we felt suicide was imminent. But the reprieve was temporary. After the person was sufficiently recovered,*

he'd be promptly returned to the cell. It reminded me of a weary swimmer treading water but starting to go under, who'd be pulled out to catch his breath, then thrown back in. It had the earmarks of torture. But I banished the word from my mind, reminding myself that I lived in a progressive country that prohibits such things. The American flag fluttered above the jail.

As we huddled to the sides of these cells, our primary concern was always suicide. Were these desperate gestures a ruse to get out – or could the person inside possibly be dead in the morning? As we struggled to make a decision, my mind flitted back to my student days of wanting to help people – to make a difference! And now, as I weighed in on life and death decisions, I had the uncomfortable feeling that far from the idealistic student I'd once been, I had become a monitor of human suffering.

These cell-side huddles were not occasional; they occurred practically every day, and as we talked to the people inside, none of them struck me as the "Hannibal Lecters" I'd been led to believe they were. They were mostly young and dark-skinned, with many suffering from impulse control disorders. Whatever infractions they'd committed seemed to pale in comparison to what we were doing to them. As I witnessed their suffering, my misgivings about solitary were only growing. Each day, I dreaded the inevitable call to a cell door. On the walk over to the unit, I always reminded myself that solitary confinement was a legally sanctioned practice carried out in jails and prisons across the county. But as I got closer to the punitive unit, my legs were wobbling anyway.

I don't know if there was a particular moment that I knew I could no longer be part of this. But that moment came, and once it did, I was at peace. My desire to help people, to treat everyone with dignity – was impossible in this setting, a place where human beings are routinely stripped of all dignity by design. My departure from Rikers Island came about ten years before the United Nations decreed that solitary confinement beyond 15 days constitutes torture. It is what I had always known.

As the country is beginning to recognize the horror of solitary confinement, the time has also come for a reckoning within the helping professions for their complicity in this practice. Health care workers are an essential component to these units – without a mental health staff to prescribe psych meds and predict and prevent suicides, and without a medical staff to patch people up following self-mutilation, the practice could not continue. It is time for the health professions to recognize that no matter how well-intended their interventions, by participating in solitary confinement, they have lost their way.

Mental health care is typically inadequate in solitary, often consisting of nothing more than a boilerplate set of stock questions, asked by mental health staff visiting them on "rounds" for a few minutes at cell-front, where there is no privacy or confidentiality. The consequences can be devastating; for example, footage from an Indiana jail recently showed that 29-year-old Joshua McLemore died of malnutrition there during a schizophrenic episode in summer 2021 after being left in solitary confinement for 20 days without mental health treatment.[6] Indeed, as already noted, 50 percent of prison suicides happen in solitary confinement.[7]

SOLITARY EXACERBATES MENTAL ILLNESS

Long-term confinement in an isolated confinement unit is well known to cause severe psychiatric morbidity, disability, and mortality, even with people who are relatively stable when they enter solitary confinement.

The most obvious risks of long-term isolative confinement are suicides and repetitive self-harm. But in addition, as a general rule, the longer an acute episode of mental illness goes untreated – in other words the longer the individual is left to be irrational and emotionally out of control – the worse the prognosis becomes. Thus, placing people prone to serious mental illness in isolation, where their disorder is exacerbated and many become acutely psychotic or suicidal, and failing to provide them with adequate mental health treatment is quite likely to result in severe and permanent psychiatric injury.

Justyna Rzewinski observed many such cases when she was a clinical supervisor for mental health on Rikers Island from December 2023 until September 2024. She recently testified about a practice called "deadlocking" that she regularly observed in the specialized mental health units. Although people with a severe mental illness are not supposed to be placed in solitary confinement in New York, she explained that with deadlocking, seriously mentally ill individuals are locked in their cells for weeks at a time or longer. When that happens, they lose access to their medications because they are not permitted to leave their cell to line-up to pick them up. Justyna describes one particular case that still haunts her:

> *I remember the day I met him. He'd come from another mental health unit and was quickly labeled a "deadlock" because the officers said he "likes to play with feces." He was diagnosed with schizophrenia, like so many others in the mental health units across Rikers Island. He was painfully thin and frail, constantly asking for chips and his lawyer's contact information. He was designated unfit to proceed with trial, and unfortunately there was no lawyer information to provide to him. Due to being deadlocked and decompensated (meaning he was experiencing a serious decline in his mental health), he could not comprehend this information. He banged and screamed around the clock, desperate to come out. His cell was covered in smeared feces, with flies swarming, and he had shredded his mattress in frustration. Trapped inside that filthy, small cell, he had no access to his medical or psychiatric medications for months. I witnessed this with so many others in my unit and the other units, and I couldn't stop wondering how, as a society, we allow this to happen. I kept asking myself why no one had ever spoken up.*
>
> *After I advocated for his release for weeks, two understanding and compassionate officers finally let him out. Those two officers always*

wanted to help the patients and did all they could in that environment. After he was out, he immediately started doing better, but when I returned after his first weekend out, he was inexplicably locked back in. No one was sure why. Of course, it was never documented since deadlocking was prohibited. But some people thought it was because a female officer who came to the unit felt uncomfortable with how close he was to her and how he looked at her. That's when I realized that I couldn't make a lasting difference at Rikers.

The echoes of his screams and those of countless others stayed with me day and night. Even on weekends, I felt intense anxiety, never knowing what might happen next upon my return to work on Monday. During our training and studies, we are constantly told never to take our work home, but how could I not? How could I go home and live my life knowing that my patients were left screaming, banging, smearing feces, and deteriorating before my eyes, and there was nothing I could do? I hadn't taken this job to witness suffering I couldn't alleviate. So, I resigned, overwhelmed with guilt, feeling like I was abandoning my patients. But I promised myself to keep fighting for them on the outside, where I can actually make a difference.

Eventually, he was transferred to a mental health state facility. When he returned, he was transformed – healthier, gaining weight, coherent. With regular medication and without solitary confinement, he was a different person. I made sure to meet with him before my last day there. He told me he was doing better but blamed himself for the time he'd spent "deadlocked." It broke me to see him carry that burden of blame. I held back tears, assuring him it wasn't his fault and encouraging him to keep up with his treatment. I ended the session quickly, not wanting him to see me cry. I returned to my office, tears streaming, fully aware that resigning was the right decision – for me, him, and the countless others who I will never stop advocating and fighting for, wherever life leads me.

Once I resigned, I testified in front of the Board of Correction meeting on October 8, 2024. The same day, the Daily News article was released detailing my experience there and everything I have witnessed regarding the "deadlocks." As a result of my testimony and exposing this practice, DOC can no longer lock any individuals in their cells, and currently, there is an ongoing investigation.

SOLITARY CONFINEMENT IS NOT CONDUCIVE TO EFFECTIVE MENTAL HEALTH TREATMENT

On my first day in solitary, I was asked: "Are you OK? Do you feel like committing suicide?"

The staff member questioning me spoke flatly, displaying no sense of compassion. This process was simply a formality.

Prisoners in solitary need to be very careful as they answer such questions. If they are seen to be at risk of self-harm, they'll be sent somewhere even worse, a cell isolated from all other prisoners where they will be stripped of absolutely everything. Even the orange jumpsuit and pink underwear would be taken away, replaced with a thick green cloth draped over them like a dress with a slit down the back. A suicide cell is not where you want to be.

Accessing mental health care in solitary confinement is fraught with obstacles, often deterring those who need it most. Marissa Potts knows this cycle all too well. In the past two years, she has been sent to solitary confinement eleven times and has attempted to take her own life on five occasions. Her experiences have left her deeply wary of seeking help from mental health counselors:

The first time I tried taking my life in prison was the closest I've ever come to death – not counting the many times before prison. Afterwards, I woke up to the mental health counselors asking, "Why didn't you just ask for help, Potts?"

See, the thing is, getting mental help in prison isn't exactly helpful. If anything, it's humiliating. First you have to tell a guard you'd like to speak to mental health. Then when you step into their office you have to be careful and not say certain words like, "I can't handle this" or "I feel hopeless." Things like that could put you on CDO (Continuous Direct Observation).

CDO is when you're moved to solitary confinement, stripped of all clothes and placed in a one-person cell to be closely monitored by a guard. Every 24 hours that same mental health counselor that deemed you unfit visits and gives you 3–5 minutes to convince her you aren't suicidal or homicidal. She'll either clear you or you remain CDO until you are transferred to Mountain View prison (nicknamed the "ice house" because of the freezing temperature inside), where they send incarcerated women in Texas for further evaluation – they put you in another empty one-person cell, totally naked, without property. Not even a ponytail holder.

In my case I skipped CDO and was sent directly to the ice house after getting my wrists stitched up at the local hospital. I was put ass naked and shivering in an off-white colored cell with feces painted on the walls.

Ms. Teague, the ice house mental health manager, decides if you are cleared to return to your prison unit or for more extreme cases if you are eligible for Skyview, a long-term prison unit for mental health treatment. "Ms. Potts are you ready to go back to your unit?" Hinting that I overstayed my welcome.

Ms. Teague asked a few more questions like, "Are you having homicidal or suicidal thoughts?" The word "No" flew out my mouth so fast, I thought she knew I was lying. I sat naked, balled up with my knees to my chest, shivering and hungry because the only thing on the menu is two sandwiches three times a day, hair matted, with wounds exposed to whatever else this filthy cell had on its floor and walls. Lucky for me, Ms. Teague didn't care if I was lying or not. I was just one out of 30 other women she had to clear.

In no time a familiar officer from my prison approached my cell door with handcuffs and gown in hand. I looked at her confused because one wrist had nine stitches and the other had four. Still, she made me turn around and bend at an angle so I could stick my hands through the tray slot to get handcuffed. After the painful and uncomfortable ride "home," they housed me in solitary confinement until a bed was available.

Isolated inside of another one-person cell, not being able to come out was the most dangerous time in my prison life. I can't count how many times suicide crossed my mind – it would have been so easy to finish what I started. The guards fail to properly do rounds, only briefly flashing a light inside your cell without looking to see if you are breathing or bleeding. Here the real battle began for me. My suicidal thoughts increased and went into overdrive as buried memories and emotions started to resurface. The things I could usually push to the back of my mind with distractions were damn near impossible to avoid with nothing to do all day but think. The only thing stopping me from trying again was the fear of failing again and being sent back to the ice house and having to do it all over again.

Many state DOCs and the Federal Bureau of Prisons require health care staff to examine incarcerated persons before they're admitted to close custody units like RHUs.[8] A clinician can recommend that someone sanctioned to RHU time should not be placed there for medical reasons.[9] But, according to incarcerated sources, mental health exams before RHU placements are cursory and superficial, often occur at "cell-front," and hardly ever prevent people from being sent to the units. Indeed, it is unclear what condition actually disqualifies an incarcerated person from being sent to solitary. As confirmed by all of the incarcerated people whose words are featured in this book, psychologists perform a perfunctory interview: As described by Marissa, they ask you a carbon copy set of four or five questions like, "Do you feel like hurting yourself," and "Do you feel like hurting anybody else," and then they take you to lockup. There is no real examination to determine whether you should be put in solitary or not.

Once in solitary, despite the proven severe harm to a person's mental health and the long-term trauma from prolonged isolation, and despite the fact that many states require regular health care assessments, people report that they are given little to no mental health support. For example, Mark "Face" Caldwell told us that he'd been trying to speak to a mental health professional in confidence since he was placed in an RHU in New Jersey, but he was only afforded rare and short visits in front of his cell door. Unfortunately, this is a common refrain.

Mental health professionals are usually accompanied by guards, and incarcerated people who want to talk are forced to share their problems on an open tier for everyone to hear. A mental health staffer might ask "Are you feeling suicidal?" Are you still hearing voices?" How is your psychotropic medication working?" These public mental health checks cause "everybody from incarcerated people to guards to joke about whatever you're expressing," Caldwell explains. "They go on to tell the next prisoner and guard and it becomes a lingering joke among everybody." In prison, where the unwritten code requires one to be tough, never show weakness, and never snitch, having a mental illness or being suicidal brings stigma and possible victimization by other incarcerated people, and also by guards. Individuals with emotional problems are viewed as "dings," or called other derogatory terms, and are often victimized once they're back in general population. It makes sense, then, that people are inhibited to speak about their mental health issues in public settings.

"Cell-front" visits, where mental health staff talk to an incarcerated person in his or her cell through the door, are a common practice. The incarcerated person is typically nervous about the visit, fearing that people in neighboring cells will overhear the conversation and the incarcerated person who talks to mental staff about the "voices," or thoughts of suicide, or the effects of psychotropic medications, will be branded a weakling. Guards passing by also overhear the conversation. In other words, there is neither privacy nor confidentiality in the cell-front mental health visit, in violation of clinical and ethical standards.

The antagonistic relationship between staff and incarcerated people discussed in Chapter 5: Cruel and Unusual Punishment: Stories of Torture, too often extends to the mental health staff, reducing the effectiveness of mental health checks even further. Incarcerated people are prone to view mental health clinicians the same way they view guards. Most of those in solitary confinement do not want to talk to the mental health staffer coming to their cell-front and asking personal questions, and are likely to say "I'm fine," hoping the mental health person will move on to the next cell and not force them to state their emotional problems and degree of suicidality in the cell-front situation where people in neighboring cells and staff walking by can overhear.

In his memoir *Finding Freedom, How Death Row Broke and Opened My Heart*, Jarvis Masters describes the lack of professionalism of a psychiatrist in his solitary unit, who didn't know anything about him, but nonetheless tried to push various drugs on him:

> *"How are you, though? The noise here must be disturbing. If you like I can give you something while I'm here, so you can get through the night."*
>
> *"No, no!" I said. "I'm doing fine, sir!"*
>
> *"Well, let's see ...," he said, reaching into one of his pants pockets. "How about this tiny blue one? This is Mellaril. But I also have ... let's see, Prolixin and Cogentin. But these here," he admitted with a doctor's frown, "I'm not so sure of. Most folks prefer these blue Mellaril to the Sinequan," he said, almost as if talking to himself. "I totally agree! So ... let's start you off here, and you can let me know how you feel. I'm usually down here twice a week. Do you have a cup?" he asked. "Because I have to see you take the medication."*

"No, Doc!" I said. "I mean, which part of 'no' do you not understand, huh? That stuff you have is for crazy people and I don't want any."

"Nonsense!" he said. "Of course, you do. Here, take two."

"No! No!" I insisted. "Why don't you take your pockets filled with syringes and funny pills some damn place else?"

"Well, sir," he said, "you don't have to get smart!"

"Of course I do, because you, sir, are not listening."

"Well, then," he said, "I'm sorry I couldn't be of any help to you today. But I'll be back on the tier later in the week – so if you happen to need any help sleeping or whatever, just let me know."[10]

Sadly, the result is that the individual in the solitary cell does not receive the mental health treatment they need. Too often, the result is a suicide where the individual who killed themself was seen by mental health staff on rounds and told the mental health staffer, "I'm fine."

Even when health screenings are part of the overall process, however, the specifics can vary based on the circumstances surrounding the placement. For example, in federal prisons, mental health staff do not always provide documentation, which leaves the Bureau of Prisons (BOP) unable to properly care for people who have mental illness, and there is often no real accountability mechanism.

Teresa Hertz describes the pain of knowing her son, who's been diagnosed with bipolar disorder, PTSD, ADHD, and obsessive-compulsive disorder (OCD), was in solitary. His last consignment to solitary was from August 2023 to February 2024:

When someone you love is in solitary confinement, it can only be described as "chronic emotional pain." I manage it as a workaholic who has become an expert at compartmentalizing. "It" I define as a dark cloud of despair that can descend at any time – on a beach or mountain where I am taken back to my son's childhood, remembering his love for nature in contrast to the reality of his cement box. Or I can be in the middle of a presentation when the call comes; I excuse myself with an apology, converse with my son, swallow my tears and return to my audience. It is an all-consuming part of my life that steals my joy and freedom. Those who don't live with this may wonder why I am compelled to pick up my phone when I see the prison number. They may not understand that I am a lifeline – that I carry the weight of his sanity. He calls and we practice breathing. When calm, we strategize and develop our next moves. He will busy himself with finding the latest DOC policy violations and I will begin drafting my next letter. This is our "hope-line." In the beginning, we appealed to human rights violations, Constitutional rights, protections for vulnerable populations – all to no avail. Now we are activists and our hope lies in ending solitary confinement. In the meantime, I will continue to pick up the phone because his father, brother, 3-year-old daughter, 15-year-old son, grandparents, uncles, aunts, cousins, nieces, nephews, and friends want him whole. He is more than #336844; he is a part of our family.

WHAT QUALITY MENTAL HEALTH TREATMENT SHOULD LOOK LIKE

In general, quality correctional mental health treatment requires that incarcerated people be treated with respect at every turn: their conditions of confinement must be conducive to mental health treatment; there need to be multiple modalities of treatment so that individualized treatment plans can be created for each individual; there need to be rewards for positive behaviors, which are proven to be more effective than negative punishments; at each level of security there need to be incremental phases wherein an incarcerated person who successfully works on their program can be advanced to higher levels of freedom and more amenities; there needs to be close collaboration between mental health and custody staff; and discipline must be handled in the context of that treatment collaboration, i.e., an incarcerated person enrolled in a mental health program must not be ejected from the program and sent to SHU for unacceptable behaviors, but rather must be disciplined within the mental health program where mental health staff have input in determining consequences for unacceptable actions.

Unfortunately, too often the very authentic mental disorders of incarcerated people are considered inauthentic by mental health staff who meet with them at cell-front for a few minutes, and then they are left to the punishments meted out by custody staff. At that point, once an incarcerated person with mental illness is consigned to isolated confinement, providing them with mental health treatment becomes just about impossible, and the isolation continues to worsen the mental illness.

Correctional mental health clinicians tend to focus exclusively on the need to keep incarcerated people with mental illness in isolation in the interest of "maintaining order," and they give too little attention to the psychological damage caused by the isolation. Research shows that super-maximum isolation units do not achieve the end of reduced prison violence.[11] In fact, studies conclude that downsizing supermax and segregated confinement while enhancing treatment and rehabilitation programming actually reduces violence in the prisons.[12]

8
Juveniles in Solitary

Chris recalls his first experience in solitary confinement, at the age of 12:

It's hard to remember what led to me being taken to solitary that first time, but what occurred there has been etched in my memory for eternity.

I was standing there – small, pale, and skinny – I couldn't have been more than 100 pounds. I remember feeling embarrassed and defeated, trying hard not to let it show. I had just been stripped of all my clothing, except my boxers, and I was yelling and screaming. I had to fight back, in some form, that's all I remember thinking. But the more I resisted, the more those guards tried to control me. This led to me being hogtied by the oversized guards. To me, at the time, they seemed large enough to be NFL players – giants next to my slim frame.

After they had achieved their goal of fully dominating me, I was left in the cold cell, laying on the dirty floor, breathing hard and crying. I was mad that I had become weak enough to let them see me cry – I knew better than to let bullies see me cry.

What seemed like hours later, my energy stripped from me, not a tear left in my eyes to be shed, and the guards returned. They asked if I was ready to follow the rules now. My ankles and wrists hurt from the restraints, and I was willing to say whatever they wanted for relief from the pain. All I kept thinking was that they had won this battle, but I would never be the same, and I would never trust anyone in a position of power again.

Released from the restraints, I stood up waiting for the clothing only they could provide. One of the large guards dropped my clothes on the floor and told me to hurry up and get dressed. I did as he said, refusing to make eye contact with him. I didn't want the guards to see the pain I felt, or the redness in my eyes from crying. When I stole a glance at them, I knew they thought they had won, but they had no clue what seeds they had planted in me.

While in various juvenile detention centers and institutions over the years, I struggled to develop the skills I needed to get my education on par with my grade level. Rehabilitation seemed to be an elusive monster I could never capture. A majority of my time was spent in survival mode; I was struggling to fit in with my peers and to deal with my issues trusting any figures of authority, after years of countless situations of mistreatment by people in positions of power.

These struggles often caused me to lash out, which resulted in disciplinary sanctions, including solitary confinement. This cycle only pushed me deeper into the isolation of only trusting myself. Each time this happened, my issues with authority figures became even more impossible to overcome. In my experience, they were an enemy I could never trust. It didn't matter if they seemed to be trying to help – in my mind, that was merely a trick to fool me into believing they were there to support me. This led to me building a towering wall – which I thought was for protection – so high that no one could penetrate it. I felt like the whole world was against me and that I alone had to protect myself. But living in a survivalist mindset makes it hard to build relationships and impossible to understand the harm you've caused. Your only focus is on the need to survive.

Accountability and rehabilitation are off the table. All your social interactions are overshadowed by this, and all previous experiences of trauma are pushed down and locked away in a tiny box hidden from the world and even from oneself.

The system was not always so hostile to juveniles. From the mid-1800s through the 1970s, the Age of Reform,[1] the system aspired to provide a place where juveniles could receive the education, mental health treatment, social skills, vocational training, and other rehabilitation services they would need to turn their lives around and become productive members of the community. Underpinning this emphasis on education and rehabilitation was the idea that youth prior to the age of 18, or even prior to age 25, were not fully formed human beings. In that context, their law-breaking and criminal proclivities were viewed as relatively transient and more amenable to correction than comparable criminality on the part of more seasoned adult law-breakers.

There is widespread consensus in the juvenile justice community that youth detention must focus mainly on rehabilitation and not punishment. As many professionals working with youth would be quick to testify, since youth are more amenable to change and transformation than older individuals, it makes sense to invest social resources into correcting their errant ways. Indeed, there are very many case histories of seemingly incorrigible youth spending time in juvenile facilities, meeting officers, teachers, and mentors who took an interest in them, and turning their lives around – and then leaving the juvenile system never to be involved further with the criminal legal system.

Tragically, even during the Age of Reform, there were many contrasting stories of inadequate rehabilitation and education in juvenile detention, often involving solitary confinement and sexual and physical abuse.

Although many states have laws precluding the placement of juveniles in solitary confinement or limiting solitary to a few hours (see Chapter 13: The Legal Boundaries of Solitude), the reality is that many are retained in solitary-like room confinement for prolonged periods, either in juvenile detention or in adult prisons if they were tried as adults. Solitary confinement can take the form of punitive segregation, but in a juvenile facility, it can also be given the innocuous-seeming name of "room confinement," as if a brief "time-out" can be utilized to help youth comport their behavior to the rules and participate productively in educational and rehabilitative pursuits. But "room confinement" too often morphs into solitary confinement, for example when the typical duration (usually two or four hours) is extended to days, weeks, or even months. When this occurs, there is very little opportunity for social engagement or to participate in educational or other similarly productive activities.

Kwaneta has confirmed the presence of juveniles in adult solitary confinement units in Texas:

> *I am perplexed to see teenagers, who are not old enough to buy beer and cigarettes, treated as grownups here. The majority of my neighbors in solitary were transferred from the Texas Juvenile Justice Department (TJJD) as teens to an adult prison. TJJD imprisons children as young as 10 years old. There, the innocuous euphemism for solitary confinement is "Security." Don't be fooled by the name. It isn't to protect an extremely vulnerable child. It's used as punishment.*
>
> *The reasons children are placed in isolation stem from immaturity, rather than deliberate so-called criminality. Youth swearing, disobedience, lying, being argumentative, insubordination, and "sexual deviancy" (being caught in bed together) are all major violations falling under the umbrella of "disrespectful behavior toward staff," which, along with assaults on staff and peers, are punishable with 30–45 days in Security at state youth prisons. Sometimes, youth return to the hole after less than 24 hours to begin a fresh 30 days.*[2]

Reports suggest that isolation is widespread in county youth facilities.[3] In 2017, reports about abusive conditions in a Dallas County facility described youth spending months and sometimes more than a year without going outdoors. Harris County's juvenile detention has also faced legal action for confining youth to their rooms for 23.5 hours per day.

Trauma is a huge problem in the juvenile justice system, both the traumas suffered prior to detention as well as the traumas of the experience in detention. Re-traumatization happens when individuals who have been previously traumatized (for example, from childhood physical or sexual abuse or parental inattention, or from violence in a low-income, inner-city neighborhood) experience a new trauma (for example, sexual assault or fights that are required to protect one's manhood or attain safety while in detention). The new trauma rekindles and exacerbates the prior trauma, and the current traumas become that much more damaging to mental stability.[4] Almost all youth in detention have serious and repeated prior traumas in their backgrounds. Youth who have been previously traumatized are very likely to suffer new and damaging traumas while incarcerated.

The multiply-traumatized juvenile is especially susceptible to re-traumatization during a stint in solitary confinement. Juveniles in solitary confinement, like adults in comparable conditions, develop massive free-floating anxiety that can trigger panic. Their thinking becomes increasingly disorganized, and they may experience paranoia. They become angry and then fearful that their anger will lead to more disciplinary problems and worse punishments. They have great trouble concentrating on a task, and they experience memory problems. If one is in an isolation cell, the activities that support sanity are reading and writing. But many incarcerated people in isolation who can read are unable to read effectively because of isolation-induced difficulty with concentration and memory.

To make matters worse, juveniles doing their time in adult prisons are especially susceptible to sexual victimization, which sadly, can lead to time in solitary "for their own protection."[5] It is well known that fair young men who cannot grow anything but "peach fuzz" on their faces are prime victims of rape and sexual abuse in adult prisons. Often staff collude in the sexual victimization of youth in adult facilities, or staff themselves are the perpetrators.

Research on brain development warns of immense psychiatric damage if juveniles are subjected to both physical and sexual abuse, along with solitary confinement, one of the worst imaginable scenarios.

The following first-hand accounts lay bare the devastating impact of solitary confinement on young people, revealing the fear, confusion, and lasting trauma of being stripped of human contact, often punished just for being children in an unforgiving system. These individuals recount experiences that no child should ever endure.

Raymond Williams, a state-raised kid with very little family support, survived several years in solitary confinement starting at the shocking age of 14:

> *The door slammed behind me. I looked across the room in confusion. This wasn't a cell; it couldn't be. There was no bed, no sink, and no toilet. There was a mattress thrown on the ground at the far end of the cell. And there was a smell. Sewage?*
>
> *I looked at the floor. It was different, covered in a rubbery material instead of the bare refined concrete I'd grown accustomed to in my cell. In the center of the room there was a barred grate over a hole in the floor. I realized with horror that the cell had a toilet after all. It was like something from medieval times.*
>
> *There is no polite way to tell this story. Imagine defecating through that barred grate in the middle of a floor. As disgusting as you imagine it, it's worse. Your waste doesn't simply fall through. It rests on top of the grate leaving you with a choice no human should be forced to make: Take the small individual squares of toilet paper they give you and push the feces through the grate into the hole, or live with the stench and horror of a log sitting in the middle of your floor like some unholy shrine. If you choose the former, like I did, you will want to be extra careful not to get any on your fingers. There is no sink to wash with, and the squares of toilet paper are perilously thin. Do not worry too much about what's left along the edges of the bars. Soon enough you will urinate, and if your aim is good enough, you can blast the remaining matter away.*
>
> *This was solitary in the Thurston County Juvenile Detention Facility in Olympia Washington in the 1990s. I was 14 years old.*[6]

Steven Nall survived five years in solitary confinement, starting when he was 17 years old:

> *I was 17 years old and 14 months into a 19-year prison sentence. I was currently in solitary confinement. Since I was so young, the guards made it their daily mission to pick on me to receive a reaction, as they knew I was always good for one given my anger issues and immaturity. In the last 14 months, I had been beaten physically and emotionally, was refused meals, showers, and my hour of recreation because I was antagonized to react by the guards.*
>
> *In the hole, I was only allowed five photos. I had 30 in my cell at the time. During a cell search, two guards took my photos and told me that I needed to mail 25 of them out. I told them that I did not have any pre-stamped envelopes to mail them out. One of the guards ripped my photos up right in front of me. Those photos were my only window to freedom and connection with my family, and the only thing I could call my own. At only 17 years old, my family was the one anchor I had to help stabilize me while in the wavering insanity that attacks the psyche of the juvenile mind in solitary confinement.*

After first being sent to solitary as a preteen, Chris Heeren basically grew up there. He became so accustomed to isolation that he purposely committed infractions in prison so that he would be sent back. And when he was released from prison, he longed to go back.

> *I started getting locked up in my pre-teens, the juvenile detention center that I grew up in kept its youth confined in one-man cells with nothing except for a book and bedding allowed in the cell. No pencils, no paper or mail allowed in the cell nor any extra clothes. For entertainment I used to write poems, spoken word, or music lyrics on my door using a bar of soap as my ink and the door as my paper. I was often placed on limited, which meant during work hours they took my mattress from me and my coveralls along with my book, leaving me with nothing in my cell except for a T-shirt,*

socks, and underwear. If you were well behaved, school was offered in the am.

The detention center wasn't meant to house us long term. Anyone sentenced to more than six months was sent up to JRA, which was the juvenile prison system. I was one of the few that grew up there, usually not even getting new charges but constantly adding to my time by fighting, which would land me another 30 days in there for a probation violation. People can adapt to anything, especially kids, and what I learned most from those experiences was that the system wasn't fair or designed to help me or rehabilitate me. It was a means of punishment. It was a source of mental abuse and physical torment. The other thing it taught me was that being locked up in isolation had a positive to it as well – there's no fear of violence when you're by yourself. Also, I learned that I was able to handle and deal with the worst the system could throw at me, and learning that at such a young age had an extremely negative effect on my mental health. It created a lack of fear of getting in trouble. For starters, the worst they had to offer didn't bother me as much as it should have, because I grew up in it. Also, the incentives to be good didn't hold much water because I saw them stripped from people for the smallest infractions. Isolation in juvenile detention not only prepared me for what awaited me in prison, but it cost me the chance to gain an education like the other kids locked up in juvenile detention received.

Later, before my 18th birthday, I was sentenced to 15 years and sent to the Washington State Penitentiary. This is scary for a kid. To make matters worse, during the first two weeks on the yard I saw someone assaulted in their cell, bad enough that they lost their teeth and the cell looked like a crime scene. I seen two staff assaults, a stabbing in the shower, and someone caught on fire. I thought I was accustomed to violence but I learned there's another level to it. I learned that if I wanted to survive I had to get used to it and be willing to do extreme violence when called upon.

I ended up doing 16 months in seg (solitary) when it was my turn to answer the call. This was in 2003. Isolation in the early days made me feel safe from the outside violence. It's a taboo in prison to ask to be in seg, so after that, my only other option was to get in trouble often and for serious stuff.

Before I knew it I'd done close to ten years of segregation out of the 13 years I was in prison. Not having regular people to talk to affected my communication skills and it cost me relationships more than once. Even worse, it made me awkward in crowded areas, which was a hard thing to overcome and contributed to me not feeling like I belonged on the streets, which made it easier to commit crimes. What is the point of being free if you feel awkward around people?

I felt nervous the whole five months I lasted on the streets – scared I'd mess up with my family, scared I'd not fit in with society or ever be comfortable around crowds. I breathed a breath of relief once I was back in county jail. I didn't hope to get caught or try to, and I didn't expect a life sentence, but I felt at home. The term they call it is "institutionalized," and it was even worse due to all the isolation time I spent in my younger days. Even now, in general population, I am in a single-man cell, isolated from people by my own choice. I can go to yard and day room to hang out with people and I do, but I feel most comfortable in my cell by myself.

The use of solitary confinement on juveniles reflects a system that has abandoned its commitment to rehabilitation in favor of punishment, despite overwhelming evidence that children are in a formative stage of development where rehabilitation and education can have a very positive effect. With brains still developing, juveniles are exquisitely vulnerable to the psychological and emotional devastation of solitary, typically emerging from isolation more traumatized than before. Instead of providing the support, education, and guidance necessary for growth and change, the system isolates and re-traumatizes them, setting them up for long-term harm.

9
Racism

When we asked Kwaneta, who is Black, if she could describe any instances of race discrimination that she endured during her eight and a half years in solitary, this is what she wrote us back, and within minutes:

Discrimination? Racism? Where to start?

On Dr MLK day, guards say "Happy James Earl Ray Day" (the man who assassinated MLK).

On Father's day, they say, "Black folks don't celebrate father's day, do they?"

I've been told, "You're pretty for a Black girl" or "You're smart for a Black girl."

In the parking lot I see pickup trucks with "Trump 2024" and "Dump Joe and the ho!" stickers, and Confederate flags on the back.

A guard too old to be working in here, called me "colored," but he just didn't know.

This county is overwhelmingly white and the guards have told me they've never been around a Black person until working here. According to the US census, Coryelle County, Texas is 57 percent incarcerated. There's tons of prisons here.

They touch my hair without asking, essentially petting me.

They ask why I don't have an American name.

They tell us the illegals are taking Black jobs.

They have tattoos that are considered STG if they were on an incarcerated man. Things like swastikas, 44, hh, lightning bolts. But you gotta look up Aryan Brotherhood, Aryan Circle and other hate groups. AB started inside Texas prisons.

We had a guard bragging about attending the insurrection. He didn't go in the Capitol but he was on the grounds showing off the photos to coworkers. This is the South and as such racism is overt. I guess that's best in a way because I know where they stand and that I can't go to them for help.

Me in particular: they get confused by battling stereotypes – do they hate me because I'm Black, a woman, or from the north? Some still call me "Yankee girl."

The Black guards are so desperate to prove they are not like us, often they mistreat us more.

It's the guards who self-identify as Redneck Rebels who have given me water, food, and pads when others refused.

The modern American prison system can be traced back to the ugly history of slavery.[1] Before the Civil War, jails in the South were mostly filled with white people. The slave owner did not need jails to discipline his slaves; he would whip them, starve them, rape family members, and sell off members of their family to other slave owners far enough away to cause destruction of the family. But after the Civil War, when Black people previously held as slaves were freed, especially during Reconstruction, the former slave owners searched for ways to keep Black people working in the fields without paying them wages.[2] So they created the Black Codes – laws in the South against loitering, vagrancy, panhandling, and such. Many of the

Black people who had recently been freed would run afoul of these clearly biased laws and be sent to prison.

Prisons, such as Angola State Prison in Louisiana, had vast cotton fields where incarcerated people were forced to toil very long hours. Soon, prison wardens started leasing out Black incarcerated people to work for former slave owners, who would put them to work in fields and houses they or their relatives had been enslaved in prior to the Civil War. Many former slaves would actually find themselves again working for their former owners and for no pay. The plantation owners would merely pay a fee to the prison for the lease of their convicts.

The plight of the leased Black field worker would often be even worse than it had been during slavery. A slave owner might beat and whip a slave, rape enslaved women, and destroy slave families, but working the slave to death would destroy his investment in the slave as chattel. But after the Emancipation Proclamation of 1863 and the Thirteenth Amendment passed in 1865, plantation owners beat many former slaves, now their leased workers, to death. Then the former slave owner merely returned to the prison warden and complained that the incarcerated person leased to him was defective because he had died. The contrite warden would simply lease the plantation owner another Black person at no additional cost.

Meanwhile, in the years leading up to the Civil War, "slave patrols" were formed to arrest runaway slaves and return them to their owners. The slave patrols would travel to the north and capture Blacks who they alleged were owned by a slaveholder – whether or not that was true, and often it was not[3] – and a large number of previously freed slaves would be returned to their owners in the South and wind up in slavery again. The slave patrols of the antebellum South would eventually morph into police operations. In fact, after the Civil War many of the same "officers" would turn from hunting and arresting runaway slaves to enforcing the Black Codes, arresting freed slaves for vagrancy and the like. Some scholars go so far as to say that this was the true origin of the twentieth-century police force.[4] The Black Codes lasted well into the third decade of the 20th century and then merged seamlessly into the Jim Crow segregationist laws and abusive police practices that would hold sway in the South until the Civil Rights Act of 1964. The cruel history of slavery, the Black Codes, slave patrols, the prison lease system, and Jim Crow were precedents for our contemporary drama of policing and mass incarceration.

The Thirteenth Amendment, ratified on December 6, 1865, abolished slavery and involuntary servitude, "except as a punishment for a crime whereof the party shall have been duly convicted." There are pending lawsuits challenging this exception to the Thirteenth Amendment.[5] For example, Colorado's state constitution bans slavery even for those who have been convicted of a crime and are serving time in prison. However, in clear violation of the State Constitution, the Colorado DOC punishes incarcerated people who refuse to work at their assigned jobs by consigning them to restrictions that constitute solitary confinement even while the DOC does not label their program solitary confinement. Similar litigation and bills before state legislators challenge the Thirteenth Amendment's exception for individuals convicted of a crime.

Robert Hillary "King" King, one of the Angola Three,[6] who was unfairly consigned to solitary confinement at Angola State Prison in Louisiana for over 30 years, provides a horrifying account of the conviction that first led to his incarceration.

It was 1970 in New Orleans. A robbery had been committed by two Black men. One, Wortham Jones Jr., was captured and pleaded guilty. His accomplice in the crime was described by a female crime victim as approximately 45 years old and Black. King was 28.

At King's trial, the prosecution called Wortham as a witness, certain he would identify King as his accomplice in the crime. Instead, and very much a surprise to the prosecutor, Wortham testified that he had never seen King before in his life, and that King had nothing to do with the robbery. He explained that at the police station, when faced with a line-up, he felt he had to identify someone to help with his defense. King had been arrested for something else he had not done, was in the line-up, and Jones randomly identified him as his accomplice in the robbery. After Wortham Jones's testimony, King recollects:

> *I was tense with anticipation, knowing I would be freed ... With the jury seated, the judge asked if they had reached a verdict. "Yes, your honor," replied the foreman. "Well," said the judge – smiling all the while – "let the court hear the verdict." The foreman said, "We, the jury, find the defendant guilty as charged." I sat there, transfixed with awe, terrified at the abuse of power I had just witnessed. The feeling then changed to indignation. I focused my anger on the jury. How could they, I thought, after all the evidence to the contrary? I then saw what "friend of the court" really meant. I learned what the district attorney had known all along. He knew he had a jury who, in the majority, were friends of the court ... I sat there in the aftermath, bathed in revulsion, while the prosecutor shook the hand of each individual juror, grinning like a wolf while doing so; the judge, from his bench, thanked them for doing such a "splendid job," a broad smile etched on his face.*[7]

Recall Albert Woodfox, another member of the Angola Three who spent his 42 years in solitary confinement on the same fabricated charges that landed King in solitary. In the gripping and profound autobiography he wrote after finally being released, *Solitary: My Story of Transformation and Hope*, he comments:[8]

> *Racism today isn't as blatant as it was 44 years ago, but it is still here, underground, coded. We have to make changes that are deeper, as a society. Without roots, nothing can grow. The systemic hatred of a human being based on his or her skin color or hair texture or cultural heritage or gender or sexual preference is pointless. These are trivial things; we are more alike than we are unlike ... Can we shift the focus of our insecurities, fears, and anger from other races and work together to deal with the unfair distribution of wealth on this planet?*[9]

It is extraordinarily impressive how Robert Hillary King and Alfred Woodfox could emerge from 32 and 42 years, respectively, of unfair solitary confinement, so free of resentment and clear in their vision of a better, less racist future. It is a testament to the way a passionate commitment to the struggle for freedom can keep people sane in a torturous environment like solitary confinement.

To this day, Black people are disproportionately stopped and frisked by police in their communities, charged with more serious crimes, more often convicted, and meted out harsher sentences compared with their white counterparts. "Three strikes" sentencing guidelines as well as the death penalty are disproportionately applied to Blacks by the courts. And that is why Black people are vastly overrepresented in jails and prisons, compared to their number in the population, making up approximately 13 percent of the population, but well over 40 percent of incarcerated people.[10] Latino people and Native Americans are similarly overrepresented in jails and prisons, and thus as one enters a jail or prison one likely sees an overwhelming proportion of the population who are People of Color. It is shocking, for example, to visit Angola State Prison in Louisiana or the State Penitentiary ("Parchman Farm") in Parchman, Mississippi, and to see vast cotton fields where hundreds of Black men in state-issued striped prison garb are sweating profusely and destroying their hands as they pick cotton, overseen by guards on horseback carrying shotguns across their laps. One has the sense one is on an antebellum slave plantation.

Inside prisons, the same disproportionate treatment unsurprisingly prevails, as Black people and other People of Color are disproportionately consigned to solitary confinement.[11] For example, a 2015 study by the Association of State Correctional Administrators and Yale Law School revealed that in California, although Latinos only made up 42 percent of the general prison population, they made up 86 percent of the people housed in solitary confinement.[12] A 2016 national survey of US prisons revealed that non-white people were 30 percent more likely to be consigned to solitary than their white counterparts, even when controlling for the type of rule violation.[13]

The link between race and solitary confinement is well-documented.[14] A 2021 in-depth survey yielding data from 33 states shows that the racial composition of solitary confinement typically does not reflect that of the larger prison population:[15] In 22 of those 33 states, the percentage of Black men who spent time in solitary was higher than the number in general population;[16] in 18 of these jurisdictions, Latinos were overrepresented.[17] Statistics such as these demonstrate that the trend is not due to chance.

Ultimately, the root cause of these outcomes is likely stereotypes used in calculations by prison officials who are exercising their discretion regarding whether an incarcerated person is acting out or being insubordinate. When corrections officers and staff have the discretionary power to send people to solitary for the smallest of violations, there is often no way to confirm the infractions. This discretionary use of solitary confinement[18] can unfairly target minority groups.

Research demonstrates that there is a racist sentiment among white guards in certain facilities, which directly translates to increased violence and write-ups of non-white incarcerated people. In a breakdown of assault charges in the New York State prison system from 2015, 61 percent of the 1,028 violations belonged to Black men, while only 9 percent belonged to white men. Concerningly, an incarcerated person need not cause an injury or even touch an officer for their behavior to constitute an assault, granting guards immeasurable discretion in their determinations. Incarcerated people note that racism is very prevalent in these facilities – guards regularly provoke altercations that are classified as assaults, including taunting them with racial slurs or touching them inappropriately during a pat-frisk. The numbers support this: overall, Black men were punished seven times as often for pat-frisk infractions as white men, and among incarcerated people under 25, Black people received 185 tickets, while their white counterparts got only 14. Incarcerated people recall racist and prejudicial statements from guards such as one who threatened to "beat the black" off an incarcerated person, and another provoking an incarcerated person with the line "monkeys don't wear glasses." Deeply ingrained racist ideology coupled with seemingly unchecked power results in these racial disparities.

A leading theory about what accounts for the racial disparity of people in solitary is the racial makeup of the corrections officers, as well as their racial biases. Authors of an investigation by the

New York Times cite research which supports the conclusion that the racial demographics of the guards contribute to the disparities in terms of who is sent to solitary.[19] From their study, researchers concluded that Black people in New York prisons were 65 percent more likely to be sent to solitary confinement than white people. Further analysis revealed that for every 100 Black incarcerated people, guards issued 56 violations for disobeying orders, compared with 32 for every 100 white incarcerated people. This was found for smoking and drug offenses in particular, which require physical evidence, white incarcerated people were only issued about a third of the tickets. In prisons where white prison guards have complete control over Black incarcerated people and other incarcerated People of Color, and where some of these guards have KKK tattoos visible to Black incarcerated people on their wrists, it becomes clear how racial bias in the discretionary issuing of disciplinary write-ups leads to a disproportionate number of Blacks in punitive segregation.

Examples of this phenomenon can be found throughout prisons in New York State. At Clinton Correctional, a maximum-security prison in New York, only a staggeringly small 0.1 percent of guards are African-American, whereas Sing Sing, another maximum-security facility, boasts 83 percent guards of color. (The average percentage of Black or Latino prison staff members in the entire New York State prison system lies between these two extremes, at 17 percent.) At Clinton, with the lowest number of Black and Brown guards, Black incarcerated people were nearly four times as likely to be sent to isolation as white incarcerated people, and they were held there for an average of 125 days, compared with 90 days for white incarcerated people. Conversely, these patterns do not exist at Sing Sing.[20] The difference in staff racial identity is in large part due to the fact that NYC and other urban areas contain a substantial number of Black residents, whereas the more rural environment of the Clinton facility is mostly white, so Blacks are more likely to apply to join the staff at Sing Sing than at Clinton.

A related explanation of these findings is rooted in the treatment of suspected gang members. Gangs provide a rationale for solitary confinement – more robustly in some states than in others. Since gangs are racialized (it's the Aryan Brotherhood for white men, the Black Guerilla Family for Black men, and the Mexican Mafia or Nuestra Familia for Latino people), the "Snitch, Parole, or Die" validation process for determining gang membership (discussed in Chapter 4: Who Gets Sent to the Hole) is also racialized. Prison gangs don't keep membership lists, so security staff are left to make informed guesses about who is in a gang. The decision is often based on nothing more than race, fanning the racism that permeates the prison culture.

Thus, a representative guard population can combat the implicit and explicit racism present in the prison systems, specifically in solitary confinement. Where guards "see the men as less 'foreign,'" as one person described the workers at Sing Sing, this mindset is reflected by a more equal distribution of violations and less abuse of subjective power. In prisons where the staff is more diverse and representative, incarcerated people report feeling more understood and seen, and the numbers demonstrate a more equal assignment of violations and infractions.

10

Sexual Assault and Gender-Based Injustices in the Hole

> For those who have endured the double cruelty of sexual violence and solitary confinement – who have been forced to heal from trauma in the very place designed to break their spirit. This chapter stands as witness to your strength. May your stories ignite the change that transforms how society treats the most vulnerable among us.

My stomach unleashed a deafening growl upon hearing the roll and rattle of an approaching food cart. Having spent the previous three out of 14 days in isolation punishment at the Texas Department of Criminal Justice, I was famished. Up until that point, my meals had consisted solely of two bologna sandwiches.

A male officer's face appeared at my cell door and smiled menacingly through the metal mesh grate as he opened the slot where the sandwiches are usually dropped, but today he produced a hot tray. Two steak-and-cheese-stuffed burritos from the officers' dining hall sat in front of me, the prison equivalent of a five-star meal. My stomach roared in agreement to the aroma, then dropped as I heard the officer utter his demand.

"Get naked and dance for me and you can have it," he sneered. Gaping at him, disbelief and hunger shone in my eyes as he added, "Or get nothing at all." So I ate my fill that day, burning in shame.

– Lanae Tipton (currently serving her second year in solitary confinement)

Sexual abuse is a huge problem in both women's and men's prisons and is exacerbated in solitary confinement. Most often the perpetrators are male staff. When the abuser is a member of staff, the abuse is termed "custodial sexual abuse."[1] It is very difficult to determine precisely how pervasive such abuse is because most of it goes unreported. The reasons for underreporting are complex, and there are many variables, but what stands out most is fear of retaliation on the part of the perpetrator or of other staff. Very many incarcerated women report such fears, including the fear that they will be consigned to solitary confinement, even if officially it is for their "protection."

Lanae Tipton, who was forced to dance naked for a meal, says that for women sexual abuse is pervasive. Many women will do whatever they can to stay out of solitary confinement. She gives this example:

> *Angela was two months away from going home after almost 15 years of imprisonment. She was so close to freedom when she was suddenly forced to defend herself against an attack by her roommate. After the altercation, Angela faced a disciplinary infraction that could jeopardize her release. When she explained to the investigating officer that her impending freedom was on the line, he offered her an ultimatum: to prove how bad she wanted to go home, she needed to perform a sexual favor. Otherwise, he would see to it that she was disciplined for getting into a fight, and therefore risk postponing her release. Angela is now home with her children.*

Many women describe their dread that, were they to report harassment or abuse, the guard who abused them, or his colleagues, would subsequently write a bogus disciplinary report and, as a punishment, they would be sent to solitary confinement and denied visits with their children. Given the "Hobson's Choice" of losing contact with their children or allowing the perpetrator of sexual abuse to go unpunished, they choose to retain visits with their children. In the cases of quite a few women who have grieved sexual abuse by a particular guard, an investigation followed, after which it was determined that there was insufficient evidence to find the guard guilty. Subsequently, that guard feels like he can approach the woman who is grieved and have his way with her with impunity.

Custodial sexual abuse in prison occurs in a cultural context of misogyny that supports or even encourages it.[2] This culture of misogyny is created and reinforced in myriad ways, such as the names grown incarcerated women are called by guards acting unprofessionally (e.g., Marissa Potts reports that her work group in her Texas medium custody unit is called the "ho squad" and she has been designated the "lead ho"), the lewd propositions they hear, and pat-down searches that take a little too long, especially those where the guard lingers over sensitive areas. In most women's prisons, guards are required to conduct a certain number of pat-down searches each shift. For example, because incarcerated people are often suspected of smuggling fruit out of the dining hall for use in their cells later in making "pruno," a prisoner-manufactured alcoholic beverage, staff pat-down women leaving the dining hall. Male staff grope and maul them in the name of pat searches, setting the stage for rape and other forms of sexual abuse. Incarcerated women report that guards perform many more of these mandated pat searches on young, good-looking women, and older women are much less frequently searched. The staff are evolving a culture of misogyny where sexual abuse can easily follow.

In the 1990s, both Human Rights Watch and Amnesty International published reports reflecting the widespread occurrence of sexual abuse in women's prisons.[3] Prior to these two groundbreaking reports, little was known about sexual abuse in women's prisons. There was widespread shock among the public as newspapers began to cover these reports, and around the same time there were a number of lawsuits that exposed the omnipresence of sexual abuse and rape in women's prison. In most of these cases, the perpetrators were correctional staff.[4]

In 2003, President George W. Bush signed into law the Prison Rape Elimination Act (PREA), outlining required steps in all jails and prisons to reduce the prevalence of sexual abuse and sexual harassment in jails and prisons. Subsequently, as mandated by PREA, there were hearings of the Prison Rape Elimination Commission about the proper implementation of the PREA requirements.

In 2012, Attorney General Eric H. Holder approved the national PREA Standards that originated in the Commission's deliberations.[5] The standards begin with a proclamation of zero tolerance for sexual abuse and harassment in jails and prisons, and direct all correctional administrations to report prohibited activities, protect women from abuse from custodial misconduct, provide confidential reporting mechanisms, adjudicate complaints of abuse from incarcerated people, and establish adequate assessment and treatment of women survivors of sexual abuse and harassment (both medical and psychiatric). The measures put in place in accordance with the standards and the instructions for filing a confidential complaint must be posted prominently in all jails and prisons.

In spite of robust attempts on the part of some correctional authorities and departments to comply with the federal PREA Standards, "staff-on-inmate" sexual abuse continues to be prevalent in women's prisons. In fact, 2023 reports of widespread sexual abuse at the Federal Correctional Institution for Women in Dublin, California (FCI Dublin), revealed that one of the main perpetrators of sexual abuse in the facility was the warden, who was also the prison's designated trainer for PREA. He, the prison's chaplain, and quite a few guards have subsequently been convicted of multiple felonies.[6]

Kwaneta provides a glimpse of the typical experience of trying to take a shower in solitary confinement:

> *At 3:15 am, both my walls vibrate from my neighbors banging to awaken me. My brain is foggy as I remember which guards are working. I want to shower today, so I must get in the right mental state to prepare. I begin by self-soothing and focusing on how good it will feel to wash my hair and body not using a sink. I love to shower but it's much more complicated than it sounds. Certain conditions must all be present to shower. Who's working? Who's escorting us to the shower? Which shower is working the best? No person in solitary confinement showers daily or even weekly.*
>
> *The reasons people don't shower vary. Many women, like my neighbor Lulu, have told me it's a defense mechanism – when it's clean, they take it, meaning that when she washes her genital area, guards will take that as an invitation to violate her. Once I overheard guards threatening to write-up a person for masturbating. This got my attention because I knew these were the type of guards who ordered women to "play wit it fo me." One guard, disgusted by*

Lulu's smell, said, "Next time she don't shave and wash it first, I'm writing her up."

This is the best time to take a birdbath. But just in case, I ask the dorm to give me "ojos" (Spanish word for eyes). Women stand at their cell door watching the tier for guards who like to hold their keys so we can't hear them approach and knock down our makeshift curtains to leer at us on the toilet or washing our body. I use two new Kotex pads to sweep my floor. We aren't allowed brooms or chemicals even in general population. Usually, the staff is too busy after lunch to knock down my makeshift curtain covering my door's viewing window. I fill my teapot with water to heat because only the cold water works in the sink. Using the sticky label from the deodorant, I cover the sink's drain. I dump the heated water in with a squirt of body wash. Refill the teapot twice more and pour the hot water in the sink. I remove all my clothes and using a big bowl I wet sections of my body, lather, and rinse with a bowlful of sink water. I do my entire body twice. Refilling the sink twice with warm teapot water and adding cold water until the temperature is tepid. Then, I pour the bowl over my hair, a beachball curly afro appears and I lather and rinse three times each before adding conditioner, rinsing, and blow drying it straight. None of the haircare products sold at the prison store are for Black people's hair. The floor is soaked. When I'm finished, I mop my floor by using my contraband bath towel (I purchased it for a ramen soup) to scoot the water out my cell onto the tier. I apply lotion and deodorant, and brush my teeth again.

The following morning at 6 am the orange girl (her face, hair, and white prison uniform were stained orange, courtesy of tear gas) ignores our warnings and demands a shower. She must remain sitting up, not laying down with the lights on, until they come to escort her to the shower. Four hours later, a female guard orders her to strip. Two male guards stand slightly aside swearing they can't see her and that they don't want to see her. Female guards are rare and she's quickly off to the next dorm. Orange girl only wears a gown and is handcuffed in the back. The narrow steps mean that one guard trails behind and usually rubs his genitalia against cuffed hands, while the other walks slowly, "accidentally" grabbing your breast with your arm.

The showers are coffin-sized with a decorative vent cover without any actual ventilation. There are only three showers for 44 people. One is cold 24/7 as the decontamination, emergency shower. One we call the prostate shower because it has no pressure and is scalding hot (we gave it that nickname after hearing radio ads for medication for people with an enlarged prostate and a "slow dribbling urine stream"). The last shower is scalding hot with a clogged showerhead so there are only two tiny holes of spray. The water is on a 90-second button timer that must be pressed over and over. The water is so hot, you can't stand directly under it. You must use your washcloth and wet it then wave it to cool it.

The door is locked and the handcuff/food slot is left open for air (and to peek). It's common to see a guard peeking through the viewing window leering. Then using his index finger to motion a circle to turn around.

In solitary, sexual abuse takes many forms. There is the "grooming," where a guard acts friendly and inquires about a woman's kids or tells her he likes her or brings her gifts. There are frequent inappropriate sexual innuendos. There are moments where a male guard stands outside a woman's cell peering through the small window in the cell door while the woman undresses or uses the toilet. There are deceptively friendly seeming pats on the buttocks. There are the inappropriate "pat searches," discussed above. Or guards conduct "strip searches," where women are stripped and guards conduct intrusive cavity explorations, presumably in an effort to find contraband drugs or weapons (ironically, most of the contraband drugs found in prisons are brought in by staff, who are not searched when they enter the facility each day). Pat searches and "counts" (guards checking at frequent intervals on the whereabouts of incarcerated people) are necessary parts of the prison regimen, but there are too many opportunities, especially in solitary, for an officer to peer lasciviously at women who are undressed or partially clad, or to touch a woman inappropriately.

Because of the level of sexual and physical abuse in their backgrounds, some incarcerated women are less able to know when their boundaries are being violated or when they are being harassed or disrespected. Often they remain confused about who was responsible for the sexual assaults in their past (children tend to think that the bad things that happen to them are their own fault, that way, they think, they can change their behavior and avoid future abuse, but if it is the fault of an evil step-father or other male, there is nothing they can do to make the abuse end). Because of the guilt, shame, and diminished self-esteem of early and repeated boundary violations, they do not have the confidence to give a clear message to halt during the early stages of an evolving sexual assault, privacy invasion, or violation of bodily integrity. Rather, they are just as likely to partially dissociate, become passive and let the abuse develop without angrily protesting. The offending staff take this as a signal, not of consent, but rather that this woman is unlikely to submit a grievance or sound an alarm when he assaults her, and consequently he may more confidently continue to make demeaning comments or move ahead with the evolving sexual assault. In fact, staff who repeatedly abuse and take advantage of incarcerated women tend to be very attuned to this pattern, so much so that they identify newly admitted women who are vulnerable and single them out for sexual assault.

In general population, women are threatened with solitary if they don't comply with the sexual abuse of guards. And if they report abuse, they are sent to seg "for their own protection." In solitary, women are punished in other ways if they complain or report the abuse. The most common thing guards do to coerce women into sexual acts is to write bogus tickets for those who won't comply. The tickets can mean cutting off visits with children and loved ones. They also cut the woman off from her in-prison support network. And phony charges leveled against them can also be used to extend their time in solitary and ultimately affect their sentences. Resisting sexual abuse or filing a complaint often results in further abuse, and most women do not think the inevitable retaliation is worth it.

In solitary confinement, women often have to choose between succumbing to sexual violence or being denied basic human rights. It is not uncommon for a guard to withhold food and other necessities unless women take their shirts off or worse. Kwaneta explains: "Just as I write this, a guard ignored a young girl's request for water. She removed her shirt and bra and he immediately got her some cold water." A common refrain you might hear from young guards is "Sho something! Fo' something!" which leads young women to perform strip dancing contests in rec cages for prizes such as a stick of gum. Kwaneta describes how women simply accept the abuse and often don't even see this type of behavior as improper:

> *"Raise your hand if you've ever been sexually abused while in prison" I say to a group of about 30 women living with me here in solitary confinement. A few people tentatively hang their arms out of their cells facing the four outdoor rec cages to indicate a "yes" response.*
>
> *"Ok, how many of you have ever had a guard watch you on the toilet or watch you take a shower?" All hands go up. "Of course!"*
>
> *"Have you ever taken your shirt off when a guard came by with the food cart so that you wouldn't get passed by for a meal?" Collective groans. "Yes!"*
>
> *"How many of you have experienced a guard knock your makeshift covering from the viewing window on your door while you were changing your pad or tampon and then just remain standing there making trivial conversation?" Everyone calls out in recognition.*
>
> *"While escorting you, has a guard ever rubbed his genitals against your handcuffed hands?" All hands go up.*

"Have you ever been called cunts, bitches and ho's by guards?" Lots of laughter. People hit the walls with handheld mirrors or bare hands in agreement.*

Finally, "how many of you have a prison 'boyfriend?'" Every woman younger than 25 raises her hand.

"That's all sexual abuse," I tell them.

Sexual voyeurism, sexual intrusion, and sexual assault in women's prisons are so rampant that they are experienced by essentially every person in here, almost on a daily basis. However, the women I was questioning did not think of certain conduct by prison guards as abuse, either because they believe they consented, because they weren't beaten or raped, or because the behaviors have become so normalized that they believe it's simply an inevitable part of their incarceration.

How do I convince these young women that such common behaviors by guards constitute abuse?

I am still haunted by an act performed by my neighbor in order to save my life, which may sound extreme but is unfortunately not that uncommon. I have a peanut allergy, which can be deadly in solitary confinement because our 24-hour medical clinic is several buildings away and nobody has an EpiPen in the hole. People living in general population are permitted to keep non-habit-forming prescribed medication like Benadryl in their possession, but in isolation, all medications are dispensed only by a med tech.

Our meals arrive in solitary pre-made, so I can never be sure if there will be traces of peanut butter on my food. Once, when I felt that familiar tingle on my lips, I banged on the door to alert my neighbors (we have an in-cell emergency button that hasn't worked since Clinton was in office). As the word spread, everyone was banging on their doors with cups and yelling out their windows. When a guard finally came, he walked right by my door.

My neighbor Lay-Lay called him to her door to tell him I needed Benadryl. Then, I heard the unmistakable bang of the food tray slot in her door open. The guard was pressed against the door as Lay-Lay fished his penis out and briefly performed oral sex with a promise to finish once he returned with the Benadryl. My back was itching and my eyes were puffy when he threw a handful of Benadryl pills wrapped in toilet paper through my door gap on his way to Lay-Lay's door. I will always be eternally grateful to Lay-Lay for saving my life. But, I will never forgive the system for putting her on her knees to do it.[7]

Another all-too-common reality involves "grooming." Newly arrived young pretty women are groomed to find a guard as a nice "boyfriend." The trick is to avoid the mean boyfriends who are renowned for demanding extreme sexual acts for their amusement. For example, Alexis, an 18-year-old who was transferred from youth to adult solitary, had a boyfriend guard who played her against her friend by encouraging both to compete for his attention by performing sexual favors. After he chose the friend, Alexis committed suicide. Sadly, young women arriving from juvenile prisons (often as young as 16) are typically already groomed. They enter prison assuming everything like requesting a shower or tampons is transactional, the transaction being about sexual favors. The worst indignity is that these young women are often eventually written up for having an improper relationship with a guard.

Over the years Kwaneta has heard countless stories of violent rapes and arbitrary beatings:

A recent example that I've seen happen far too many times: My neighbor Elizabeth was left with two black eyes and stitches to her right temple after she rejected the sexual advances of a guard here in solitary. Usually when staff flirted she ignored them but this time she said it didn't work. She found herself the focus of two male security staff and had to choose between them. In exchange for a relationship, the chosen guard helped her mother financially until he was terminated and escorted off the prison grounds. Liz's punishment was a disciplinary infraction: Establishing an inappropriate relationship. The rejected guard didn't take her decision well, and in February 2024, she says he beat her up. After she followed the protocol and filed a grievance that included nine witness statements, an investigation determined her "allegations were unsubstantiated." Shortly after the alleged assault, Liz was charged with "Assault of a Public Servant." This charge carries a sentence enhancement of 25 years to life. As word spread by some staff that Liz assaulted the rejected guard, the witnesses asked, "How could she? Her hands were handcuffed behind her back before she exited her cell, per policy."

People here call me Mama Detroit. As a former nurse and someone who has been incarcerated for a long time, I am like a mother to many young women trying to survive solitary and I do what I can for them. After more than eight years in the hole, I am still deeply disturbed by what I witness on a daily basis and I feel an obligation to report abuse. But then I remember, "Who the hell am I supposed to tell?"[8]

Of course, not all staff sexually abuse incarcerated women. In fact, there are many exceptions to the culture of misogyny. For example, quite a few women report that the only way they survived imprisonment was with the support and encouragement of women staff members. But staff who take a stand against custodial sexual abuse, disproportionately women staff, face severe retaliation themselves. A female CO who was brave and ethical enough to speak out about ongoing sexual abuse at FCI Dublin recently stated in a news clip, "the way they [male guards] referred to them [incarcerated females], they are 'bitches,' … um, those are the nicer terms that they used."[9] She continued, "When we leave, these sexually abused women are left here alone with these perpetrators … 90% of these women have serious trauma in their backgrounds." She had tried to report abusive guards, and said in the newscast that not only was nothing done, but she was punished for reporting the sexual abuse. "I got called into my supervisor's office, for the first time in 25 years. I got a letter of reprimand." After she made public statements about the ongoing abuse, she was abruptly transferred to a federal prison in another state. Another female correction officer at FCI Dublin, who spoke during the same newscast said, "We've been reporting this stuff for years, and they still work there."

In men's prisons, sexual assault is similarly pervasive and deeply entrenched. Incarcerated males generally ascribe to an exaggerated notion of masculinity and put a lot of energy into establishing their dominant station in a cruel and violent dominance hierarchy on the prison yard.[10] Ambiguity in gender identification is not tolerated, with weak, feminized men at the bottom of the pile.[11] An incarcerated person who does not fit the mold of a "real man" is likely to be attacked and raped.

Trans women are at extraordinarily high risk of sexual abuse and rape in male prisons. A California study concludes 59 percent of trans women in California's men's prisons are subjected to sexual abuse and rape, and that figure is an underestimate because many trans women do not report sexual abuse for fear of retaliation or consignment to solitary confinement.[12] Trans women routinely seek transfer to women's prisons where they would feel safer, but prison authorities typically insist they remain in men's prisons claiming that they would pose a security risk in women's prisons. Now, the Trump regime's mandate that transgender individuals be housed according to the sex assigned to them at birth, makes transfer impossible. In men's prisons, they are raped by a man, for example a cellmate they were forced to share a cell with but did not select, or they are housed in solitary "for their own protection," exposing them to all the harms discussed above.

Dr. Kupers testified on behalf of a trans woman who was locked up in Folsom Prison for Men in California. The CDCR required that she be housed in a men's prison because she was pre-operative.[13] In other words, she still had male genitalia even though in every other way she was a woman and had been for years. Because of crowding, she was required to share a cell with a man. A tough incarcerated male "talked nice" to her and convinced her to "cell with him." But as soon as she was locked into the cell with him, his personality changed. He became angry and controlling. He began to grope her and then he raped her repeatedly. She complained to a guard who responded to her complaint, "What's the matter, you like dick!"

Rather than being offered meaningful protection, people at risk of sexual assault or rape are often placed in solitary confinement "for their own safety," where they face a new range of severe risks. Trans women are often denied hormone therapy and other necessary gender-affirming care while in solitary, exacerbating gender dysphoria and mental distress. In addition, once they're placed in solitary "for protection," they may remain there indefinitely, especially if there are no alternative housing options or if guards view them as a continued risk in general population. As in women's prisons, isolation removes incarcerated people from witnesses, making them more vulnerable to abuse by guards, including physical violence, sexual assault, and harassment. In many cases, solitary confinement functions less as a protective measure and more as an additional form of punishment, worsening the harm already experienced by LGBTQ+ individuals in the prison system.

11

Environmental Injustice and Its Effect on Solitary

Recently, Chris woke up at 5 am, coughing:

It felt like I'd smoked a pack of cigarettes the night before. Careful not to awaken my cellmate, I climbed off my top bunk, found my cup on the shelf, and made my way to the bathroom to get some water. Still groggy, I wondered if I was getting sick. But then I remembered the wildfires.

They had been burning out of control for several days in the area surrounding the prison. Smoke had rolled in both from the city of Spokane to the east and from Canada to the north. That morning, it was too dark outside to see if the sky was still hazy, but the unmistakable smell of smoke was enough to tell me things were not good.

By now, itchy eyes and a burning throat are familiar sensations to people all over the country, whether inside or outside prison. We've all been forced to contend with an ever-expanding wildfire season and the devastating air quality that accompanies it. But unlike people in the free world, those of us who are incarcerated have very little control over our physical environments. We're usually trapped in poorly ventilated buildings. We cannot purchase air purifiers to make our living space more habitable. We cannot flee to somewhere safer for the weekend. And as the smoky air fills our lungs, one question lingers: If we get caught in the path of raging flames, what will be the plan for those of us locked behind bars? And what will happen to those hidden away in solitary confinement?

When Hurricane Katrina hit Louisiana almost two decades ago, guards in a New Orleans jail panicked.[1] With no guidance from management or the state and a rapidly worsening storm building around them, they abandoned hundreds of incarcerated people in their cells while floodwaters rose, forcing them to drink the putrid water that seeped into their cells.[2] Back then, it was an exception. Now, such scenarios are happening with increased frequency around the country.

Climate experts predict that climate change will continue to cause larger, more frequent, and more devastating impacts that will test the limits of our social and ecological systems. Prisons are already at that limit. Even without climate change, prisons around the country have billions of dollars worth of deferred maintenance just to stop the walls from crumbling and keep the lights and the heat on. Now, climate change is turning already miserable conditions inside of prisons into life-threatening ones.[3]

During the record-breaking heat waves of recent years, prisons in the usually temperate Pacific Northwest were overwhelmed. Incarcerated people were trapped in cells that reached up to 114 degrees Fahrenheit (45 degrees Celsius) with no air-conditioning and no fans, covering themselves with cool washcloths and lying on the concrete floor to avoid heat stroke. During this time, floods devastated prisons in Dixie County, Florida, leaving incarcerated individuals stuck in ankle-deep, fetid water with human waste swirling around in it.[4] All the while, wildfires ripped through California, leaving several prisons without power for a month – shutting down ventilation systems, access to cooked food, and multiple other necessities.[5]

Often located in remote, rural communities, frequently on brownfields or near Superfund sites, prisons are dangerously underprepared for the increasingly severe impacts of climate change – but they're uniquely susceptible to them. According to The Intercept's analysis of 6,500 prisons, jails, and detention facilities across the US, half of all prisons will be in places with more than ten days annually over 105 degrees Fahrenheit (40 degrees Celsius) by 2100,[6] and 621 facilities have major-to-extreme flood risk.[7] The same analysis showed that at least 54 jails, prisons, and detention centers nationwide holding more than 1,000 people are already above the 95th percentile for wildfire risk,[8] meaning that they will, sooner or later, be forced to evacuate.

As the planet continues to warm as a result of climate change, conditions in prisons, and specifically in oppressive solitary confinement housing, continue to worsen. For now, heat waves – already the deadliest climate hazard worldwide – are also the biggest hazard for prisons. Shortly after the Texas Senate denied funding that would have seen air-conditioning installed in all prisons in Texas, the state was hit with another heat wave, and the heat index soared to 120 degrees Fahrenheit (49 degrees Celsius) in some prisons, trapping thousands of people in inhumanely hot cells.[9]

"The tablet is malfunctioning due to the heat. Soda pops are spontaneously exploding," Kwaneta explained from solitary confinement during one such heat wave. "Two girls had seizures, a guard fainted, and I have had a dizzying headache. It's horrible." At least 41 people died in Texas prisons between June and August 2023; experts say most of those deaths were heat-related.[10]

Kwaneta has been a fearless advocate for environmental justice, fighting for years for adequate temperature conditions in her solitary confinement unit in Gatesville, Texas, where temperatures regularly rose to levels that are not livable during parts of the year. She was finally successful in getting air-conditioning, only to then be moved to medium-security, where she was again faced with no air-conditioning. After being moved back to solitary two months later because of a shortage of beds (see her shocking story in Chapter 4: Who Gets Sent to the Hole), she actually felt relief to be back in solitary confinement, able to enjoy a brief respite from temperatures of up to 120 degrees Fahrenheit (49 degrees Celsius).

According to Kwaneta, "Prisons are literally heating people to death," leaving incarcerated people with no option but to strip down:

> *Because of my history of sexual victimization, I had never undressed in front of others. But in the last few weeks, survival has won out. I and others in solitary have tried to stay cool by donning "prison*

> *bikinis": wearing only our underwear in our cells. I felt "violated and demeaned" by officers leering and making comments about the "flatness of her stomach," but faced with the unrelenting heat, I felt I had little choice. I wrapped myself in a wet sheet, like a mummy, to avoid their comments.*
>
> *One woman incarcerated with me describes her plight as "whack-a-mole"; she ties her breasts up halter style around her neck to heal the rash underneath, which leads to a rash on the back of her neck. Another woman ties her breasts to a cloth and to the window bars, like a pulley. One night, she slept with a breast hanging out of her window through the bars. She was awakened by a male officer pinching her nipple.*
>
> *The women whom I'm incarcerated with swap ideas to stay cool: flood your cell with toilet water, lie on the floor on your back with your heels up, and point your fan toward your body. Women go anywhere to get into air-conditioning, taking visits with people they don't want to see, asking doctors question after question just to remain in air-conditioned areas. At worst, a few women have attempted suicide just to get into the emergency room to wait in the air-conditioning until a bed is available. In response, the guards have used pepper spray, making the already steamy, thick air that much less breathable, burning the lips and nasal passages of everyone within its reach. Being in solitary feels like being cooked alive.*[11]

Lanae Tipton highlights the discrepancy between the prison's official claim of air-conditioning in her solitary confinement unit as compared to the reality she experiences. She paints a grim picture:

> *A chorus of strained shouts and frustrated cries echoes down the vacant hallway outside of my cell door. The chorus of angry voices is validated by the waterfall of sweat pouring from my pores. We are all suffering under the unbearable heat and are highly distressed, not only because of our extreme discomfort, but also because of the silence that our complaints are met with. But here in the Patrick*

O'Daniel unit, where I'm incarcerated, unless something's fatal, we will continue to be ignored.

The heat is absolutely brutal living in a Texas prison. Out of the 15 women's prisons in Texas, only four are equipped with air-conditioning. According to the Texas Department of Criminal Justice website, there are 32 fully air-conditioned units and 55 partially air-conditioned, with the agency implementing "enhanced procedures to lessen the effects of hot temperatures for those in our facilities." The O'Daniel unit is supposed to be one of the fortunate units, but I can attest that my living area is neither equipped with AC nor implemented with provisions to combat the heat.

I'm incarcerated in the restricted housing area of the prison, which is where people who are in solitary confinement are. In this area we aren't offered many options for relief and due to staff shortages or the officers' preference to be as active as a brick, the salubrious shower we are supposed to have access to once a day is often denied. There is an existing policy in place to ensure that the people who are in solitary have access to ice-cold water hourly, but this is also seen as a burden by the officers, so they ignore our pleas and instead sip from their own containers of cool water and lounge in front of the huge industrial fan that's meant to cool down our hallway.

Through my door of metal mesh, bars, and plastic plexiglass I am frequently forced to watch uselessly as my friend Kira, who occupies the cell across from mine, passes out from the heat or is so delirious from dehydration she can hardly function. The torturous heat in these cells combined with the meager options for relief ultimately disables our energy and leaves us immobile and suffering alone in our cells. In addition to the harm Texas heat causes physically, it creates burdensome obstacles around our cell. Humidity will condensate on our floors and other surfaces and has caused me many falls, as well as injuries to others. Lotions, ointments, and toothpaste melt and liquefy, air-sealed bottles and soda cans will randomly combust, and packaged meats spoil quickly in the heat.

At TDCJ, there is a policy known as "respite," which requires that all people incarcerated in non-AC units must be offered relief in extreme heat. We can either get a short break in an AC-equipped area or have a cold shower. Since the O'Daniel unit claims to be a unit that's equipped with AC, respite provisions aren't offered nor are they provided when requested, even if our health depends on it. By residing in restrictive housing, the only building on O'Daniel without AC, we are not offered respite luxuries, leaving the people in solitary confinement to face the constant and torturous heat alone. Both the officers assigned to our area and the people who occupy the cells suffer from the inequality presented by the absence of AC. Complaints can reach soaring crescendos at times, with the hopes that our grievances won't be ignored and that high-commanding officers will be dispatched to help improve our situation. Some officers advocate that AC should be provided in the inhumane Texas heat, but other officers remain unsympathetic and even antagonistic. Many attempt to justify our suffering, believing we deserve the crueler conditions since we've been sent to prison.

Our already miserable cells turn into torture chambers in the summer. Upon request a sweat-riddled officer did a temperature check in a barren cell in the wing where I am located. The request was made at 12:27 am and the cell was 99.6°F. Midday temperature checks are refused, probably because sweltering waves of invisible fire fill our 5-by-10-foot cells at all hours of the day, and the staff knows it. Suffocating air overheats all electric devices including the 7-inch personal fan that I purchased from the commissary. From constant use, the motor will quickly reach a scalding temperature and further intensify the hot air being blown around. When the sun overpowers the cell anything metal in the cell will absorb all of the heat causing blisters and burns when touched. For example, the metal toilet, which gets piping hot in the high afternoon, makes it unusable or curse-worthy when accidental contact is made from urgency.

Often profuse with sweat, even in minimum clothing, and covered with painful and swollen scarlet-red sweat rashes in the creases of our bodies with sensitive-to-the-touch peeling patches of skin, we're forced to find DIY ways to stay comfortable. Options include keeping our thin white undergarments, shirts, and shorts wet throughout the day, leaving nothing to the imagination and attracting unwanted lingering attention from male officers who freely offer cringe-worthy sexual comments. We also flood our cell floors then lay sprawled in the water or take bird baths in our cell's sink. But since covering your door results in disciplinary action, we perform these attempts at cooling without any privacy, and with showers offered only once a day, if that, it makes the risk of exposure or disciplinary action worth our need for relief.

The people incarcerated in TDCJ are kept hidden and ignored as we suffer from heat exhaustion year to year. Even in a unit advertising that all of its buildings have AC, it is kept secret that the only people who actually have full access to AC are the staff – leaving us begging for reprieve against the heat and equality.[12]

Xandan Gulley is a trans writer who has been incarcerated in the same solitary unit as Lanae for over seven years because of his gender identity and likely as retribution for his advocacy and writing about the inhumane conditions that transgender incarcerated people face. He confirms the brutal reality described by Lanae:

I'm sweating profusely in my 9 x 6 cement and steel solitary confinement cell. My heart is pounding! And my heartbeat is racing against my chest! It's hot! Sweat drips down my forehead onto the concrete as I lay on the floor. I'm drenched in sweat all over as I lay under a commissary-purchased fan that is uselessly blowing the hot air that circulates repeatedly inside my cell.

Another day of triple heat-indexed weather this week. Another day of hell. Another day of unbearable heat. It's hot everywhere all over Texas! And Texas prisons are feeling the heat the worst.

With no air conditioning and limited channels of respite I feel like bacon frying in a skillet. Sometimes it's hard to breathe. Sometimes I want to cry because I'm so hot and my body feels like it's melting. Every day is a battle against heat exhaustion, heat stroke and dehydration.

To appease the courts and pacify activists protesting the heat-induced illnesses and deaths inside of Texas prisons, last year, the Lane Murray unit decided to experiment with gasoline-fueled portable air-conditioning units that run feeding tubes through the ventilation systems of the prison's century-old buildings. To no avail, the heat has not been alleviated.

For one, the gas-fueled portable air-conditioning units do nothing but push exhaust fumes throughout the vents, bringing more heat into the buildings with the already pre-existing boiling temperatures. For two, the windows are bolted and nailed shut and closed, denying incarcerated people the opportunity of fresh air and evasion of toxic air and poisonous oxygen.

These highly toxic fumes which cause headaches, migraines, stomachaches and regurgitation, are the detrimental effects of Texas's futile appeasements of attempting to modify the heat-hazardous obstacles inside the prisons.

With billions of dollars sitting idle in the treasury of the Texas Department of Criminal Justice's budget,[13] *what is the excuse as to why air-conditioning has not been permanently installed in the prisons? Instead of utilizing the funds allocated to modify, reform and rectify the prisons collectively, the Texas Department of Criminal Justice has been avoiding for years to fix the problems concerning the safety of incarcerated people, extreme temperatures and health protocols.*

Not only is the heat a hazard, but access to cold water is all but non-existent! Water runs conducted by SSIs are supposed to be run

> *throughout the buildings at least once an hour. These water runs are scarce and far in between. Water runs, where an SSI (unpaid incarcerated worker) whose job description involves janitorial cleaning along with pouring water through an Auto Zone purchased a motor oil funnel through the mesh and/or tray slot of the cell door. Many times the funnel is dirty as if motor oil was poured before the water. Sometimes the water cooler is dirty. Sometimes the water has plastic particles floating in it from the ice where the kitchen made bags of water and placed them in the freezer to make ice. Unsanitary means of water access is the norm among solitary confinement.*
>
> *Fact of the matter is, Texas heat is like a cancer slowly snatching the life out of incarcerated people. Heat and toxicity from the gas circulating through the ventilation systems is like the AIDS virus slowly killing the immune system of prisoners. With little to no access to cold water, respite and/or cool or fresh air, I along with other incarcerated people suffer grotesquely in the horrific living conditions inside Texas prisons.*[14]

As hot as it is in the summers, the winters can be just as unbearably cold. Kwaneta explains the elaborate routine she engages in in preparation for the long cold winter:

> *Women in solitary confinement repeatedly lack heat during winters. The Arctic Blast was predicted to hit us on Sunday but as usual, the solitary confinement building didn't have heat. I'm used to this. Every year in October I begin collecting blankets from people transferring to the hospital, psych center, and other prisons. I tell the young new arrivals to collect blankets. They don't listen.*
>
> *Sunday, my cell felt like a walk-in freezer. I checked to see if I can see my breath. I'm from the Midwest, so I know how to prepare to survive the cold. I begin with taping cardboard over the vent blowing cold air using sanitary pads. Then, I prop my travel-sized blow dryer on high setting in my toilet tissue hole as a portable heater. While placing cardboard over my windows I notice my peers*

outside quickly pushing food tray carts to us which is always cold by the time we're served. State-issued socks are tied around their ears and on their hands. Winter protective gear like hats and earmuffs aren't available for free or purchase in Texas. Because Texas doesn't pay its incarcerated people to work, only those who have outside financial support can purchase thermals and gardening-type gloves from the commissary.

Several blow dryers are heard in the background as I create a sleeping bag. One blanket is laid directly on the thin lumpy plastic mat for cushion. Then I tie on a flat sheet (fitted sheets aren't permitted in prison). I am only supposed to have one blanket. Nine folded blankets are sandwiched between two sheets and securely tucked around the mat.. I fill three empty water bottles with hot water and place each one in a sock to warm the bed. One toward the foot of the bed, one in the middle, and one at the head to warm it. No pillows in prison but a soft pack of commissary-purchased pads wrapped in a few t-shirts serves as mine.

Everything I wear I've purchased because the state doesn't provide anything except undergarments, shirt, pants, socks, gown, one blanket, and two sheets. We're in the hole, so we aren't assigned jackets. We weren't allowed shirts and pants, only gowns until I told NPR reporter Paul Flahive. He did a story asking, "Why are women in solitary forced to only wear gowns?"

I layer a T-shirt, top and bottom thermals, shorts, two pairs of socks, and a bath towel (which is prohibited for solitary folks to have in our cell) wrapped around my head. The overwhelming majority of my neighbors are indigent. Thus, when temperatures fall below freezing they are stuck with only a threadbare blanket and two flat sheets. If they were in general population, other incarcerated folks would give or loan them items, though that's against the rules. They would have heat and could ask a laundry worker to sneak in thermals from lost and found in exchange for braiding their hair. Down here, there are no options.

The night before last it was the freezing staff that wore hats, gloves, scarves and heavy ski coats, whose complaints were heard. They demanded a solution after being reminded that when we get sick, they often get sick, too. A call to the warden yielded an additional blanket distributed to us. But still no heat.[15]

The lack of adequate heat and air-conditioning that is customary in prisons is especially dangerous to people who are restrained in solitary confinement, who tend to be especially vulnerable to heat-related illness. As detailed in Chapter 7: Mental Illness and Solitary Confinement, the population in solitary is disproportionately folks with serious mental illness. Most of the psychotropic medications taken for various mental illnesses make people more vulnerable to heat-related problems and crises.[16] In addition, after years in solitary, just about everyone has multiple serious chronic medical conditions, including heart and cardiovascular disease, hypertension, kidney disease, and diabetes – primarily from eating only starchy food and getting very little exercise. All of these conditions make a person vulnerable to heat-related medical problems and risk of death. This is a big part of the reason that, as studies show, after being released from prison, individuals who spent significant time in solitary have a much higher one-year mortality rate than individuals released from prison who were not in solitary.

A 2002 motion by plaintiffs' attorneys in *Willie Russel v. Christopher Epps*, a class action lawsuit about the unconstitutional harsh conditions on death row in the Unit 32 Supermax Unit at Mississippi State Penitentiary in Parchman, where the entire facility is solitary confinement, contains this account of heat-related problems:

From May through September, Unit 32 swarms with clouds of mosquitoes, gnats, horseflies, and many other kinds of insects which breed in the cesspool outside the Unit, and harass the inmates every moment of the day and night. In many cells, swarms of beetles, mosquitoes and other insects cover the inmates' bodies and the inmates' food and water. The mosquito and insect infestation is so severe that inmates are forced to close their window and cover themselves up as much as possible with clothes and bedding despite the sweltering heat.

Even with cell temperatures routinely reaching well above 90 degrees Fahrenheit during the summer months, the prisoners are permitted to shower only three times per week and are routinely denied access to showers for four or even five consecutive days. In their desperation to find relief from the intense heat, some prisoners use the toilet bowl for drinking water and to wet down their bodies. Conditions such as these, which subject the prisoners to prolonged exposure to high ambient temperatures and humidity, pose a life-threatening health risk as well as a significant risk to the prisoners' mental health.

Heat-related illnesses seriously exacerbate respiratory, circulatory, and many other chronic illnesses. Sleep deprivation, resulting from prolonged exposure to high temperatures, compounds other emotional stressors that lead to mental breakdown. Heat stroke is a life-threatening emergency and, unless promptly and energetically treated, can result in convulsions, renal failure, circulatory collapse, and permanent brain damage. The primary risk factors for heat stroke during heat waves include prolonged stays in non-air-conditioned places; age (the risk increases with age); and a number of interactive medical conditions and medications. These conditions and medications cause hyperthermia, heat stroke or heat death by incapacitating a person's ability to control body temperature during periods of high ambient temperatures. Among the many medical conditions that diminish the body's ability to regulate its temperature are hyperthyroidism, heart disease, kidney disease, vascular insufficiency, obesity and mental illness. Among the many medications that impede the body's ability to adjust to high ambient temperatures are most psychiatric medications, many anti-hypertensive medications, diuretics, antihistamines, and several heart medications.

All of the plaintiffs have one or more of these high-risk characteristics; many of the prisoners have multiple high-risk characteristics for heat stroke and are at acute risk.

Air-conditioning is one of the best ways to keep people from dying during a heat wave, but many prisons still lack it. Forty-four states don't have air-conditioning in all of their prisons, including ten states in the South, where temperatures in prison have reached as high as 145 degrees Fahrenheit (63 degrees Celsius).[17]

Even with air-conditioning, many prisons still lack a functioning electrical and plumbing system. Facilities around the nation, many more than 100 years old, face billions of dollars in inferred maintenance costs.[18] A recent investigation into climate change and prison infrastructure in Washington State showed that because of deferred maintenance and outdated HVAC systems, heat and air-conditioning don't actually reach many cells even when the system is present. Under normal conditions, that is simply cruel and inhumane - and during a powerful snowstorm or heat wave, it can be lethal.

Washington isn't an outlier. Reports from other states around the country show an epidemic of crumbling prison infrastructure. A DOJ inspector general report found that every single one of the 123 federal prisons, which collectively house nearly 160,000 incarcerated people, needed maintenance, requiring at least $2 billion.[19]

Prisons also perpetuate and exacerbate the very climate hazards they are woefully unprepared to face. As a result of being built on or near wastelands, prisons constantly expose those inside and outside to tainted water, harmful air pollutants, and other environmental hazards. Panagioti Tsolkas, head of the Prison Ecology Project, states that prisons produce waste and pollution far beyond[20] local and federal standards, often in under-resourced communities[21] and their environments. A 2020 study on how mass incarceration contributes to climate change showed that increasing incarceration rates between 1997 and 2016 were correlated with increases in industrial emissions due to expanding industrial prison supply manufacturing operations.[22]

Most prison agencies have no climate adaptation plans and scant plans for dealing with the mass calamities that climate hazards like floods or wildfires are already bringing. When plans do exist, they are largely inadequate. For example, the California Department of Corrections and Rehabilitation Plan, developed as part of an Executive Order mandating all state agencies develop climate adaptation plans, outlines primarily how the state will improve existing infrastructure to stave off the worst effects of climate change[23] with almost no information about mitigating impacts to incarcerated people[24] during a climate hazard. Last year, the Ella Baker Center for Human Rights released a 166-page report[25] looking at the impacts of climate change on incarcerated people in California prisons, finding that even with the plan in place, the California carceral system is not prepared to respond to climate hazards in or near prisons and that aging infrastructure, lack of emergency response plans, and overcrowding in prison are contributing to the problem.[26]

De-carceration is the humane solution that should be applied on a national scale to combat climate crises in prisons. Locking fewer people up and letting more people out is not only a criminal justice issue but also our best bet at adapting prisons to climate change. It also works. After Hurricane Katrina devastated New Orleans and left hundreds of incarcerated people trapped for days forced to drink sewage water in their cells, the city managed to slash its jail population by 67 percent.[27] Yet, both crime and recidivism rates have fallen.[28] Evidence is increasingly showing that de-carceration – coupled with policies and services like supported housing and public mental health, programs that keep people out of prison – is a much better option for society.

The pandemic unmasked the horrors of what happens when prisons – crumbling, unprepared, and overcrowded – are hit with a crisis. Climate change is such a crisis. We are at a fork in the road. We can continue to turn a blind eye to the harms of mass incarceration and our crumbling prison infrastructure that will be painfully amplified as climate change worsens or choose the humane option: investing now in de-carceration and criminal justice reform, with ultimately lower costs to our economy, our society, and the people who sooner or later will become full members of our society. We need to act now, while we still have a choice.[29]

12
After Solitary

Back in my general population unit, I'd look out the window into the dark forest, made darker by the bright lights shining on the nearby fences. Sometimes I didn't sleep at all. The noises were different. In solitary everything happened at almost the same time, and I could tell where I was at in the day based on the sounds. Here, even though I had a clock now, I was still listening for those sounds. And the light ... I'd grown accustomed to the constant glare of light in my cell. Now when I turned the light off, it was almost dark. Except for the light that crept in through the windows or the count light during count time, it was dark. That was unsettling. I got yelled at for turning the light on and going to bed with it on. I was so used to communicating with just myself that sometimes when I spoke to other people I genuinely thought they should be already informed about the thing I was thinking about. That was a difficult thing to overcome.[1]

– Jonathan Kirkpatrick (endured 18 months in solitary)

So much trauma in such limited space and time does irreparable harm to mind, body, and soul, even beyond the prison walls. The severe neurological effects of extreme isolation and confinement often last long after the end of the isolation and can be permanent. Numerous studies have warned of poor health outcomes, increased risk of death while incarcerated and during community re-entry, and lifelong side-effects caused to those forced to endure the hole's harsh conditions.

In 2019, the *Journal of the American Medical Association* published a study[2] of 229,274 people who were released from imprisonment in North Carolina from 2000 to 2015. The findings were striking:

all else being equal, people who spent any time in the hole were 24 percent more likely to die within one year of release than those released who weren't placed in solitary; the leading causes of death in that group, according to the study, were suicide (78 percent more likely) and homicide (54 percent more likely); and those who spent time in solitary were found to be 127 percent more likely to die of an opioid overdose within two weeks of release from imprisonment.

Dennis Hope spent 27 years in solitary confinement in Texas, 15 years of which were on death row, even though he was not under a sentence of death. He reflects on trying to adjust to general population after being released from segregation and the severe symptoms and lasting harms he still suffers:

> *In June of 2022 I was released from Solitary Confinement after having spent 27 years in solitary and a long court battle. It is hard to explain that all has changed in those 27 years. In February 1996 all televisions were removed from solitary. It had been 26 years since I had seen a television. The bright colors hurt my eyes at first. The fast-moving images made it hard for me to keep up with the movement on the screen. It took a week for my eyes to adjust and for me to adjust to how fast things moved on the screen.*
>
> *All of my senses were in overdrive. I kept my back to any wall and was apprehensive about being around people. I didn't want anyone touching me, shaking my hand, patting me on the back or anything. I was not given a cellmate for four months while I tried to adjust to being around people again. When I was given a cellmate I had extreme difficulty going to sleep. I am still not comfortable with sleeping and someone else being in the cell. I have awoken startled with my heart racing a number of times because my cellmate made a noise or flushed the toilet.*
>
> *I have had to adjust to walking with my hands in front of me rather than handcuffed behind me with a guard on each side of me. Several times I have tripped by taking shorter steps than needed. Several weeks after being out of solitary I felt pain in the backs of my legs. I*

had dark purple bruises that were solid and running from the back of my knees to the lower part of my buttocks. The medical department had not seen anything like it before. An online search revealed it's called "sprinter's leg." Although I hadn't been running, I had been taking longer strides and walking longer than I had done in almost 30 years.

The first time I walked out on grass I found it hard to maintain my balance. I hadn't walked on a soft surface in decades and my leg muscles had to adjust to it. It felt good to walk on a soft surface. I took my shoes off and walked barefoot on the grass.

Now that guards don't sit in on my medical appointments I am able to be more open about my medical issues. Many times I avoided sharing things with medical providers because officers were sitting there listening and would go back and tell others about issues you were dealing with.

There are times I see an inmate in handcuffs being escorted. It immediately causes me to flashback and know what he is feeling. Not long ago I was called over to see a SCC [State Classification Committee] member in the segregation building. There were inmates lined up against the wall with officers beside them waiting to be seen by the SCC. I made eye contact with one and he looked at me like I thought I was better than him because I wasn't handcuffed. I thought to myself, "If you only knew how long I went through that." I knew exactly how he felt.

The unit I am currently assigned to is about a four-hour drive from the prison hospital. When I am transported to the hospital, I am shackled down (like in solitary) and transported by myself in a van. For about 15 hours it feels like I am in solitary again. My back goes stiff and my hands swell and go numb. I can only count the hours until I will be out of the restraints.

Although I'm out of solitary confinement I still periodically struggle with depression. Each day is a continuing adjustment, but I will never forget the time I spent in solitary. Some things we cannot remember, then there are some things we will never forget.[3]

Kwaneta struggled with many of the same issues as Dennis. She explains that in some men's prisons, people coming out of solitary confinement get to live alone and slowly reintegrate back into general population. There is no such transition program in her prison, and, she says, women are just "thrown to the wolves" by being immediately placed in a cell with a roommate, putting them in a "constant state of hypervigilance":

After eight and a half years of living in solitary confinement, I was finally returning to general population. The dorm was filled with a silence that's normally reserved for after a person commits suicide, as I walked past friends, who have become family, to say goodbye. We placed our palms on opposing sides of the mesh window of their door. A lump in my throat formed and was followed by tears. We silently mouthed "I love you." It was strange to say this to women I've never seen. For many, this was the first time I could attach a face to the voice I recognized from the heating vent. With each step an albatross of survivor's guilt weighed me down.

Unlike in the men's prisons, we are not automatically enrolled in the four-month Administrative Segregation Transition to General Population program. Instead, the state forces people coming out of solitary to live with a cellmate, and I ended up with a series of severely mentally ill roommates. My first roommate constantly dipped the cardboard tampon applicator in toothpaste and pretended it was a cigarette. My second one wore a handkerchief filled with chicken bones around her neck. My last one slept in every piece of clothing she owned, despite the brutal Texas summer heat. I felt paranoid and in a constant state of hypervigilance.

Returning to general population was much more challenging than I anticipated. I expected difficulty with noise and crowds. What floored me was relearning to walk and talk. I had over eight years of only walking handcuffed with ankle shackles. I'm used to taking small shuffling steps, stooped over my handcuffed hands grasping metal links attached to a belly chain leash. I still walked as if invisible chains were attached. Guards and friends constantly reminded me: Stand up straight! Pull your shoulders back! Take big steps! Mentally, I repeated these commands with each step. I had no idea what to do with my hands. I put them at my sides, clasped them behind my back and mimicked the swing of others. I was so preoccupied with making eye contact and nodding during discussions that I couldn't follow the conversation. I held my breath, whenever well-meaning friends embraced me while silently screaming, "Stop touching me!"

Three months later, I was doing better. People weren't yelling at me to take big steps. I realized I could put my hands wherever I chose. I was following and contributing meaningfully to conversations. Panic attacks during mealtimes stopped. I didn't cringe whenever someone touched me. I still was getting in trouble for stealing dandelions. I was progressing until I was reassigned to return to solitary confinement.

This prison is overcrowded. The roommate rule stipulates that both occupants must be within a decade of age and 50 pounds of weight to be considered compatible with one another. After my last roommate was sent to the psych center, I was alone. They returned me to solitary confinement because my cell was needed for younger compatible folks. Returning to solitary was a mind trip. I was there for administrative not punitive reasons but still subject to handcuffs and shackles when leaving my cell. I only stayed a week but I easily slipped back into my isolation mindset.

But this time when I returned to general population, I had a harder time readjusting. Everyone was yelling commands at me again.

The invisible chains returned. I was embarrassed that I couldn't maintain eye contact and preferred to self-isolate in my cell. Now, two months later, progress is still stunted. My brain is still stuck in isolation mode. Will I ever return to the extroverted me? Now, I realize the only solution for coping with the trauma from solitary isn't a program. It's never to go.

Gail Brashear shares what it was like to return to general population in the Washington DOC after three years in segregation:

Back in 2007, I spent three years in segregation and during that time of isolation I felt normal. Well, as normal as one could feel being isolated from human contact and having limited time outside of a small, boxed cell. But I didn't have too many concerns about my mental well-being. I spent the days writing or educating myself through books, and on those few occasions when I did speak with others, I didn't feel like there were any issues. This wasn't the first time I had been placed in long-term segregation, so I assumed when I was released back into population, it would just be like every other time. Yeah, there would be some anxieties at first, like getting used to being around so many people again, but within a few days, everything would feel normal again. But oh, how wrong I was. There was no preparing me for what I was about to endure once I was finally put back into population.

I can still remember that first morning once I was released into population, walking into the kitchen and grabbing my tray of food. There were so many women around me and everything was so loud. It was too much and my body just shut down. I just stood there in the middle of the kitchen physically and mentally paralyzed. I couldn't move or speak if my life depended on it. I can only remember the feeling of the tears that were running down my cheeks and having this overwhelming sense of fear that was flooding my body. Thankfully I had friends that were able to walk me outside and with their help I made it back to my room where I spent the rest of the day trying to figure out what had happened to me.

> *Those first few weeks are a bit of a blur. I couldn't sleep at all, not even for a few hours. Every time I closed my eyes my brain was flooded with my pictures and sounds as if I was watching TV in my head, and I was incapable of turning it off. I had chronic amnesia and couldn't remember basic events throughout a single day, such as whether I had used the phone to call home. I found myself walking down to the mental health unit every day in a state of crisis, begging and crying for them to help me. Trying to explain that something was wrong, as if my brain was legit broken. But of course, there was nothing mental health could do to help me. The response was always the same, "Gail you either need to figure it out, or you're going back to segregation."*

> *I learned that because I was isolated for so long, my brain wasn't getting the necessary stimuli that it needed to function properly. So, when I was finally put back in population after three years, I was overstimulated, and I no longer knew how to process all the information my brain was being flooded with. Those weeks were terrifying for me because I was alone in this. No one was able to explain to me what was happening to me or if I could be "fixed." I wasn't sure I would ever feel normal again.*

Kevin Light-Roth describes the process of becoming habituated to solitary confinement, then the process of leaving solitary to return to general population.

> *After nine months in the hole, maybe a year, your psychological rhythm shifts to match the tempo of solitary. You lose all desire to get out of your cell. Five days out of the week you are allowed one hour in the concrete dog run that serves as a recreation area, but you decline that time out more often than not, only leaving your cell if you need to make a phone call. At length you start skipping those too. People won't hear from you for weeks on end. They will assume you're being mistreated.*

When you shower three times per week in a 4 foot by 4 foot cage at the end of the tier – you finish quickly and flag down the guards to take you back. Returning to your prison cell feels like returning to sanctuary.

You can feel yourself slipping toward total dissociation, becoming unmoored from the physical world. And you want it to happen. You will not be able to admit it, least of all to yourself, but you want to let go of reality. You don't want to deal with the world anymore and you don't want to get out of solitary.

One day they release you. You never know ahead of time when it will happen. Early on a random morning, guards appear in your cell window and tell you to pack your things. Everything you own fits easily inside a paper sack. They handcuff you and take you down the hall to a holding cell and they strip-search you, as if there is anything in solitary worth smuggling out. The guards throw your jumpsuit and rubber sandals into a bin and give you a standard prison uniform. Pants feel oddly restrictive. Shoes are heavy and cumbersome to wear, and your feet are sweating from the instant you put them on. Your toes will hurt for days.

You step out alone onto a main prison walkway. The open expanse of the sky disorients you. The sunlight stings your eyes, and they will water continuously any time you go outside this first week. Walking without handcuffs feels bizarre – you aren't sure what to do with your unrestrained arms. They dangle awkwardly at your sides like a chimp's. Making your way to a living unit, part of you is exhilarated. The rest is a churning knot of anxiety and apprehension and jumbled, careening thoughts.

In general population, every social interaction makes you uncomfortable. Friends want to shake hands and embrace you. The physical contact puts you on edge. Eye contact produces tension in you. People stand too close and their movements seem spastic and combative. Their voices are too loud. You feel like a forest animal dropped in the middle of a carnival. Something dangerous is spring loaded inside you and you don't know what might trigger it, or what might result. You are perpetually afraid that you will come unhinged in some unpredictable way.

Looking in a real mirror for the first time in however long, months or years, you discover yourself physically diminished in ways that border on frightening. You're skinny. You have aged, with furrows carved into your face and gray seeping through your hair. Your skin is dull and taut over your skull, the bone structure of your face made stark. You don't look like a prisoner, you look like a warzone refugee. Meeting your reflected stare, you see something wild and unfamiliar in your own eyes.

It will take weeks for you to mentally reset and become a recognizable version of yourself. In that time, you will think of all the people you have seen permanently and horrifically altered by solitary. Men were psychologically shattered, their core personalities disfigured. You have an overriding fear that you will never recover. That an essential part of you is irretrievably lost. And you will wonder, well after you achieve the feeling of recovery, whether recovery is even possible. Because if who you are is the sum of your personal experience, the grand total of what you've seen and felt and learned over your lifetime, then a large component of yourself is, and always will be, the years you spent in solitary confinement.

You will begin to understand that recovery from solitary is an illusion. A lie necessitated by the perceived loss of the person you imagine you could have been. You can never go back to what you were, and what you could have been will always be out of reach. The version of you that might have come to be without solitary confinement – without disadvantage, without all the destructive decisions and cruel luck and tragedies you wish you could undo – is not something that can be reclaimed. It's something that never existed, and never will. You will come to accept, after extensive struggle, that to mourn its loss is to mourn nothing at all. But from time to time, you will mourn it anyway.[4]

After surviving ten years in isolation Ralph D. Dunuan III still feels the effects years later:

I always knew the direction of my criminal lifestyle would ultimately lead me to one of two places, dead or in prison. I came across a quote by Aristotle while doing my third long-term program in the hole at the Clallam Bay Correctional Center, a 23-hour-a-day solitary confinement unit: "The man who is content to live alone is either a beast or a God." I found myself in a unit surrounded by my opposition, rivals of my gang. There was no one to socialize with outside of myself because of this. All I had was some books and my own thoughts. Still, I found myself perfectly content.

Even today, after I have been in general population for over two years, it is an everyday struggle to not want to end up back in the hole. To date, I have been in prison for 18 years straight, and ten of those years have been spent in solitary confinement. I am still anti-social and I struggle being around people. Will that ever go away? I have no clue. I sure hope that it will. What is important is that I am coping though and I am doing what I can to rewire my brain. In the end, I know that I am not a God, but I also do not want to be the beast any longer …

Jonathan Kirkpatrick describes with great self-awareness his mental and physical state after his return to general population:

I looked out my window. It was still early. I might have been able to see the sunrise, but my cell window didn't have a view that far east; the trees were in the way. No one else was awake, only me. I had just been released from almost 18 months in solitary confinement.

Now that I was back in my general population unit, I was having a hard time sleeping. It wasn't the noise – our tier was generally quiet.

The problem was I was having a hard time winding down. The days were filled with so many sights and sounds that I wasn't used to. When people tried to talk to me, I just heard meaningless babble, like the adults in a Charlie Brown cartoon.

Everything seemed so large and oppressive: a walk to the chow hall was an ordeal that required the preparation of a road trip. I would lay in my bunk at night just trying to catch up with the day. A few minutes of conversation could take me hours to process, as I tried to figure out what everyone wanted. And so I couldn't sleep.

In my mind, I knew I probably had some sort of post-traumatic stress disorder. A lot had happened. Two summers before, I had been brutally stabbed due to a gang conflict. My lung collapsed and my carotid artery nearly severed. I was airlifted from the remote prison in Clallam Bay on the northwest tip of Washington to Harborview Hospital in Seattle 100 miles away, where I underwent surgery. I spent the next year in solitary, which was the prison's way of protecting me from my assailants. During that time, I received no counseling to address what had happened to me, just dead time for my mind to race with negative thoughts. I spent all of that time nursing my grudge against the people who had stabbed me, promising myself some sort of retribution. Someone had to pay for the harm I suffered.[5]

There is a veritable decimation of life skills during time in solitary, which impedes rehabilitation and re-entry. Individuals who have been in prolonged solitary confinement tend to stay to themselves in their cell in general population after being released from solitary, or in their room or home after being released from prison.[6] They continue to experience many of the symptoms they had first experienced in solitary confinement, including anxiety, insomnia, problems concentrating, paranoia, hyperawareness, strong startle reaction and so forth. And their social interactions are quite constricted. They do not want to be in a crowd or wait in a line. They do not go to entertainment or sporting events where there might be a crowd. They sit with their back to a wall facing the door, and they lack the humor, gregariousness and spontaneity they had enjoyed prior to their time in solitary confinement.

Paris Whitfield tells the story of a friend they encountered in prison right after the friend had done a lengthy time in SHU:

> *Sadly, I have witnessed many people who have gone to the box and returned: it isn't pretty. In a way, a bit of light from their eyes always appears to be gone.*
>
> *Prison is strange. I was on the Island [Rikers] for two years and many months. A guy I met there, I'll call him Brooklyn, because that is where he was from and rep with pride (also Puerto Rico), as Brooklynites are known to do.*
>
> *He was my big brother, teaching me how to survive the Island and how to stay out of jail politics, and he helped me prepare my mind for the worst-case scenario: going Upstate to prison.*
>
> *We spent many days playing spades, reading case law, and outdoing one another in making the biggest and strangest ingredients sandwiches.*
>
> *Fast forward many years: I hadn't seen anyone in the cell next to me when I walked past. It was a cell reserved for people coming back to population from the box.*
>
> *Normally, I would keep magazines, snacks, hygiene products, and cigarettes on hand – to dole out when a new neighbor arrived.*
>
> *When I heard "Paris" in his unmistakable Brooklyn and Puerto Rican accent, I knew it was him – my Rikers Island mentor/comrade/brother.*
>
> *I had class that night, so I couldn't really get caught up properly, but I had time to warm up a can of ravioli. I added a bit of flavor, warmed some breadsticks, and made some green tea.*

I handed over the "care package" items.

He whispered a "thanks," and things were quiet for a few seconds. I assumed he had started eating, or lit a cigarette.

I tapped on our shared wall to let him know I was "coming over," which meant I was asking for permission to reach my hand outside the bars with my mirror, so we could simulate talking face-to-face, through our reflection.

I saw my old comrade sniff over the food with animal-like instinct, and with an alertness not normally witnessed in humans: the pinched-up nose, the animal-sized eyes, and hunger.

He later told me he didn't think I had done anything to his food, but he questioned it out of habit, after having experienced so many cops and their "attachés" (other prisoners in cops' favor) do things to his and other people's food, who were locked up in SHU.

The only food he trusted while being in the box, it turned out, were the Jewish meals, because they were hermetically sealed.

The worst meal in the box was the "loaf," which is stale bread with bits of vegetables baked in it. This meal was often given to "unruly" prisoners.

He ate the food I had prepared, as if he had never eaten before. It was just a can of ravioli, breadsticks, and tea, but it was made with love, kindness, and familiarity, and those were ingredients he hadn't had in some time.

In our travels, throughout the state prisons, I've only seen him that one time. We have mutual comrades, and he tells them I'm the best cook in the state. I'm surely not. But my warming skills are unmatched.

13
The Legal Boundaries of Solitude

The degradation and deprivation wrought by prison conditions, particularly solitary confinement, are so stark that the Eighth Amendment's prohibition against cruel and unusual punishment must be held to reach them.

– Justice William Brennan in a 1981 dissent in *Rhodes v. Chapman*[1]

Despite the move by prison administrations away from the term "solitary confinement" to more bland descriptors such as "restricted housing," today the practice remains as entrenched in our prison systems of punishment as ever. Federal law and most state laws permit solitary confinement as a form of punishment when it is necessary to protect staff or other incarcerated people, or for the so-called protection of the person subjected to it. People's Constitutional rights are diminished when they go to prison, and wide discretion is given to corrections officers to make the determination to send someone to solitary with very little oversight or accountability. Under current federal law, even if conditions in solitary are viewed as inhumane, they can still be justified if a variety of other factors converge in favor of solitary, such as the dangerous conduct of the incarcerated person and the good intent of the corrections officers.

Federal laws curtailing the use of solitary confinement vary and can be complex. They often fall under either the broader umbrella of Constitutional protections against cruel and unusual punishment, the Constitutional right to due process of the law, or the Americans with Disabilities Act.

Additionally, the use of solitary confinement is regulated by specific federal statutes and policies, including those outlined by the

Federal Bureau of Prisons (BOP). States have statutes and policies controlling the use of solitary confinement, but here the example is the federal system, the BOP. Notably, these policies do not refer to the term *solitary confinement* but instead use various terms encompassing different types of restrictive housing.[2] This can make an understanding of the process of isolating incarcerated people difficult for those outside the BOP.[3] The BOP often communicates policy guidance to wardens through internal as opposed to public memoranda, which further obfuscates an outsider's understanding of the policies governing solitary.[4]

The BOP generally uses three types of restrictive housing: Special Housing Units, Special Management Units, and Control Unit Programs.[5] While each facility type has specific placement criteria, all three share policies that establish common conditions of confinement.[6]

As previously discussed in Chapter 4: Who Gets Sent to the Hole, the BOP has generally used two rationales for isolating incarcerated individuals: (1) administrative detention, which is considered non-punitive and is used to isolate individuals in protective custody, pending an investigation, or for general administrative security concerns;[7] and (2) disciplinary segregation, which is considered punitive and is used as a sanction for violating the BOP code of conduct.[8] However, these distinctions have blurred, particularly with the proliferation of different types of restrictive housing, and the use of a variety of terms to describe solitary confinement,[9] as discussed in Chapter 15: Solitary by Any Other Name. And regardless of the reason a person is sent to solitary confinement, the conditions and their treatment once there are generally the same.

CRUEL AND UNUSUAL PUNISHMENT IN VIOLATION OF THE EIGHTH AMENDMENT

The Eighth Amendment of the US Constitution prohibits cruel and unusual punishment, which, according to the Supreme Court, implies "something inhumane and barbarous, torture and the like."

Some forms of punishment are hence simply considered inhumane and may never be used as a penalty for any crime.

The determination of what exactly counts as cruel and unusual is largely determined based on the social mores of the time. In 1910, the Court in *Weems v. United States* took a progressive view of the punishment clause: "The clause of the Constitution ... is not fastened to the obsolete, *but may acquire meaning as public opinion becomes enlightened by a humane justice*" (emphasis added). The Court recognized that as a society, our thinking evolves over time, and that courts should have the flexibility to modify and adapt their interpretation of the Eighth Amendment alongside evolving contemporary societal morality or "evolving standards of decency."[10]

In that case, the Court found that a 15-year sentence for a crime similar to embezzlement was cruel and unusual punishment.[11] With this holding, the *Weems* Court broadened the "cruel and unusual punishments" clause by establishing the proportionality principle – the Court held that the clause applies not just to torture, but "against all punishments which, by their excessive length or severity, are greatly disproportioned to the offense charged."[12] The Court conceded the possibility "that imprisonment in the State prison for a long term of years might be so disproportionate to the offense as to constitute a cruel and unusual punishment."

In 1958, the Court expanded on this progressive view in *Trop v. Dulles*, where it again refused to read the punishment clause as static, declaring that the Eighth Amendment "must draw its meaning from the *evolving standards of decency* that mark the progress of a maturing society."[13] Instead of interpreting "cruel and unusual" in a literal way, the court focused on human dignity.

In 1970, the Eastern District Court in Arkansas found the entire prison farm system in Arkansas to be unconstitutional. The court noted that if conditions of confinement "shock[s] the conscience of a reasonably civilized people," then they should be found to be cruel and unusual punishment, regardless of the specifics of the particular situation.[14]

Consistent with the many stories recounted in this book, and by all accounts throughout the history of the practice, it seems clear that prolonged solitary confinement should shock the conscience of a civilized people. But the determination of cruelty in the context of solitary confinement is a complex legal matter that is made on a case-by-case basis.[15] Legal interpretations of individual cases to assess whether the conditions of solitary confinement meet this Constitutional standard may vary, and challenges to the use of solitary confinement often involve considerations of the duration, conditions, and impact on the individual's mental health.

Though federal courts don't all agree, the most common reason for an Eighth Amendment violation based on duration has been the absence of a firm duration upon which to measure.[16] Some Circuits lean toward finding shorter periods of time in isolation an Eighth Amendment violation, while others allow shockingly long durations. For example, the Second Circuit, in *Colon v. Howard* acknowledged that duration is relevant, holding that 305 days of solitary confinement was unconstitutional.[17] On the other hand, the Tenth Circuit's decision in *Silverstein v. Fed. Bureau of Prisons* shockingly held that 30 years in solitary confinement did not violate the Eighth Amendment, since there was no showing of psychological harm.[18]

As for the living conditions themselves, specific conditions alone are generally not sufficient for a finding of cruel and unusual punishment; rather, courts generally look to the cumulative effect of a combination of factors:

> Segregation may be harsh and unpleasant, but basic sanitation and nutrition is required. Inadequate lighting, ventilation, heating, cleaning, bedding, nutrition, medical care, or opportunities to wash are all factors which bear on a finding of cruel and unusual punishment.[19]

Courts rarely find poor living conditions alone amount to a Constitutional violation, as it seems understood that living conditions in solitary confinement will be unbearable, which is the unspoken reason for sending a person there. For example, in *Novak v. Beto*, the Fifth Circuit Court of Appeals held that deprivation of light and bedding and minimal access to food did not meet the standard of cruel and unusual punishment because it was not accompanied by "deprivation of basic elements of hygiene."[20] Likewise, in *Hawkins v. Hall,* the solitary confinement cell was unfurnished, except for a seatless hole-in-the-floor toilet with an outside flush and one bare lightbulb fixture. Although the court acknowledged that the conditions of the cell were "unpleasant," they were not "so barbarous as to constitute 'cruel and unusual punishment' as a matter of law."[21] Despite the absence of a toilet, the court reasoned that the conditions did not constitute cruel and unusual punishment because the cell provided adequate shelter, as well as satisfactory ventilation, light, and heat.[22]

Courts are particularly hesitant to find that the extreme psychological impact of solitary confinement rises to the level of a Constitutional violation. Despite the Supreme Court's early recognition of the effect of solitary confinement on mental health in *Medley*, courts tend to concentrate on physical needs rather than the psychological consequence of isolation,[23] and some courts have explicitly declined to consider the psychological impact of solitary confinement altogether. For example, in *Newman v. State of Alabama*, with respect to a claim brought by someone who had endured solitary confinement for over twelve years, the Fifth Circuit Court of Appeals acknowledged that "[t]he mental, physical, and emotional status of individuals .... do deteriorate and there is no power on earth to prevent it ...."[24] However, that court declined to consider the psychological impact, holding that "[i]f the State furnishes its prisoners with reasonably adequate food, clothing, shelter, sanitation, medical care, and personal safety, so as to avoid the imposition of cruel and unusual punishment, that ends its obligations under Amendment Eight."[25] The court reasoned that "the Constitution does not require that prisoners, as individuals or as a group, be provided with any and every amenity which some person may think is needed to avoid mental, physical, and emotional deterioration."[26]

Under current law, even if the conditions of solitary confinement were to rise to the level of cruel and unusual, it does not mean that there is necessarily an Eighth Amendment violation. In *Farmer v.*

Brennan, the Supreme Court laid out a two-part inquiry. First, the alleged deprivation must be "sufficiently serious,"[27] meaning that "[t]he prison official's act or omission must result in the denial of the minimal civilized measure of life's necessities."[28] Second, to violate the Eighth Amendment, the prison official must have "a sufficiently culpable state of mind." In prison conditions, this requires "deliberate indifference to inmate health or safety,"[29] such as where prison officials applied force "maliciously and sadistically for the purpose of causing harm" or where officials used force "with a knowing willingness that harm could occur."[30]

In addition to that two-part inquiry, recent Supreme Court cases have focused on whether an incarcerated person's misconduct was more than "trivial" so as to justify the punishment, rather than simply on the effect of the punishment on the incarcerated person. For example, just recently, the Supreme Court refused to hear a case about the prolonged denial of outdoor exercise brought by a person who was in solitary confinement in Illinois for three years, because he had assaulted staff members, damaged property, and disobeyed prison guards, which the Court said justified the harsher punishment.[31]

In a searing dissent, Justice Jackson wrote:

> During that time, Johnson spent nearly every hour of his existence in a windowless, perpetually lit cell about the size of a parking space. His cell was poorly ventilated, resulting in unbearable heat and noxious odors. The space was also unsanitary, often caked with human waste ... And because Pontiac officials would not provide cleaning supplies to Johnson unless he purchased them from the commissary, he was frequently forced to clean that filth with his bare hands. Johnson was allowed out of his cell to shower only once per week, for ten brief minutes.[32]

The dissent focused on the extremity of the punishment, pointing out that justifying the punishments based on Johnson's behavior toward corrections officers was misguided, especially since it likely occurred because of his profound mental illness.[33]

There are two conditions for which some courts have recognized the inhumanity of solitary confinement in all instances: it is fairly well established that people with certain types of mental illness as well as juveniles should not be held in solitary confinement. Unfortunately, though, in practice many juveniles and people with mental illness are still sent to solitary confinement regularly, even when the law prohibits it.

Although the Supreme Court has yet to rule on the issue, many state and federal courts have held that prolonged solitary confinement is cruel and unusual punishment for incarcerated people with mental illness. In *Ruiz v. Johnson*, a federal district court in Texas noted that it is "deplorable and outrageous" that so many people with serious mental illness are held in solitary confinement:

> Persons who, with psychiatric care, could fit well into society, are instead locked away, to become wards of the state's penal system. Then, in a tragically ironic twist, they may be confined in conditions that nurture, rather than abate, their psychoses. The United States Constitution cannot abide such a perverse and unconscionable system of punishment.[34]

Nonetheless, the Supreme Court has repeatedly refused to hear appeals on the constitutionality of solitary *per se* for people with a mental illness. For example, in 2023, the Supreme Court refused to hear an appeal brought by Michael Johnson, a man with a severe mental illness who was in solitary confinement for more than three years.[35] A CNN report noted that Johnson was classified as "seriously mentally ill and diagnosed with depression, bipolar disorder, among other disorders."[36] He was in an endless loop of being punished for misconduct he engaged in because of his mental illness. The more he was punished and the longer he was left to languish in solitary confinement, the deeper he fell into mental distress and the more severe his behavior became.

On January 25, 2016, President Obama declared an Executive Order banning solitary confinement for juveniles in federal prisons, based on convincing scientific evidence of the destructive effects on the mental health of minors.[37] Several years later, in December of 2018, Congress passed the First Step Act,[38] and reauthorized the Juvenile Justice and Delinquency Prevention Act (JJDPA),[39] with the Juvenile Justice Reform Act of 2018,[40] enshrining Obama's solitary ban in federal statute. The First Step Act federal juvenile solitary ban is in effect unless the minor's behavior presents an immediate risk of harm to themselves or others, and in that case, solitary is only permitted for a three-hour maximum.[41] The 2018 JJDPA incentivizes states to implement similar bans on youth solitary. It requires states to regularly report data on their use of solitary confinement as well as their strategies and plans to reduce isolation. The law also requires the Office of Juvenile Justice and Delinquency Prevention to provide training and technical assistance programs to support eliminating solitary.[42]

Recognizing the need for specialized care and alternatives that consider the unique vulnerabilities of young individuals, 24 states plus the District of Columbia have taken steps to limit or prohibit the use of solitary confinement for minors, while other states have limited its use through administrative code, policy or court rules.[43] In addition, the American Civil Liberties Union (ACLU) and the American Academy of Child and Adolescent Psychiatry (AACAP) both oppose the use of solitary confinement for juveniles, saying it can cause serious psychological, physical, and developmental harm.

But as with mental illness, the laws aren't unified and there are loopholes that result in juveniles being subjected to solitary confinement in large numbers. Minors continue to suffer in isolation in many US counties and states: Eleven states (Alabama, Georgia, Kansas, Minnesota, Mississippi, Missouri, Rhode Island, South Carolina, South Dakota, Wisconsin, and Wyoming), have no limits at all on the use of solitary confinement for juveniles.[44] Some state DOC policies actually demand that youth admitted to adult prisons be held in solitary until they reach the age of 18, and then they are released into general population.

FOURTEENTH AMENDMENT RIGHT TO DUE PROCESS OF THE LAW

While the complete elimination of solitary confinement remains an elusive goal, the hope is that this brutal form of discipline is used sparingly and only in the most egregious cases when no reasonable alternative exists. But far too often, and arguably more often than not, incarcerated people are being isolated from the general population for minor violations of rules at the whims of the guards (see Chapter 4: Who Gets Sent to the Hole), with no real or meaningful way to challenge that decision.

This is not to say that there are not at least *theoretical* means of challenging the segregation decision. But this of course assumes that an incarcerated person has the capacity, awareness, and means to do so. In addition, the fear of retaliation often prevents a person in solitary confinement from complaining – angry guards translate to worse conditions and longer amounts of time in isolation.

But legally, even the theoretical possibility of challenging a decision by prison authorities is extremely limited based on legal precedent that gives broad discretion to prison officials based on their purported public safety needs.

The Fourteenth Amendment to the US Constitution protects individuals from having their life, liberty, or property deprived without "due process of law." So, as a threshold matter, incarcerated people who seek to make a due process challenge to a decision of prison officials to place them in solitary confinement must show that the prison officials deprived them of a *constitutionally protected* liberty interest.

The first problem here is to determine what liberty interests incarcerated people actually have. Once a person is incarcerated, their liberty interests are obviously limited in certain ways – they clearly and by design don't have the freedom to move about as they wish. As the Supreme Court stated in *Wolff v. McDonnell* in 1974, due process means something different in prison than in the free world: "one cannot automatically apply procedural rules designed for free citizens in an open society ... to the very different situation presented by a disciplinary proceeding in a state prison."[45] A few years later, in 1979, in *Bell v. Wolfish*, the Supreme Court noted: "Maintaining institutional security and preserving internal order and discipline are essential goals that may require limitation or retraction of the retained constitutional rights of both convicted prisoners and pretrial detainees."[46] But the extent of that limitation is the issue.

The Supreme Court has clarified that incarcerated people do not have a Constitutional right under the due process clause to challenge a decision by prison officials to be placed in solitary confinement *unless* such enhanced punishment amounts to an "atypical and significant hardship on the inmate in relation to the ordinary incidents of prison life."[47] To complicate matters, the standard for determining if a solitary confinement sentence is "atypical" or poses a "significant hardship" has never been clearly defined. In *Wilkinson v. Austin*, the Supreme Court noted that a "baseline from which to measure what is atypical and significant" has not been identified for any prison system and that the decision should be made by lower courts.[48] Notably, lower courts are not in agreement about how to make this determination. Some lower courts focus strictly on the length of the confinement in relation to the infraction or the reason for being sent to solitary.[49] Other lower courts focus more on the actual conditions relative to the conditions under which the general prison population resides.[50] Still, other lower courts examine one or both of those questions in connection with the infraction for which the punishment is imposed.[51] In any event, while a state or prison system can go beyond what is required by the US Constitution, it is not required to do so – and the complexity and case-by-case variability of what qualifies as "atypical and significant" often leads courts to adhere to the minimum legal standards rather than grant a right to review segregation.[52]

Even if the incarcerated person has a right to have the decision reviewed, the ability of an incarcerated person to challenge the decision often only arises *after the fact*, depending on the legal framework, the due process rights involved, and the jurisdiction – proactive challenges are difficult unless the person can show a clear violation of Constitutional rights.

Further, there is no right to a "speedy" appeal of a segregation decision. Rather, the circuits are all in agreement that no procedures are required before placing an individual in solitary confinement for a "short" period of time, which can leave a person to languish for weeks or months before they are permitted to show that they are not guilty of whatever violation they are accused of or that the sentence is too harsh in relation to what they did.[53] While the Supreme Court has held that meaningful periodic review of segregation decisions is necessary to satisfy due process in certain circumstances, that does not guarantee immediate or rapid review – only that reviews must happen at regular intervals. Courts have generally recognized that unreasonably prolonged segregation resulting from undue delays in appeals may violate Constitutional rights, but litigation is rarely fast enough to qualify as a "speedy" resolution.

In *Wolff v. McDonnell*, the Supreme Court made it clear that under the procedural protections of the Fourteenth Amendment, prison officials need only abide by certain minimal procedures.[54] The requirements are slightly different for administrative versus disciplinary segregation, but generally incarcerated people are entitled to written notice of the charges at least 24 hours prior to the hearing, the opportunity to present a defense with evidence and witnesses, and a written statement detailing the evidence and reasoning behind any disciplinary actions taken (the *Wilkinson* Court, however, upheld a process for administrative segregation that didn't include the right to present witnesses). They are not, however, afforded the right to counsel, or the opportunity to confront and cross-examine adverse witnesses.[55] The Court noted that "inserting counsel into the disciplinary process would make proceedings more adversarial, undermine correctional goals, cause unnecessary delays, and create practical problems in sufficiently providing counsel at every disciplinary hearing."[56]

Some years later in *Hewitt v. Helms*,[57] the Court found that procedural due process could be satisfied through an initial hearing and *some* form of periodic review, without specifying an exact frequency. This leaves the timing for subsequent reviews largely up to the discretion of prison officials, allowing them flexibility based on the needs and policies of their facilities.

In a dissent, Justice Stevens criticized the majority's due process analysis, saying that its minimal review procedures "fail[] to provide adequate protection against arbitrary continuation of an inmate's solitary confinement," and that in his view, "the Due Process Clause requires a more searching review of the justifiability of continued confinement."[58]

Perhaps most importantly, according to David Fathi, Director of the ACLU National Prison Project, although the procedures upheld in *Wilkinson* provide for considerable process before someone can be transferred to solitary, in the end the reviews are often "a meaningless rubberstamp." Even when a person's segregation is "atypical and significant," and they are successful in getting the decision reviewed, Supreme Court jurisprudence mandates deference to prison administrators' penological concerns, making it increasingly difficult for lower courts to accept challenges to prison conditions. An incarcerated person raising a challenge to their segregation at the prison level will hardly ever be successful, and successful challenges in the courts are equally few and far between due to the extremely broad discretion that rests in the hands of prison officials.

As an example, according to the Texas prison policy for when/how someone gets sent to solitary, guards have near-complete discretion, with "offenders" assigned to single-cell housing "for health, safety, and security reasons." There is a review procedure: The Unit Classification Committee (UCC) considers the characteristics of the incarcerated person in relation to the person's current institutional record, as well as current attitude and behavior and rules on the need for continued single-cell housing. But rules for assigning someone to single-cell housing are ambiguous, leaving custody staff a lot of unchallenged discretion in the matter.

In the end, while there are a few circuit court decisions that have given some actual teeth to the procedural due process requirements for solitary confinement,[59] there is a troubling level of unchecked authority that leaves incarcerated individuals with few meaningful protections against prolonged confinement.

14

Reform, Advocacy, and Activism by Impacted People and the Community

How can we subject prisoners to unnecessary solitary confinement, knowing its effects, and then expect them to return to our communities as whole people?

– Barack Obama addressing the need for solitary confinement reform in 2016

We won't stop until solitary confinement is eradicated from this country.

– Unlock the Box, a national advocacy non-profit dedicated to ending solitary confinement in all US prisons, jails, detention facilities, and juvenile facilities

Forty-four states are considering or have already passed laws greatly limiting solitary confinement in jails, prisons, and detention facilities, an important sign of the success of the struggle to end solitary confinement.[1] Meanwhile, families of incarcerated people, formerly incarcerated people, and social justice activists in the community have joined together to put pressure on the legislatures and the departments of correction to ban solitary confinement altogether. We do not have space in this volume to discuss every instance of social activism, every reform effort, and every legal campaign, but we will mention a few that are representative and deserving of further study.

ADVOCACY, ACTIVISM, AND ORGANIZING IN THE US

Legislation limiting solitary confinement never comes out of the blue, nor is it alone sufficient to halt the practice. Every successful legislative campaign to reduce solitary confinement has been preceded by activism by impacted people and communities, as well as by related lawsuits. The lawsuits help expose what is going on inside jails and prisons, and the activism brings about the community consciousness necessary to pass legislation and change policies. There has been robust, courageous activism on the part of incarcerated people, families of incarcerated people, and activists in the community to end the torture of solitary confinement.

Many of the state and federal efforts to reduce the use of solitary confinement have been driven by grassroots campaigns across the country led by people who have lived through solitary confinement, community activists, people who have family members inside, and reform-minded legislators. The national Unlock the Box (UTB) campaign, National Religious Campaign Against Torture (NRCAT), and others have helped support and spur on those grassroots efforts. Created in 2017 and launched in 2018, UTB was founded by a coalition of solitary survivors, advocates, and watchdog groups who envision a unified strategy to tackle the complex state and federal policies that perpetuate state-sanctioned torture. Collaborating with key partners like NRCAT, the ACLU National Prison Project, Solitary Watch, disability rights organizations, California Families Against Solitary Confinement, Social Workers and Allies Against Solitary Confinement, the Federal Anti-Solitary Taskforce (FAST), the HALT Solitary Campaign, and civil rights law groups including the Center for Constitutional Rights, UTB works to shift the public narrative, follow the leadership of survivors of solitary and family members as movement leaders, and champion legislation to ban solitary confinement and challenge the carceral system as a whole.

UTB, NRCAT, Solitary Watch, FAST, and other national allies have also helped support policy change, consciousness-raising, and shifts in the narrative about the need to end solitary confinement, by publishing reports and amplifying mass media attention. Recent polling shows widespread, bipartisan public support for banning solitary, including a ban on solitary beyond a maximum of four hours for emergency de-escalation.[3] National news media, from *NBC News*[4] to *Teen Vogue*[5] to *Last Week Tonight with John Oliver*,[6] have all highlighted the horrors of solitary confinement and the need to end it.

Vincent "Tank" Sherrill writes about advocacy that can be done from prison, suggesting that incarcerated people have more power than one might think. He explains how incarcerated people are "superorganisms," like ants and bees, which can come together to perform actions that they wouldn't be able to perform individually:

> *Organism*
>
> *Superorganisms are a collective of single organisms coming together to perform actions that they wouldn't be able to perform individually. Ants and Bees are superorganisms. Prisoners and their free world allies are also superorganisms, and prison structures are transformed into Ant-holes or Beehives, whereby the natural beauty and genius of its captors' imagination to strategize and organize toward liberation are realized.*
>
> *The prison structure is a highly hostile and volatile ecosystem, but subject to climate and cultural change by organisms committed to doing "the work." How is it possible for trauma-impacted captives to re-calibrate their unnatural biosphere to a natural one conducive to their transformation and ultimate liberation?*
>
> *Organizing*
>
> *Antcraft and Antwork are my imaginative language to describe organizing. Ants are considered colonizers and as a superorganism, they cooperate with the biosphere they occupy under some super-extraordinary circumstances. Ants can educate us – in a natural way – on how to colonize or occupy spaces on the ground and how to cooperate en masse. Imagine if prisoners were organized collectively like we organize separately in our silo-ed ecosystems, how much*

cultural and social capital we can Harambe (pull together) under the flag of freedom, justice, and equality in the spirit of abolition.

When we come out of our individuality to support each other, or someone in deeper crisis than our own, we are practicing abolition. When we "fish" (unravel the thread from our underclothes, to make fishing line to reach a fellow prisoner's cell-front) to deliver or receive a care package (food, coffee, hygiene items etc.), which are considered contraband and a violation of the prohibition against borrowing, lending, or trading policy, we are practicing abolition. And, when we engage in dialectical argument on the tier about spirituality, relationships, politics, or favorite free or carceral cuisines, we are practicing abolition.

I Fathered, Brothered, Uncled, and Friended the young men in my pod (from behind closed doors), because that's what I would want an older gentleman to do for my son or nephew.

Unnatural are the structures and conditions people build and place other people in. But if we can build it we can abolish it. Dedicated to all who are organizing on these Ant Hills. We are many millions of ants on thousands of colonies. We are Siafu, the elite warrior/soldier class of the Ant world.

Nothing illustrates Tank's theory about superorganisms more than the hunger strikes at Pelican Bay Prison in 2011 and 2013. Todd Ashker, a key organizer of the hunger strikes, the lead plaintiff in the *Ashker v. Governor of California* class action, and an author of the Agreement to End Hostilities,[7] wrote on January 7, 2021:

"Carpe Diem: *The time is now to seize the day by doing what's right and just for all." The "prisoner class" is nearing a historical time – that ten-year anniversary (of the first Hunger Strike at PBSP) which stands out as an example of the power of the people. I am referring to it being ten years since similarly situated prisoners, subjected to decades of the state-sanctioned torture of solitary confinement,* *set aside our differences and united in our collective stand against our common adversary. We referred to ourselves as the PBSP-SHU Short Corridor Collective as we helped to educate the world via our focused writing campaign about our plight, exposing decades of California's torture of thousands in the CDCr system. We let our adversaries know that we were drawing a line. We were not going to accept being treated as less than human and demanded the end to our torture: the decades of torture of the entire similarly situated prisoner class, including our outside loved ones who experienced our pain – often more so. I believe that three of the key elements which together proved an unstoppable combination and, beyond our wildest hopes, made possible what many of our adversaries believed impossible:*

We said "Enough!" and meant it … ***The prisoner class is not powerless. We have proven this!***

Jack Morris, who was in the SHU at Pelican Bay State Prison for many years, and another leader of the hunger strikes, explains:

We all understood that if there wasn't something done, we would all simply die inside those cells. I look at the ticker tape at the bottom, and right there it said on national news, "30,000 California prisoners on hunger strike," and it was – it was amazing. We were fortunate to have litigation taking place and family members yelling at the top of their lungs on the street corners and we finally got legislators to listen when the news broadcasted that 30,000 prisoners were not gonna eat no more.

After three hunger strikes (the first lasting 21 days, the second 17 days, and the third and biggest, involving 60,000 incarcerated people, lasting 55 days), the incarcerated people leading the hunger strikes launched a class action lawsuit, *Ashker v. Governor of California,* and eventually entered into the Ashker Settlement, which finally succeeded in getting the people who had been consigned to a lifetime in solitary confinement out.

Brant Daniel, who has endured 28 years and counting in solitary confinement, did a long stint at Pelican Bay SHU from 2000–2015, and was another organizer of the hunger strikes. As Brant tells it, they were ready to do the hunger strike "until the end." He describes that extraordinary act of advocacy and non-violent resistance like this:

Here we all sat year after year, the same men all going through the same things together. We learned who we are in our souls an how much we can endure mentally, spiritually, an physically too. Everyone was sick of sitting here rotting away, even though we hadn't broken no rules, no laws, no CDCR policy – nothing more than a prison rat lying an trying to use his lies to get himself outta this prison.

Then some of us started talking about this life an how can we unite an reach across these boundaries that exist an create change. We agreed if we don't do something we'll rot here. All of us will rot having broken no rules of the prison.

Then, we all got ready to go on strike. We signed do not resuscitate forms. Then on the big day, boom we started. The CDCR head guy, the Director of Corrections Scott Keenan, on day 20 had flown up there from Sacramento California to talk to the main strike leaders we had chosen to go talk for us. Then we all agreed to show good faith an the strike was called off with their promise of our release.

In two months, we didn't see any movement an we felt we were duped, so in September we resumed our strike. My wife Liza (who I met in 2008) was very helpful to get word to the public an attorneys an the media on how humans were done on our own American soil by our own Americans. I went all the way 18 days (the first one I went all 21 days). We were threatened by staff all the time, our mail would be lost, thrown away etc. It was ugly. Then more promises were made an we stopped the strike.
We waited an seen a little movement but it took over a year to just start CDCR's review of the gang associate files an comb through

them to determine who would be released to general population. In six months they only sent back five guys an then stopped for five months. We felt bamboozled again. So in 2013, over 40,000 inmates in CDCRs started another strike, still protesting the conditions in the SHU, an did not stop. No talking, no games, no bullshit!!!

This one went 57 days an then CDCR agreed to release us over the next year or two. We had many attorneys on board now an filed lawsuits and in November 2013 the strike ended. In October 2015, the big Ashker lawsuit was settled with CDCR an our strike attorneys an we got outta solitary. We felt we won! They streamlined the process an in December 2015 I was transferred to general population in Salinas Valley.

I remained there for only ten months and then I went back to solitary on October 29, 2016. I've been here ever since then. Nine years almost an still in solitary. The CDCR manipulates information against us and call us the deadliest men in the country so it almost doesn't matter what anyone says after that.

The sad thing is that after all the hunger strikes, and all the lawsuits, and all the media attention, I'm still in solitary confinement and they still continue to put humans in concrete boxes. Nothing really changed in the end.

Brant is not the only one with such a horror story. Although there is supposed to be a limit on SHU terms to a few years since *Ashker*, the 9th Circuit Court of Appeals terminated monitoring, and the CDCR seems intent on retaliation against the leaders of the hunger strikes. The CDCR filed a RICO case against alleged gang members, including Brant, and convicted them of new charges of organized crime, which puts them in the federal system, where they can then be sent to ADX, as is happening with Brant. Brant claims the CDCR is punishing him for refusing to "rat" anyone out by naming gang members.[8]

The men who participated in the hunger strikes engaged in peaceful resistance against oppressive systems, drawing on a long history of non-violent protest. They took a courageous stand against conditions designed to break the human spirit. Even from the confines of solitary confinement, men of all races were able to work together with a common cause. They made their plight public, and were ultimately successful in effecting change. In doing so, they were able to reclaim their dignity and humanity. By risking their health and their lives, these men made profound sacrifices in the hopes of sparking reform, highlighting the urgency of their demands and the severity of the conditions they faced.

The story of prison reform involves twists and turns in the road. But in spite of reports of setbacks and retaliation against some of the hunger strikers and plaintiffs in the Ashker litigation, the hunger strikes and class action litigation did bring about significant improvement *vis a vis* solitary confinement in California's prisons. And there are many other successful reform movements, internationally as well as in the US. We list a few examples in the following paragraphs.

INTERNATIONAL REFORM

Although solitary confinement is used by many nations around the world, its use in the United States far surpasses that found in other democratic nations in both the extent and length of isolation.

The UN Standard Minimum Rules for the Treatment of Prisoners (also known as the Mandela Rules)[9] prohibit solitary confinement for longer than 15 days. The *UN Rules for the Protection of Juveniles Deprived of their Liberty*[10] and the *Bangkok Rules for the Treatment of Women Prisoners*[11] prohibit the use of solitary for children and pregnant women, and the UN Basic Principles for the Treatment of Prisoners[12] encourage the efforts to abolish solitary confinement completely.

In Northern Europe, there are countries that have taken a "human dignity" approach to incarceration. Those countries employ what is known as an open-prison model. Finland is the poster child for open prisons, but they can also be found in Germany, Denmark, Ireland, Norway, and Britain.

The overall philosophy of the open-prison system is very progressive. While it does not advocate for prison abolition, it focuses strongly on rehabilitation. The open-prison model is predicated on small prison populations, which allows the facility to offer the inhabitants individual guidance and programming. "Gentle justice" is the focus; both the incarcerated and the guards address each other by first name, contrary to the prison cultures in most countries, where incarcerated people are addressed by numbers, last names, or other dehumanizing identifiers. Solitary is not an option in open prisons, as it would undermine the concept entirely. Instead, resources are poured into positive programming, demonstrating what rehabilitation can truly look like.

Not all northern European countries have successfully integrated incarcerated people into open-prison systems, but there are still other approaches to reforming the solitary model and its conditions. In some Finnish closed prisons, for example, people in solitary confinement may still take part in visits and outdoor exercise. The maximum mandated duration is 14 days, and, in practice, solitary confinement lasting more than 72 hours is very rare. Absent unique circumstances, pregnant or breastfeeding mothers and people with mental illness are excluded from solitary confinement. Finally, guards try to avoid sending people to solitary confinement when they can, by first talking out the problem with the offending person to see if there is an alternate solution. This is de-escalation, something that is too often absent in American prisons.

Another novel idea is found in Norwegian closed prisons, which comprise a majority of their prisons. In many of these closed facilities, there must be a written decision explaining why solitary confinement is necessary. This requires documentation and evidence, which decreases discrimination from the corrections officers in power. The Halden Prison in Norway, for example, makes such efforts to limit the use of solitary confinement. The facility has a mental health team composed of psychologists and psychiatrists who implement early treatment programs to prevent acts of aggression. The nation is also vocal about increasing education about solitary confinement. In addition to the distribution of informational brochures to guards, facility members, and visitors of the prison, all prison staff in Norway must complete a course for credit on solitary confinement – how to use it, when to use it, the effects of it, and alternative measures to take first.

In Denmark, solitary confinement can now only be imposed for a period of no longer than two weeks. Additionally, there are stricter guidelines for placing minors in solitary than in previous years, and guards have been instructed to use it only as a last resort.[13]

AMERICAN REFORM

American activists have been working tirelessly to import European models to the United States. Here in the States, some jurisdictions are starting to pull back on the use of solitary confinement, especially for individuals with serious mental illness, incarcerated youth, and pregnant people. Since 2017, more than 120 state bills have been introduced to restrict or prohibit solitary confinement, with at least 16 states and the federal government enacting laws that limit or ban its use in the last four years.[14]

Federal Reform. In 2018, the federal First Step Act[15] fully banned the use of solitary confinement in youth facilities (referred to as "room confinement" and defined as the "involuntary placement … alone in a cell, room, or other area for any reason") in all circumstances other than for up to a maximum of 30 *minutes* in instances where there is a risk of self-harm and up to a maximum of three hours in instances where there is a risk of harm to others. In 2023, Congress introduced the End Solitary Confinement Act (ESCA), a bill that would ban solitary in federal custody and incentivize states and localities to do the same. Specifically, among other provisions, the bill would end solitary confinement by all names beyond four hours for purposes of de-escalation and emergencies, and otherwise require that all people – including people in alternatives to solitary – have access to at least 14 hours of daily group out-of-cell time, with group programming, recreation, and activities. ESCA offers a powerful legislative path for ending solitary at the federal level. Unfortunately, ESCA was not passed in 2024, and with Donald Trump back in office, the prospects for passing such a bill are considerably diminished, as his administration has generally opposed prison reform efforts.

State Reform. An Unlock the Box report notes five key trends in legislation across states and localities to restrict or end solitary confinement.[16] Those trends are: ending solitary confinement for young people, ending solitary for vulnerable groups, aligning legislation with the UN Mandela Rules prohibition on solitary confinement beyond 15 consecutive days, creating reporting and oversight mechanisms, and ending solitary completely.

With regards to ending solitary for young people, the Unlock the Box report counts 16 states (including Arkansas, Colorado, Connecticut, Hawaii, Illinois, Louisiana, Maryland, Massachusetts, Montana, Nebraska, New Jersey, New Mexico, New York, Tennessee, Virginia, and Washington D.C.) that have either banned or restricted solitary for young people since 2018. Notably, laws ending solitary for pregnant women and during the postpartum period appear to be more successful than those protecting other vulnerable groups – and have passed in 26 states. New Jersey has prohibited solitary for those with developmental disabilities, with "a serious medical condition that cannot be effectively treated in solitary," with "a significant auditory or visual impairment," who "are pregnant or in the postpartum period or have recently suffered a miscarriage or terminated a pregnancy," or who identify or are perceived to be LGBTQI+.

Since 2018, four states – New York, Connecticut, Nevada, and New Jersey – have passed legislation to align with the Mandela Rules' prohibition on more than 15 consecutive days in solitary confinement. (Subsequent to passage of legislation limiting the number of days individuals can be held in solitary, however, the actual practice of solitary confinement has not changed entirely in these states. In New Jersey and some of the other states, individuals are still retained in solitary confinement for periods much longer than 20 days, but their solitary confinement is called something else, as discussed in Chapter 15: Solitary by Any Other Name. Finally, as of the 2023 Unlock the Box report, at least twelve jurisdictions have introduced legislation aimed at ending solitary confinement altogether, including New York City, the District of Columbia, Kentucky, Pennsylvania, Virginia, West Virginia, Maine, Connecticut, New Hampshire, and Maryland.

In North Dakota, after officials from the North Dakota DOC toured prisons in Norway, the DOC instituted reforms modeled on Norwegian approaches to corrections, which reduced the number of people subjected to solitary confinement by 74 percent in the state's two largest prisons between 2016 and 2020.[17] David Cloud and his colleagues at AMEND, along with corrections officials from North Dakota, share a poignant report of developments in the North Dakota DOC subsequent to their implementation of a Norway-informed program. Essentially, the success of the North Dakota reforms hinges on a critical principle: in order to safely and effectively reduce or end solitary confinement in a prison system, there needs to be concurrent expansion of the appropriate rehabilitation, substance abuse treatment, and mental health treatment programs. Best practices require providing people with the programs and treatments that support their continued well-being and rehabilitation. In North Dakota's evolution of creative rehabilitation and treatment programs, there is a model for enhancing rehabilitation opportunities in general population while decreasing reliance on solitary confinement. There have been very positive results, including the fact that, with the downsizing of solitary confinement and expansion of rehabilitation and treatment programs, prison violence has decreased.[18]

The Colorado DOC revised its solitary confinement policy in 2017 after Rick Raemisch, then the DOC secretary, had himself put in one of the solitary cells for a day in order to better understand the practice.[19] Afterwards, he declared that Colorado would stop the practice. The new policy limits a person's isolation to 15 days or less, but the Director of Prisons can extend that limit. While correction officers at first opposed the reforms, many ended up supporting the limits on solitary once they saw the benefits of implementing the changes.

In New York, legislation has been passed in both the state legislature and the New York City Council limiting the use of solitary confinement in correctional facilities. The results to date have been mixed. At the state level, following years-long efforts of the Mental Health Alternatives to Solitary Confinement (MHASC) coalition, the #HALTsolitary Campaign was launched in 2012. The HALT campaign has been carrying out grassroots education, organizing, and advocacy across New York State to end solitary confinement, promote alternatives proven to reduce violence and better protect people's health, and build on those changes to dismantle the racism and punishment paradigm that undergird the entire carceral system. Members of the #HALTsolitary Campaign poured their hearts and energy into drawing attention to the devastating and deadly harms of solitary confinement, the need to end it, and the benefits of alternatives.

In 2021, supermajorities of both houses of the New York State legislature passed, and the Governor signed, the HALT Solitary Confinement Act. In effect since March 31, 2022, the HALT Solitary Law has had tremendous positive impacts on people's lives. For instance, as a result of the law's passage, the state closed Southport Correctional Facility, an all-solitary supermax prison with a long history of abuse; the New York Department of Corrections and Community Supervision (DOCCS) officially ended "keeplock," one of the prevalent forms of solitary confinement where individuals are simply locked in their cells almost 24 hours per day; and the number of people in New York's Special Housing Units (SHU) dropped from thousands of people on a given day to hundreds. Moreover, DOCCS is now required by the legislation to limit SHU confinement to 15 consecutive days. Several individuals who had spent decades in solitary – some for more than 25 or 30 years – have been released from solitary and have subsequently been released to the community.

But sadly, DOCCS continues to systematically violate some of the core components of the HALT Solitary Law, causing grave harm. For example, prisons and jails lock people with mental health needs and physical and cognitive disabilities in solitary[20] despite the HALT Solitary Law's ban on solitary for those special subpopulations. In early 2025, thousands of prison guards initiated a strike in protest of the HALT Act. Officers argued that this legislation compromised their safety and hindered their ability to manage the behavior of people in their charge effectively. The strike led to severe understaffing in prisons, prompting Governor Kathy Hochul to deploy National Guard troops to maintain order. After weeks of negotiations, a tentative agreement was reached on February 28, 2025, which included the temporary suspension of certain provisions of the HALT Act and increased overtime pay for officers.

Meanwhile, the New York City Council passed legislation prohibiting all forms of solitary in NYC jails, including Rikers Island, beyond 15 days, and requiring all people in custody to have access to at least 14 hours of daily out-of-cell time with group programs and activities. Subsequent to passage of the NYC Council's legislation, Mayor Eric Adams declared a state of emergency and suspended parts of the law. The City Council launched a legal challenge to the Mayor's order, demanding full implementation of the Council's resolution.

GOING FORWARD

The torture that is solitary confinement symbolizes what is terribly amiss about our social priorities. We tend to allow the population harmed by broader social problems to be disappeared behind bars. But for solitary confinement to end once and for all, we need to make profound changes in our social arrangements that go far beyond solitary confinement and far beyond the prison industrial complex. We need sentencing reform to reverse years of excessive harshness, the bail system must be made fair, we need expansion of diversion programs that give individuals facing criminal charges an opportunity to change course and live productive lives in the community, we need wrap-around services including housing for folks who are diverted from jail and who are released after serving time, we need robust public mental health programs, and we need to expand employment opportunities and re-build the social welfare safety net programs that have been incrementally slashed since the 1970s when neoliberal policies took control of governance. For those who remain behind bars, there needs to be adequate mental health treatment and enhanced prison rehabilitation and treatment programs, and incarcerated people need to be treated with respect and asked to voluntarily do jobs that are fairly remunerative.

In the end, the complete abolition of solitary confinement and eventual massive de-carceration and rebuilding of social welfare safety net programs in the community are the only real answers. De-carceration has proven repeatedly to be more effective in ensuring citizen security, reducing recidivism, and lowering costs than mass incarceration. It is also imminently possible. For example, between 1999 and 2020, when New York more than halved its prison population, the state's violent crime rate fell by 38 percent, a much greater drop than the national crime rate, which fell by only 24 percent.[21] During the pandemic, we were able to release 100,000 people from state and federal prisons, an eight percent decrease in the entire prison population.[22] Today, incarceration rates are slowly starting to rise again. We must seize the chance we have now to enact laws that would reduce the number of people going into prisons. Stopping juvenile adjudications, focusing on re-entry and restorative justice, and investing in evidence-based policies that lower sentencing lengths have all been shown to be effective.[23]

Many other industrialized countries have found humane, dignified ways of reducing incarceration, with recidivism and crime rates that are far lower than ours. The US prison system in comparison has been called an "affront to human dignity," and represents the "worst version of a racist criminal legal system," according to a UN report published in September 2023.[24] We need to follow science and evidence rather than outdated "tough-on-crime" narratives and notions of what public safety is.

Solitary confinement casts a long shadow over the carceral space when all incarcerated people are constrained in their freedoms and aspirations by the constant threat of being sent to "the hole." It is time for all of us to get involved in the struggle to end solitary confinement. Here are a few things readers and their networks can do:

1. Follow the stories in Solitary Watch (https://solitarywatch.org/), a website dedicated to ending solitary confinement, where most stories are written by authors in solitary confinement.

2. There are a number of organizations that organize educational panels, demonstrations, support services for incarcerated people, and so forth. Find organizations and join their activities.

3. Lobby legislative bodies.

4. Support political prisoners, most of whom languish in solitary confinement.

Artie Gonzalez, incarcerated in solitary confinement for eight years, is now out of prison and doing advocacy work as a producer, speaker, and writer. He shares valuable insights and advice for those on the outside who are working in this area. His perspective is rooted in his lived experience, and while his words may feel direct or challenging at times, they reflect the urgency and importance of amplifying the voices of those who have endured solitary confinement. He emphasizes the need for advocates to listen, learn, and humbly acknowledge the central role of lived experience in driving meaningful change.

If you are currently involved in – or considering joining – the social/criminal justice space and have never actually been incarcerated yourself, welcome, and thank you. Here are some things you should consider:

"We are vehemently opposed to your limiting or speaking with our voices."

This is, without a doubt, my main inspiration for deciding to enter the arena as a voice for the system-impacted in the first place. Too often, those without actual lived experience are deferred to on subjects such as social and criminal justice, especially when it comes to high-profile individuals, like celebrities. I have personally witnessed several speaking panels and events having both system-impacted and high-profile individuals coming together in a common cause, only to be greatly disappointed at the sight of the impacted individual being made to "wait in line" to be heard.

Let me state this very clearly: No matter how well-intentioned a non-system-impacted individual may be, limiting or speaking with our voices is tantamount to a traumatic event. Yes, you read that correctly. Once again, we are made to feel second-class, less than, even bullied. We are made to feel that what we have to say is less significant, just as it was throughout the length of our system involvement. Our self-expression, most of which comes from long histories of pain, fear and abuse, is diminished, its light dimmed by being supplanted in these moments. Our voices, what ought to be the driving force of changing the narrative, of change, are once more overshadowed. This is unacceptable, and it happens daily in the social justice space.

"We want you to be mindful of our trauma."

One of the most insensitive things that I hear from non-system-impacted friends in the space is that I "seem so normal." What does that even mean? How am I supposed to present? This is meant as a compliment, but can be highly insulting and degrading to hear. Yes, I spent over 20 years in a cage, seven of which included being buried in Pelican Bay's notorious solitary confinement unit. Yes, I have been witness to, and participated in, many real-life horrors most only experience vicariously or watch on television. Is the expectation here that I am now condemned to living the rest of my life as a mentally broken, emotionally damaged, inarticulate, practically helpless shell-of-my-former-self? Is this expectation – grounded in bias – the source of your being confounded by my "normal" habits and intellect? Whatever the cause, this attitude is divisive and harmful. It dehumanizes. Furthermore, it reveals deep misunderstandings of what trauma is and looks like for the system-impacted. It also spotlights the sense of "apartness" so many of the inexperienced bring into the space.

There is nothing more empowering than having the freedom to live in our truths, to have ownership over our own identity and expression. Anything which falls short of that equals imprisonment in another form.

The robust national campaign to end solitary confinement has hit a big bump in the road during the second Trump Presidency. Donald Trump and his enablers are intent on applying their cruelty to people who find themselves behind bars, including increased utilization of solitary confinement in federal prisons. ICE detention facilities, mainly run by for-profit corporations contracting with ICE, enlarge their profits by reducing staff and programs at facilities. And private corporations contracting with ICE are well known for their excessive reliance on solitary confinement. Meanwhile they provide inadequate mental health treatment, on average, and the suicide rate in ICE detention facilities is remarkably high. There are also very many credible reports of, and lawsuits about, sexual abuse of detainees in ICE detention facilities.

Now, with the Trump administration rapidly multiplying the number of immigrants in detention, the ICE detention facilities are overcrowded and new facilities are planned. Meanwhile, immigrants are being sent to Guantanamo Bay Detention Camp, where solitary confinement is prevalent; and hundreds of immigrants from Venezuela and elsewhere have been sent to CECOT, the prison built in 2022–2023 in El Salvador to incarcerate alleged terrorists. The Trump administration is considering sending US citizens to CECOT.[25] Human Rights groups are alarmed about conditions in CECOT, where most prisoners are confined in large dormitories, there are no outdoor recreation areas and no family visits, and there are credible reports of torture. Solitary confinement is a significant part of the program at CECOT, along with another form of cruel punishment that involves placing many prisoners in a crowded "dark cell" where there is almost no light, nothing to do, and prisoners must sleep standing up because of the crowding.[26]

The cruelty of the Trump administration means we need to put even more energy into the multi-faceted campaign to end the torture.

For information about how to get involved in the growing movement to end solitary confinement in your state, please check out these links:

Unlock the Box, https://unlocktheboxcampaign.org/action-center/#:~:text=GET%20INVOLVED%20LOCALLY&text=It's%20vital%20that%20we%20connect,campaign%20to%20people%20in%20solitary

National Religious Campaign Against Torture, https://www.nrcat.org/get-involved

15
Solitary by Any Other Name

When they promoted me to medium custody, I thought I was leaving solitary confinement behind. Instead, I found myself in a strange space not quite solitary, not quite general population, but somehow managing to combine the worst aspects of both.

On paper, in Texas, medium custody is supposed to have outdoor recreation twice a week, Tuesdays and Thursdays, for one hour each time. In reality, staffing shortages mean we often go weeks without seeing the sky. It's like being teased with more freedom. Here's what you could have, if only we had enough guards to watch you.

Then there's the 23:59, a bureaucratic sleight of hand that would be almost impressive if it weren't so cruel. Texas has regulations against 24-hour lockdowns, so they lock us down for 23 hours and 59 minutes instead. One single minute of theoretical freedom makes it legal, makes it not-technically-solitary-confinement for the 86 people in medium custody. Someone in an office somewhere must have felt very clever when they thought of that.

The worst part isn't even the confinement. It's the psychological game they're playing. In solitary, at least the rules were clear. You knew you were locked down. You knew what to expect. Here, they dangle the promise of more freedom while holding the threat of lockdown over our heads. It's like being given a longer leash but still feeling the collar just as tight. Now, I understand why most of the people promoted to medium-security ultimately returned to solitary. At least solitary didn't dress up torture in a promotion or play games with minutes and regulations. This "medium custody" feels like gaslighting, telling us we're more free while finding new ways to emulate solitary.

Someone raises their voice in the dayroom? 23:59. Short of staff? 23:59. An argument in the chow line? 23:59. One person's infraction becomes everyone's punishment. During these lockdowns, which happen weekly and can be extended indefinitely, life becomes a mirror image of solitary. Meals arrive through the food slot. Medications are delivered to our cells. Laundry appears and disappears without us ever leaving our rooms. The teargas drifts through corridors just as frequently as it did in solitary – a burning reminder that control here is maintained with the same tools of force. I was supposed to feel grateful for this new "freedom." But, sometimes, the only real difference I can see is that they've painted the walls a different shade of white.

We do get daily showers without guard escorts or handcuffs now, which sounds like an improvement over solitary where broken plumbing and predatory guards make showering rare and risky endeavors. But this small mercy feels almost mocking in the face of everything else that remains the same.

The cruelest part is that medium-security is supposed to be my transition period, 20 months of "preparation" for general population, which I won't reach until January 2026. But even this uncertain progress isn't guaranteed. The prison regularly sends me back to solitary when they need my bed space, treating me like a human chess piece to be moved at their convenience.

Sometimes I wonder if this is what purgatory feels like, that theological space between heaven and hell where souls await judgment. It's a waiting room with tear gas, a transition period that feels suspiciously permanent, a "promotion" that keeps dragging me backward.

I realize now that I never really left solitary confinement after eight and a half years. They just rebranded it, added a roommate, and called it progress. This isn't freedom or even a step toward it. Some days, watching the sun through barred windows during another extended 23:59 lockdown, I wonder if they've just found a more palatable way to keep us in solitary by another name.

– Kwaneta Harris (moved to medium-security after eight and a half years in solitary confinement)

As I woke up for my daily job at the Washington State Reformatory on September 30, 2021, I drank a cup of freeze-dried coffee and watched the local morning news. One story instantly caught my attention: The reporter said the Washington Department of Corrections, or WDOC, had decided to stop using segregation as punishment.[1] Could this even be possible? I convinced myself that I must have misheard something.

The department claimed it had already stopped using disciplinary segregation for two weeks and had no plan to use it in the future. But, as someone who lives in the violent and oppressive US prison system and has experienced solitary first-hand, I knew the truth: solitary confinement wasn't over – they had just decided to call it something else.[2]

Despite some public claims that states are moving away from solitary confinement, legislation is often no more than window dressing, and in practice solitary is still used liberally as a tool to control incarcerated people. Corrections departments may continue to consign people to solitary confinement long after county resolutions or state laws mandate sharp restrictions. The name for solitary is changed to "restricted housing" or "special programming," but the practice remains the same.[3]

The first deceiving thing about the Washington DOC's announcement that it would end the use of "disciplinary segregation" is that it addresses only a small fraction of the people in solitary confinement and leaves hundreds in conditions that the international community has deemed torture because the vast majority of people in solitary confinement in Washington are in administrative, not disciplinary, segregation.

Although people in administrative segregation can no longer be sentenced to solitary confinement as punishment *after* a hearing, under the DOC's changes people can still spend extended periods in those barbaric conditions while they *await* a hearing. According to a report by the Vera Institute, a national body the WDOC contracted with to help reduce its solitary population, as of September 2020 incarcerated people in Washington spent on average almost 29 days in administrative segregation, with many much longer.[4] In August 2021, the Office of the Corrections Ombuds issued a report on administrative segregation which found that many people remained in solitary for well over 100 days.[5] The WDOC change does nothing to address this reality.[6]

In addition to administrative segregation, there are many other reasons that can land someone in solitary apart from "disciplinary segregation." There are many people in maximum custody, which is often indefinite long-term solitary, and many of those people have been there for more than 500 days, some for a decade or more. As discussed in Chapter 4: Who Gets Sent to the Hole, there are also people serving time in solitary for medical isolation, suicide watch, protective custody, and the like. The state's new law does not affect the use of solitary for any of these reasons.

The second deceiving thing about the WDOC's proclamation that it will end "disciplinary segregation" is that "disciplinary segregation" is just one of the many phrases that corrections departments use to describe solitary confinement. What's to stop the WDOC from using a different label as a way to continue the use of isolation as a form of discipline?

The press response to the WDOC's announcement was overwhelmingly positive. Some outlets claimed the state was ending solitary confinement entirely, prompting the department to issue a clarification to its own press release, noting that it "continues to utilize segregation for non-disciplinary purposes such as investigations, safety, protective custody and classification."[7]

We need to take a much deeper look into what is actually being changed. From where we sit, this policy shift falls far short of the massive reform that the department is claiming. In its press statements, WDOC actually admitted that the numbers were deceiving by explaining that the actual number of days individuals spent in designated disciplinary segregation was seemingly small only because many people had often already served time in solitary under administrative segregation while awaiting their hearings.

The WDOC has not yet specified what forms of punishment will be replacing disciplinary segregation, other than providing four out-of-cell hours per day, rather than only one hour. One troubling possibility is confining incarcerated persons in their regular cells, a practice often used as a disciplinary sanction. In some cases, people find themselves in cell confinement for a month or even longer. This approach is really no different from being placed in a separate, empty cell designated for solitary, with nothing but the concrete walls to keep them company.

Last year, a bill was introduced in the legislature that would have affected a real change in Washington State, but the WDOC did not support it. Passing that legislation, SB 5413/ HB 1312, would ban long-term solitary and prohibit its use entirely against vulnerable populations, including people with mental illness.[8]

A similar effort failed in New Jersey in 2016 – a revised bill passed in 2019, but subsequent accounts indicate that its implementation has been widely ineffective at limiting isolation.[9] Consider Nathan Gray's story. He often found himself pacing his cramped cell, barraged night and day by the sound of other men's screams. The cell was chilly, with a paper-thin mattress, a small shelf for his belongings and a combined sink and toilet. In this small space, he ate his meals, read Frantz Fanon and Angela Davis, and slept when he could. When depression overwhelmed him, he had no one to talk to. He didn't tell his family about the conditions he was forced to endure; he didn't want to worry them.

Gray and his neighbors were permitted to leave their cells for only a handful of reasons each week: to take three showers, for example, or make five 15-minute phone calls, or use an email kiosk to send messages to friends and family on the outside. Sometimes, they were allowed to hang out in one of the holding cells in the unit, known as "cages," or in outdoor enclosed spaces.

In short, Gray's description of the living conditions in his unit sounds like those experienced by people held in solitary confinement across the US: severe restrictions on movement, moratoriums on physical contact, and nearly 24-hour spans spent in cells about the size of bathrooms.

But Gray, who is known as "Freedom" to friends and family, was not in solitary confinement, according to the New Jersey Department of Corrections. Instead, he lived in one of New Jersey State Prison's Restorative Housing Units, or RHUs, where people are sent as punishment for breaking prison rules.

In New Jersey, a 2019 law put strict limits on the NJDOC's use of solitary confinement, which is referred to as "isolated confinement." Instead, New Jersey now sends people to RHUs as punishment for breaking prison rules. RHUs are in theory a less restrictive alternative to solitary confinement, but in reality they are barely different at all.

Gray, who was released from prison in May 2023, spent more than 370 days in RHUs across two facilities, mostly in New Jersey State Prison. He said that people in his unit at New Jersey State Prison spent more than 20 hours in their cells most days. He was later transferred to an RHU at South Woods State Prison, ahead of his release from prison in May. The conditions there, he said, were even worse than what he experienced at NJSP.

The Department of Corrections created RHUs in response to the 2019 passage of the Isolated Confinement Restriction Act (ICRA),[10] a law intended to reform the use of solitary confinement in New Jersey correctional facilities.[11] At the time, ICRA was the most progressive solitary confinement reform law in the nation. The law put strict limits on NJDOC's use of solitary confinement – which is referred to as "isolated confinement," and is defined as holding a person "in a cell or similarly confined holding or living space, alone or with other inmates" for 20 or more hours per day "with severely restricted activity, movement, and social interaction." The limits included capping the practice at 20 consecutive days or 30 days in a 60-day period. The law also restricted the placement of vulnerable groups, like LGBTQ+ people, in isolated confinement. Isolated confinement can still be used as a punishment in some cases, but people placed there are afforded some protections, like frequent health exams.

RHUs are meant to be a "less restrictive" alternative to isolated confinement. Incarcerated people held in RHUs should have access to recreation, education and out-of-cell activities that allow for social interaction, per departmental regulations.[12] And most importantly, unlike in isolated confinement, people held in RHUs must be offered the opportunity to spend at least four hours each day outside of their cells. People found guilty of violating prison rules can be placed in these units for up to one year per disciplinary incident.

But Gray was dismayed at how little conditions in his new unit differed from what he had endured in solitary confinement. Gray and several other incarcerated people who have lived in RHUs told us that they were not regularly offered at least four hours of daily out-of-cell time, they often spent their out-of-cell time in confined spaces they compared to dog kennels, and they received little to no mental health care.

An 18-month investigation by *Type Investigations* and *HuffPost* – which involved interviews with more than a dozen individuals, including incarcerated people, advocates, and lawyers, and a review of hundreds of pages of public records – found that conditions in some of these Restorative Housing Units may qualify as isolated confinement under the department's own definition and defy state regulations, and appear at times to violate the law.

Two years later, in July 2021, the state appeared to have reduced its solitary population drastically. NJDOC reported in response to an annual survey that it was holding only 49 individuals, or 0.4 percent of all incarcerated people in the state, in solitary confinement.[13] But these numbers are misleading. After passing the reform law, it appears the state has simply replicated the conditions of solitary confinement in at least some of the RHUs.

Advocates told us that in some prisons, they've been informed that the main difference between ad-seg and RHUs is a new sign on the door of the same unit. And those RHUs are not classified as solitary by the department, meaning that people held there do not receive the protections, like the 20-day limit on isolated confinement, that ICRA provides.

Other states have imposed watered-down bans on the practice[14] but have refused to abandon it completely.[15] For example, Massachusetts's 2018 Criminal Justice Reform Act limits placement in "restrictive housing" to no more than six months and prohibits it for anyone with a release date of fewer than 120 days (unless that person posed an immediate threat),[16] among other restrictions. However, in response to this Act, the Massachusetts DOC simply created new units – "Behavioral Adjustment Units" and "Secure Adjustment Units," which are, for all intents and purposes, the same as solitary. Likewise, Michigan has claimed to reduce its use of solitary, touting a 70 percent decrease in the number of people "administratively segregated" from 2008 to 2024.[17] However, the activist group Open MI Door claims that this alleged decrease only exists because of a narrow definition of what constitutes solitary confinement.[18] In February 2023, the Virginia General Assembly passed similar watered-down legislation reforming solitary confinement.[19] In 2024, Senate Bill no. 719[20] would have placed a 15-day limit on solitary along with many other pretty progressive reforms, but this bill was vetoed by the Governor.

Despite claims and pledges to end solitary confinement for many years, the New York City Department of Correction repeatedly introduced various forms of solitary confinement by many names.[21] For example, even after the HALT Act, the New York DOC continued to lock people in solitary confinement in tiny shower cages,[22] where people were surrounded by caged walls without even the ability to sit down, leading to devastating harm and even death. The DOC also locked people in solitary confinement for 23 to 24 hours a day, for days, weeks, months, and more than a year, with fake so-called out-of-cell time taking place locked alone in an extended part of the cell.[23]

Regardless of what name officials give it, when the social isolation is replicated, and people are locked alone in cells without meaningful human touch, interaction, or programming, they will continue to suffer all of the harmful and well-known consequences of solitary. These experiences demonstrate how critical it is for legislation to explicitly prohibit all forms of solitary by all names and require that people have access to full days of out-of-cell time with group programming and activities.

16

The Case Against Solitary Confinement

We pass through a gate, and I recognize the large concrete steps that lead to the living units in the main part of the prison. My heart starts to race. All I can think is that this nightmare is finally over. Once we pass through the gate, the guards tell me to stop. I do as I'm told, and they remove the cuffs from my sore wrists. I wait for instructions, afraid of upsetting them. After about 30 seconds, the guards instruct me to go back to my unit. I take the stairs two at a time as if I'm trying to escape capture from an enemy combatant, as if they might change their minds at any moment and haul me back to solitary.

This begins the end of my story in solitary, which encompassed hundreds of days of my life.

In my new cell, I remove my shoes and place my phonebook on the desk. I listen to the silence of the unit. What a beautiful thing it is – no banging, no yelling, no toilets flooding, just the eerie silence of prison at night. I'm ready to get back to my family, to go to school again, to not let myself slip back into a pattern of disruptive behavior. Meanwhile, I know this could easily happen again in a week, a month, a year – after all, in prison nothing is guaranteed. But one thing I know for sure is that I won't let this story go untold.

I was perhaps one of the lucky ones. For many, this has been their existence for years, even decades, and these barbaric conditions lead to harm, fear, and anger that can last a lifetime. Solitary confinement must end if we want people to leave prison healthy, productive, and ready to integrate into our neighborhoods.[1]

Solitary confinement should be *per se* unconstitutional. It is cruel and unusual punishment that violates the Eighth Amendment in *every* instance. Research has confirmed what the Supreme Court initially saw in *In Re Medley:* that solitary confinement not only exacerbates existing mental illness, but it also *causes* mental illness: "After decades, if not centuries, of research, there is not a single published study of solitary or supermax-like confinement lasting for longer than 10 days that failed to find negative psychological effects."[2] The very nature of the harm and deprivation caused by isolation, regardless of services provided and number of hours of "exercise" allowed, violates contemporary standards of decency.

Because of the severe and long-lasting harm likely caused by solitary confinement in every instance, case-by-case analysis is unnecessary and the nature of the incarcerated person's infraction should never justify the torture. Decisions about solitary confinement should be taken out of the hands of prison guards because it is likely that prolonged isolation will actually cause severe harm in almost every instance.

Solitary confinement cannot be justified as being vital to the safety and security of the prison. Most people sent to solitary have not even been "officially designated as exhibiting violent or serious and disruptive behavior while incarcerated."[3] As we have shown, the vast majority of people being sent to solitary aren't even being accused of posing any threat to the safety of others at all.

There is no evidence that solitary confinement actually reduces violence. Instead, there are research findings that point strongly to the opposite conclusion, that solitary confinement worsens the problem of violence, both within prisons and in the public. Most incarcerated people are eventually released either back into the prison population or sometimes right back into the public after spending significant amounts of time in solitary confinement, often with little or no preparation for reintegration.[4] They often re-enter general population or society more dangerous than they left due to the psychological torture they went through. On top of that, the decimation of life skills caused by their stint in solitary means they have fewer non-violent ways to settle disputes.[5] The result, proven clearly by statistics, is that the longer a person is in solitary confinement, the more likely they are to commit a new crime once released from prison.[6]

When use of solitary confinement is diminished in a corrections department, and at the same time rehabilitation programs, drug treatment, and mental health treatment programs are expanded, the rate of violence diminishes, suggesting that the way to reduce violence in the prisons is not more solitary confinement, but rather bolstering treatment and rehabilitation programs.

Solitary confinement also cannot be justified by the surges in prison populations since the 1980s, which have left prisons ill-equipped to handle the sheer volume of people in custody. Certainly, torture cannot be justified based on convenience. There are far better ways to deal with overcrowding and violence in prisons, including robust efforts to reduce the population through improved access to mental health treatment and revisiting lengthy sentences.

Other common justifications for the use of solitary confinement also fail: solitary doesn't save money; it costs three times more than standard incarceration.[7] It doesn't make guards safer;[8] it makes them more prone to mental and physical health issues.[9] And solitary doesn't teach people a lesson or prepare them for release; it makes them angry, isolated, and more likely to be re-incarcerated.[10]

As so wisely put by solitary survivor and activist Johnny Perez, "every day we allow solitary confinement to exist is another day we legislate loneliness, normalize cruelty, and postpone the future we claim to believe in." The extremity of conditions in solitary forces its inhabitants into survival mode, and in survival mode it's impossible to be accountable or to think clearly about the future. We need to get beyond survival mode to be able to process the traumas, only then can we reflect on the harm the crimes we committed have caused others.

We like to believe that rising from the torture there is always hope, as found in the corners. We think of the following poem, "The Corner," by Lanae Tipton, who is currently serving her second year in solitary confinement:

I sit by the slit in the corner of my door
Hours at a time I dare
to listen to stories and tales
from anyone willing to share.

Captive in solitary confinement
I have found life in these corners.

I'm not in this corner
by punishment or by force
One small choice in my life
Made with no remorse.

A hypothetical escape or an exciting adventure awaits
The promise of relief lies ahead
When I'm left alone with my own thoughts
I'm swallowed in darkness instead.

The simple sound of a stranger's voice
coming through the cracks
is everything
when I'm enslaved in this box.

With good neighbors the connection revives and uplifts
and allows light to seep into the void I know
when I forget that the abyss of ad-seg swallowed me up
a long, long time ago.

Something as simple and common
as communication
is the hand that has pulled me out
time and time again.

Conversations in the corner remind me
of dreams long forgotten
of the identity of a person I once knew
that was forced into hiding.

One that handcuffs and barbed wire effectively turned
into an unrecognizable defensive shield
now unable to drop its guard
or be fully revealed.

I don't have to hide anymore
when I'm in these corners.
Hope glimmers once again
when I'm in these corners.

I'm stored away like food
in a pantry waiting to rot
forcing myself to remember I'm alive
when everyone else forgot.

Yet, here is where I am able to shine
with a light that once freely shone
when I'm sitting in these corners
I'm no longer alone.

If hurt people hurt people, we must reconstruct a prison system that rehabilitates our fellow citizens, as opposed to further harming them.

I have found that one of the greatest solaces in staying hopeful is reading about the experiences of others who have survived solitary confinement. I return often to the words of Wilbert Rideau, who endured twelve years in solitary confinement. He wrote in "In The Place of Justice":

> *The sensation passes and an old longing surfaces – a longing to escape this harsh, ultra-masculine jungle unsoftened by love or beauty, where everyone is engaged in a perpetual battle to prove who is the toughest, the strongest, the cruelest. I long to get away from this field of pain and misery. Not to the city; that's just*

another jungle. I want to flee to the country, where I imagine there is no madness, no hate, no war, no animal save those that walk on four legs. Out where life is simple, peaceful, and clean. Where rippling creeks feed open meadows and green leaves dance on soft breezes to the chirpings of gaily colored birds. I long for the fragrance of honeysuckle in my nostrils, the air of innocence. And alongside the creek, clover matted from tender lovemaking. This is freedom – to work, to love, to aspire. To find my place in the world.[11]

Glossary

Active Gang: Incarcerated persons that are actively representing a gang in the prison. An example would be Crips, Bloods, or racial gangs.

Administrative Segregation ("ad-seg" or "seg"): When incarcerated persons are held in solitary confinement for safety or security reasons, rather than as punishment. This can be because an individual poses a threat to themselves or others, because there is an investigation or transfer from the prison pending, or because protective custody is required, such as for a high-profile incarcerated person or someone who is vulnerable to harm.

Birdbath: Where an incarcerated person takes a bath in a small sink in their cell.

Cell Search: When guards come in a search through an incarcerated person's cell and belongings.

Cell Warriors: Incarcerated persons who insult and threaten others while in solitary confinement, knowing they can say whatever they want and others cannot get to them while they are locked in a cell.

Closed Custody Facility: The maximum-security prisons in Washington State.

Control Booth: Where our calls are answered when we push our emergency call button.

Counselors: Staff that are assigned to each incarcerated person to deal with their classification and any other needs that pertain to their placement within the prison system.

County Jail: Where individuals are held while in the process of awaiting trial for the crime they were accused of committing.

Cuff Port: Another word used for the slot/tray door/hatch on a cell door that is used to give items to incarcerated persons.

Cultural Groups: Individuals that stick together because they relate to each other through their cultural backgrounds.

Custody Unit Supervisor (CUS): The administrator that is in charge of the living units. They are in all living units where incarcerated persons are housed.

Department of Corrections (DOC) Administration: High-ranking staff that run the prison. Examples are Superintendent, Associate Superintendent, Custody Program Manager (CPM), and Custody Unit Manager (CUS).

Disciplinary Segregation: When incarcerated persons are held in solitary confinement as a punitive measure as a result of a disciplinary infraction or rule violation.

Dog Leash: Exactly what it sounds like – a short lead that has a metal clip on it. These are used to control incarcerated persons' movements while in transport in the hole.

Emergency Call Button: This is placed in each cell in case an incarcerated person needs to contact a guard at any time, as there is not a consistent staff present in the living unit.

Extraction: When guards go into an incarcerated person's cell to remove them forcefully.

Fishing: A way for incarcerated persons to communicate or get something from their cell to another incarcerated person's cell despite being physically isolated. It involves creating makeshift lines, often from torn clothing, bed sheets, or other materials, and sliding them along the floor to pass notes, food, or other small items between cells.

Flooding a Cell: Where an item is used to block the toilet from flushing allowing the water to spill out onto the cell floor, and eventually into the unit.

Four o'clock count: A daily count the guards do in the prison to make sure all incarcerated persons are present.

General Population: The main population of the prison.

Goon Squad: A term used by incarcerated persons and DOC staff for the guard's response team. This team is called in when a situation is out of control and past being handled by the regular floor guards. This squad is suited up in full riot gear and equipped with weapons, such as large cans of OC spray, shock shields, electric tasers, and shotguns with rubber bullets.

Green Smock: A small dress-like gown to cover the body with an open back. This is used when incarcerated persons are under threat of suicide, or when an incarcerated person is being punished and has had all their property taken.

Hatch: Another word used for the slot/tray door on a cell door that is used to give items to incarcerated persons.

Holding Cell: Small rooms designed to hold an incarcerated person for a short amount of time.

Hourly Check: The guards do these in the units, as a way of making sure we are safe and in good health.

IMU Counselor: Staff that are assigned to each incarcerated person to deal with their classification and any other needs that pertain to their placement within the prison system.

Initial Review: Done for every incarcerated person upon entering solitary confinement, mostly as a formality as it is rare to actually get any information from this review.

Intensive Management Unit (IMU): The same place as solitary confinement, just a different name.

Intercom: The speaker that is placed in cells to allow incarcerated persons to communicate with guards in the control booth.

Internal Investigations (I&I): The staff tasked to investigate incarcerated persons and guards that are thought to be involved with illegal behavior, within the prison grounds.

Isolation Cell: Rooms that are stripped of everything. Incarcerated persons are put into them when they are under observation of self-harm.

Jumpsuit: A one-piece suit that incarcerated persons are given to wear while in solitary confinement.

Juvenile System: The system where individuals are confined if they are not of age to enter the adult system.

Lifers: Incarcerated persons with life sentences.

Living unit Sargent: The guard that is in charge of all the regular guards in each living unit.

Main Prison: The regular main line outside of solitary confinement.

Medium/Long-term Minimum Custody: Prisons that incarcerated persons have earned their way to through good behavior.

Incarcerated persons have more time out of their cells and extra privileges compared to closed custody prisons.

Mental Health Staff: Staff hired by the prison to work with incarcerated persons on areas surrounding their mental health. There are not a ton of them working at the prison and they are not all that readily accessible.

Mentor Programs: Positive programs where older incarcerated persons help younger ones to work on positive change within their lives.

Offender Store: Where incarcerated persons are able to purchase things like toiletries/hygienic products (also called "hygiene") and writing materials.

Pad: What some people call the mattress, as it is very thin, and nowhere near the thickness of a mattress.

Phone book: Incarcerated persons carry small phone books with them, most all do this in case they are sent to solitary confinement. This way they are able to have friends' and family member's addresses handy.

Postage Transfers: Slips used to send out mail that would be overweight when using a regular pre-stamped envelope.

Prison Kites: Carbon copy papers that are used for incarcerated persons to send messages to administration, counselors, medical staff, mental health staff, and any other prison officials.

Prisoner Grievance: This is meant to be an avenue for incarcerated persons to highlight complaints and mistreatments.

Programs: These are designated amounts of time incarcerated persons are given to do in solitary confinement, because of their deemed misbehaviors. These amounts of time can range from six months to an indefinite sentence in solitary confinement.

Reviews: These are regular reviews incarcerated persons are given on a timeline to keep them updated on the process of the investigation.

Riot Gear: Face shields, helmets, and thick plastic armor to cover the rest of the body.

Safety & Security of the Prison: This term is often used to put incarcerated persons in solitary confinement under investigation.

It allows the administration to bypass any real proof that there was actual wrongdoing by an incarcerated person.

Security Threat Group (STG): A group of incarcerated persons that are actively involved in a gang within the prison system.

Self-help Programs: Programs that involve restorative justice, addiction, anger management, parenting, and any other area that helps an individual address areas of need within themselves.

Sent of Missions: A term used by incarcerated persons when an incarcerated person is sent to attack another individual by an incarcerated person.

Shock Shields: Shields that are close to body length, have electricity running through them, and are used as weapons against incarcerated persons.

Shot Callers: Incarcerated persons that have been raised to lead their gangs and groups within the prison.

Shower Shoes: Slippers that incarcerated persons are given in solitary confinement, as no shoes are permitted. They are open-toed slippers.

SHU: The accepted acronym for solitary confinement.

Slot: The small tray door on each door for every cell in solitary confinement. They are about one and a half feet wide, by 7 inches high.

Small Flexible Pen: The pen that we are given to write content while in solitary confinement. It is about 4 inches tall and very flexible, which makes it extremely hard to write with.

Spray You: A term used by guards when they are threatening to use OC (pepper spray) on an incarcerated person.

STG Activity: Incarcerated persons that are involved in activities that are gang-related.

Strip Cells: When an incarcerated person's cell is stripped of "everything."

Strip Down: When an incarcerated person is stripped of all their clothing and a guard inspects their body from top to bottom. No place is left unseen.

Suicide Cell: Rooms that are stripped of everything. Incarcerated persons are put into them when they are under observation of self-harm.

Suited Up: A term used by guards and incarcerated persons when the goon squad is about to be called in to deal with a situation.

The Beaver Tail: A nickname for the toothbrush that we receive in solitary confinement.

Ticket: A disciplinary report or infraction notice issued to an incarcerated person for violating a prison rule. Consequences can range from loss of privileges to solitary confinement.

Tier: A walkway for the guards to walk in front of the incarcerated person's cells.

Top Tier: The second floor of cells in the unit.

Transferred: When incarcerated persons are moved from one prison to another prison.

Under Investigation: When incarcerated persons are put in solitary confinement pending the outcome of their involvement in behavior that is against prison policy, while the administration is looking for evidence to link them to the actions the incarcerated person is believed to be involved in.

Unit Staff Member: The same as a guard. In most juvenile facilities this is what guards are called.

Unit: Where all the cells are.

Using the Doorbell: What some incarcerated persons call banging on their door.

Written Up: A term used by guards and incarcerated persons referring to a guard writing an infraction on an incarcerated person for something they saw as a misbehavior. Incarcerated persons can receive time in solitary confinement, loss of good time from their sentence, and many other loss of privileges if found guilty of the write-up.

Yard: A small concrete room, not much larger than the cell an incarcerated person lives in. There is a small opening for fresh air to enter, but no sunlight to bathe in. There is typically a phone to make collect calls, and a pull-up and dip bar for exercise.

Yellow Line: These are lines within the prison that we are not allowed to cross, or lines that we are meant to stand on in order to receive a meal.

About the Authors

Christopher William Blackwell is an award-winning journalist currently serving a 45-year prison sentence in Washington State for taking a human life during a drug robbery. He has been incarcerated since 2003 and was incarcerated for the first time at the age of 12. While incarcerated, Chris earned a college degree in political and social sciences, created multiple mentor programs, and became a facilitator for restorative justice circles. He is the co-founder, with Dr. Chelsea Moore, and Executive Director of Look2Justice, a grassroots organization of system-impacted organizers and researchers who work to cultivate justice, fairness, and accountability in Washington State's criminal legal system. With co-author Deborah Zalesne, he founded and runs a Writers Development Program that uplifts the voices of incarcerated writers in the mainstream media.

Chris has published well over 100 essays and articles in outlets such as the *New York Times*, the *Washington Post*, the *Boston Globe*, *HuffPost*, *Mother Jones*, the *Nation*, *BuzzFeed*, and the *Seattle Times*. He has written and co-written many articles about the harms of solitary confinement, including "Prisoners Say New Jersey's Alternative to Solitary Confinement is Pretty Much the Same (*HuffPost*); In the Hole" (*Jewish Currents*); "The Unceasing Noise of Solitary Confinement" (the *Progressive*); "End Solitary in All Its Forms" (the *Progressive*); "Prisons Said it was COVID Isolation. The Incarcerated Describe Torture" (*HuffPost*); "Quarantined in Solitary is Still Solitary" (Prison Journalism Project); "Voices from Solitary: Fighting the Coronavirus in Prison with Transfers, Isolation, Threats, and Game Boys" (Solitary Watch); "The Harms of Solitary Confinement During COVID" (*Counterpunch*); "Abolish All Forms of Solitary Confinement in Washington State" (*Seattle Times*); "Voices from Solitary: Everyday Torture" (Solitary Watch); and "Voices from Solitary: Why Did They Choose Antonio" (Solitary Watch).

Chris is a contributing writer with Jewish Currents and a contributing editor with The Appeal, where he writes a monthly newsletter. He was awarded the Galaxy Leader Fellowship in 2024 with his wife, Dr. Chelsea Moore. He was the Grand Prize winner of Narratively's prestigious 2023 Memoir Contest, and he was awarded the 2024 Incarcerated Journalist of the Year award by Prison Journalism Project through their Stillwater Awards.

Email: christopherwilliamblackwell@gmail.com
Website: www.christopher-blackwell.com
Blue Sky: @chriswblackwell.bsky.social
IG: @christopherwblackwell
X: @chriswblackwell

Look2Justice:
Website: www.look2justice.org
X: @Look2Justice
IG: @look2justice
FB: @Look2Justice

Deborah Zalesne is a Professor of Law at the City University of New York School of Law where she has been teaching contract law from a social justice perspective since August 1997. With co-author Christopher Blackwell, she founded and runs a Writers Development Program that pairs aspiring incarcerated writers with inside and outside volunteer mentors who support their writing and help pitch it to media outlets.

Deborah has published extensively in the areas of criminal justice, race and gender justice, legal pedagogy, and issues relating to the use of contracts to empower disenfranchised groups. She has authored/co-authored two books and over 40 scholarly articles for legal publications such as the Yale Journal of Law and Feminism, the Columbia Journal of Race and the Law, and the Harvard Women's Law Review, and her work has been cited as legal authority hundreds of times in law journals, books, and state and federal court opinions. She has published several articles focused on solitary confinement, including co-authored pieces with Christopher Blackwell in The Appeal and Kwaneta Harris in The Marshall Project. Chris and Deborah are currently co-editing a book along with Jamie Beth Cohen, entitled *Dear Teenage Me: Voices from Beyond the Barbed Wire*, that will include essays by incarcerated people in the form of letters to their younger selves.

zalesne@law.cuny.edu
X: @DebbieZalesne
CUNY Law faculty page: http://www.law.cuny.edu/faculty/directory/zalesne

Terry A. Kupers is a psychiatrist and Professor Emeritus at the Wright Institute in Berkeley, California. His leadership and expertise have shed light on the intersection of mental health and incarceration, challenging outdated paradigms, and advocating for humane and effective solutions. Dr. Kupers's research illuminates the detrimental effects of solitary confinement on mental health, the inadequacy of mental health treatment behind bars, and the terrible human damage caused by sexual abuse in jails, prisons, and immigration detention facilities. He testifies as an expert witness in class action and other litigation. Dr. Kupers is a Distinguished Life Fellow of the American Psychiatric Association, recipient of the Exemplary Psychiatrist Award from the National Alliance on Mental Illness (NAMI), and the 2024 Judge Stephen S. Goss Lifetime Achievement Award from Judges and Psychiatrists Leadership Initiative (JPLI). Among the five books he has authored are *Prison Madness: The Mental Health Crisis Behind Bars*, and *Solitary: The Inside Story of Supermax Isolation*. He is co-editor and contributor to *Prison Masculinities*.

Faculty spotlight: www.wi.edu/news-faculty-spotlight-dr-kupers

Kwaneta Harris is a former nurse, business owner, and expat, and is now an incarcerated journalist and Haymarket Writing Freedom Fellow. In her writing, she illuminates how the experience of being incarcerated in the largest state prison in Texas is vastly different for women in ways that directly map onto a culture rooted in misogyny. Her stories expose how the intersection of gender, race, and place contribute to state-sanctioned, gender-based violence. Through her writing she offers a peek inside the brutal criminal legal system, with hope to reimagine effective non-carceral solutions for those who harm. She writes about censorship, healthcare, climate and how they affect systems-impacted people.

Her writings have appeared in a wide range of publications including *Solitary Watch, Cosmopolitan, Rolling Stone, The Marshall Project, Scalawag, Prism, The Appeal,* and *Teen Vogue,* among others, and she publishes the Substack newsletter *Write or Die.* Harris authored a segment on This American Life and was interviewed for a documentary by Al-Jazeera about solitary confinement, in which she was detained for 8.5 of her 17 years incarcerated. She is currently working on a book about the teenagers from juvenile who were her neighbors in adult solitary confinement.

kwanetaharris@gmail.com
Personal website: www.kwanetaharris.com
Bluesky: @kwanetaharris.bsky.social
X: @kwanetaharris
Substack: Write or Die: kwanetaharris.substack.com

Acknowledgements

We are deeply grateful to those who generously gave their time, expertise, and wisdom to help shape this book.

First and foremost, without the courage of the incarcerated and formerly incarcerated contributors who shared their profoundly traumatic stories, this book would not exist. There would be no way to truly understand what takes place inside the dark, hidden corners of solitary confinement. Those who speak out from prison, knowing very well that telling their stories exposes them to great risk of retaliation while they remain behind bars, are no different from reporters who risk their lives to report from a war zone. You are reporting from behind enemy lines. Thank you to the following people for trusting us with your stories, and for the immense courage it took to share them with the world: Todd Ashker, Stacy Berry, Jeremiah Bourgeois, Gail Brashear, Jason Burdett, Jeremy Busby, Dolores Canales, Augustus E. Cooper, Brant Daniel, Frank De Palma, Ralph D. Dunuan III, Paul Fuentes, Artie Gonzalez, Nathan Gray, Xandan Gulley, Lacino Hamilton, Chris Heeren, Juan C. Hernandez, Dennis Hope, Tomiekia Johnson, Amber Kim, Robert King, Jonathan Kirkpatrick, Kevin Light-Roth, Jarvis Jay Masters, Michael Moore, Jack Morris, Matthew J. Murphy, Steven Nall, Aaron Olson, Timothy Pauley, Marissa Leanne Potts, Marc Ramirez, Willie Russell, Sean Ryan, Vincent "Tank" Sherrill, Kunlyna Tausch, Lanae Tipton, John ("Divine G") Whitfield, Paris Whitfield, Raymond Williams, Samantha Wohlford.

We also thank other contributors who were never incarcerated themselves, but nonetheless took significant risks to share their experience and insights, especially Mary Buser, Liza Daniel, Teresa Hertz, Summer Knight, and Justyna Rzewinski.

We received important editing suggestions from New York's #HALTsolitary Campaign and the Unlock the Box Campaign for the

"Reform and Advocacy" and "Solitary by Another Name" chapters. We are especially grateful to Jessica Sandoval, National Director of the Unlock the Box Campaign, and Scott Paltrowitz, a member of New York's #HALTsolitary Campaign and Unlock the Box, for reading and editing drafts and for their real-time updates on the Halt Act and other legislative efforts around the country.

We received crucial support on the legal and historical dimensions of the book from several people in the anti-solitary legal community. In particular, David Fathi, Director of the ACLU National Prison Project and one of the leading legal scholars on solitary confinement, read and provided invaluable feedback on the legal and history chapters; Michael Jaffe contributed significantly to earlier drafts of the section on due process and offered steadfast support throughout the writing process; and Professor Jeffrey Kirchmeier, Debbie's colleague at CUNY School of Law, provided thoughtful insights and careful commentary on the legal chapter.

We can't say enough amazing things about Jessica Sandoval, Jane Bloom, Sarah Kissel, Anisah Sabur, Della Maggio, and the rest of the incredible team at the Unlock the Box Campaign, who worked closely with Chris and so many others to organize the *Journey to Justice* bus tour, a nationwide campaign to end solitary confinement. It is a creative and powerful way to raise awareness about this human rights crisis. From the life-sized replica of a solitary cell to the virtual reality goggle experiences, the exhibit featuring some of our writers photographed in solitary units at Alcatraz, Eastern State, and other sites, and a range of other interactive and entertainment-based events – the bus tour has been truly extraordinary. Thank you for centering our book in these powerful events.

We want to acknowledge the tremendous support of many others from the prison justice and solitary confinement communities for their unwavering dedication to the movement to end solitary confinement, including: Victor Pate, Jerome Wright, Anisah Sabur, and Jennifer Parish from #HALTsolitary, Jean Casella, Juan Moreno Haines, and Valerie Kiebala from Solitary Watch, Jules Lobel, past president of the Center for Constitutional Rights, Emily Nonko of Narrative Change Lab, Jessica Schulberg, senior reporter at HuffPost,

Glenn Ruga, founder of Social Documentary Network, Nina Zweig, Research Editor at Type Investigations, Kristine Bruch, Director of Development and Special Programs at Type Media Center, Justyna Rzewinski, licensed clinical social worker and Rikers Island whistleblower, Mary Buser and Nicole Capozziello from Social Workers & Allies Against Solitary Confinement, Mari Cohen from Jewish Currents, Dolores Canales and Jack Morris of California Families Against Solitary Confinement, and Johnny Perez, Director of U.S. Prisons Program for the National Religious Campaign Against Torture.

Thank you to Danielle Squillante of the Prison Policy Initiative for your tireless efforts in providing statistics and sources we needed – helping to show that our experiences are not anomalies, but part of a broader, systemic pattern.

We greatly appreciate the support and partnership of the following organizations, whose work and collaboration helped move this project forward: The Appeal, California Families Against Solitary Confinement, Jewish Currents, the National Religious Campaign Against Torture, the Oz Effect, Posco Publicity, Social Documentary Network, Solitary Watch, Social Workers & Allies Against Solitary Confinement, and Unlock the Box.

We give huge thanks to our good friends Camille Sweeney and Rachel Zarrow, who read earlier drafts of the manuscript, gave generous feedback, and contributed many thoughtful ideas that helped refine the book's direction.

We would also like to thank our publicist, Megan Posco of Posco Publicity, who has helped us get the word out about solitary confinement and continues to elevate our visibility. A book is only meaningful if people read it, and Megan's work is central to ensuring that our message reaches the public. Because the purpose of this book is to educate people about the harms of solitary confinement, her role in amplifying that message is not just important – it's essential. And thanks to John J. Lennon for sharing Megan with us and cutting a path for incarcerated writers to make it in mainstream media. With both our books releasing in the same month, it's been an unexpected and powerful reminder of how solidarity and shared platforms can amplify voices that need to be heard.

We are indebted to Kate Becker, Danielle Brinberg, Ava Reilly, Jill Reilly, and Rebecca Ger for their invaluable research assistance. We especially want to thank Debbie's outstanding CUNY Law research assistants – Claire Thomas, Isaiah Yehros, Stacy Berry, and Sarah D'Ambrosio – whose dedication and hard work were essential to this project. We also thank CUNY Law students Sarah Petrick, Alex Vivas, Evie Wolfe, and the CUNY Law Abolitionist Law Organization for their support in hosting events relating to solitary confinement and the book.

We are deeply grateful to the entire Pluto Press team for believing in this book and for making space for incarcerated voices. David Shulman, thank you for taking a chance on this project and helping bring a message from inside prison walls to a broader public. It has also been a pleasure to work with Patrick Hughes and the rest of the Pluto team, including Robert Webb, David Castle, Jonila Krasniqi, Dave Stanford, and Martin Pettitt. A special thank you to Melanie Patrick for designing such a powerful and dynamic book cover. Its brilliance lies not only in its striking imagery, but in its unique versatility – turn it upside down, and it reveals a whole new layer of meaning, equally compelling.

It is also important to acknowledge all the people who helped bring the Writers Development Program to life, as many of the program's writers contributed to this very book. Emily Nonko invested in the development of this program and Kwaneta Harris developed our next chapter in her prison in Texas and brought women's voices into our space – thank you both! Beth Saidel, Nina Simmons, Robert Jensen, Sarah Sax, Catherine Stupp, Jasmine Faustino, Emma Jacobs, Julia Wick, Eileen Livers, Laura Pellicer, Ella Jaffe, and so many others deserve credit for the love and time they invested in our writers. You helped them publish over 200 pieces since we started this a couple years ago. Look at our writers now! Our inaugural writers, Antoine E. Davis, Darrell Jackson, Dustin Kelley, Jonathan Kirkpatrick, Kevin Light-Roth, Aaron Olson, Timothy Pauley, Marissa Potts, Lanae Tipton, and Raymond Williams, are doing the most, and hats off to all of you for being the next wave of incarcerated journalists.

Finally, we are thankful to the individuals and organizations whose generous financial support made this work possible. You play a key role in the change we must create in our communities. Thank you to everyone who has always supported our vision, including Jay Aronson, Alexander Bernstein, Anne Bernstein, Jamie Bernstein, Deborah Carstens, Harriet Charney, Carey Francis, Teresa Hertz, Wendy Katzman, Dinesh Khosla, Wendy Lichtman and Louis Hagler, Andrea McArdle, Gilbert Newman, Connie Palmersheim, Thomas Palmersheim, Karen Peacey, Stephanie Penalver, Randal Sable, Beth Saidel, Nina Simmons, Jonathan Zalesne, Kinney Zalesne, and Rachelle Zalesne.

We especially thank Donald Ger, Ken Goldman, Marlo Hyman, Terry Kupers, Langeloth Foundation, Look2Justice, Susan Retik, Retik-Mello Foundation, Seattle Foundation, Solitary Watch, Unlock the Box Campaign, Vital Projects Fund, Harvey and Judy Zalesne, Maxine and Jack Zarrow Family Foundation, and our private donors who asked not to be named, for their financial support.

A note of thanks from Debbie:

I'd like to extend my heartfelt thanks to those who have stood beside me throughout this journey. First and foremost, I want to thank my daughter, Ella Jaffe, who was the reason I first became involved in prison justice work. It began when she took a high-school class on mass incarceration and wanted to volunteer for a program with incarcerated writers. We ended up doing it together, and that experience opened a door I didn't even know I needed to walk through. Ella, your presence brings light, clarity, and conscience to everything I do. Your quiet strength, deep compassion, and unwavering sense of justice continue to teach me – not just about the world, but about the kind of person I strive to be. You listen with care and you ask the questions that matter. Watching you grow into yourself has been one of the greatest privileges of my life.

I am very grateful to Michael Jaffe, who supported me through the writing process, both intellectually and emotionally. His contributions to the book – and to my life – have been significant in every way.

In this new chapter, I am also thankful to Randy Sable for his encouragement, compassion, and grounding presence as I brought this work to completion.

I'm endlessly grateful to my friends and family for allowing me to bring solitary confinement into just about every conversation over the past two years. Your patience has been heroic. Each time I reread the stories in this book or speak with my incarcerated friends, many of whom are still in solitary, I'm reminded of how fortunate I've been to have such a strong and enduring support system throughout my life.

Mom (and Dad), thank you for setting an example of how to live a life grounded in gratitude. I could not have asked for better parents or role models. Whether you realize it or not, your involvement in that remarkable prison program, and the deep loving relationship you had with Paul Perry, laid the foundation for my interest in this work. Sheryl Levin, Jonny Zalesne, and Susan Retik, you are my best friends. Thank you for always being there.

Thank you Carol Caesar, Carey Francis, Amy Fried, Lisa Godek, Kim Hall, Jonathan Kowit, Corinna Lamb, Jacki Moline, David Nadvorney, Beth Saidel, and Camille Sweeney for decades of true friendship. I love that I can tell you anything! Amy, Lisa, Kim, and Jacki, thank you for tolerating my endless talk about solitary confinement during our long walks. Thank you Beth and Camille for your camaraderie and steadfast support in this vital prison work, as well as for generously sharing your writing and editing expertise. And thanks David for literally making this work possible for me by taking my Contracts class at a crucial time. I love you all!

I would like to give a special thanks to Nazia Hanif for her steady presence and support over the years and throughout this project. Her reliability and professionalism made a real difference.

Finally, I want to thank my amazing co-authors.

Kwaneta, your strength and resilience inspire me every single day. The way you fiercely protect and uplift the young women who were in solitary with you, while holding space for laughter, joy, and honesty, sets a powerful example of what it means to fight with both grace and fire. You show us not only how to survive, but how to rise, how to heal, and how to lead with compassion. Your voice is necessary and your vision is transformative.

Terry, you are simply brilliant. Working with you has been one of the most intellectually rewarding experiences of my career. Your insight, rigor, and clarity pushed this work to be sharper, stronger, and more impactful. But beyond your brilliance, it's your generosity of spirit, time, and thought, that makes you such an extraordinary colleague and friend. You made this journey not only smarter, but lighter.

And finally, the deepest thanks go to Christopher Blackwell. Chris, you have truly changed my life. Your courage, honesty, and unwavering commitment to truth-telling have challenged me, moved me, and expanded the way I see the world. You write with a clarity that cuts through silence, and a heart that refuses to turn away from the hardest truths. Collaborating with you has been a profound privilege. Your friendship is a gift, your voice is a force, and your presence in this work has made all the difference. I am endlessly grateful for what you give to the writers we support in the Writers Development Program, to the communities that benefit from your tireless work, and especially to me, both professionally and personally. I hope we can continue collaborating and making change!

A note of thanks from Chris:

So many people have helped me with this project in ways big and small. I am grateful for every last one of you. The position and voice I'm honored to hold in this moment is due to all of your love, support, mentorship, and willingness to invest in me in some way or another.

First, I have to thank my incredibly smart and beautiful wife, Dr. Chelsea Moore. Chelsea, you are my rock, best friend, and the person who has pushed me to become who I am today in many of these spaces. You never gave it to me easy. You challenged me along the way to make me a better writer, activist, and overall person. And you continue to do so each and every day. I would never be the leader I am today without all the water you shared to help my seed grow. You are what nourishes me to be who I am.

You are the person who's helped me work through my many emotions as I pressed forward with this book – fighting through the anger and frustration about the harm caused to others and myself throughout my decades of incarceration. I know there were moments where I was not easy to be around while working on this deeply traumatizing project. But you stood by and supported me throughout it all. When I needed to process my emotions, you always provided a safe space to do that. You have handled my broken self with care and love from the day I met you. You never judge me for my past or try to make me something I'm not. You simply love me with all my flaws. You are my world and without you I would never accomplish even a small portion of what I do. Thank you for always providing the love and support that you do, and for challenging me when others don't.

Right next to my incredible wife is my loving mother, Connie Palmersheim, who has stood by me throughout my decades of incarceration – starting at the age of twelve. What a rollercoaster I've put you through, yet you have never left my side. I am so very grateful for your love and support. I know you have not had an easy life, but the way you keep your head high and heart filled with love for the world has always been a guiding path for me to emulate. You could easily be such a bitter human, but you refuse to take that path. Thank you for always teaching me to love people and to fight against injustice. You are a strong human, and I am deeply proud to call you my mother.

I must also thank Lauri Moore, Chelsea's mother. I know it wasn't easy to support your incredible daughter going into a relationship with a man in prison for such a horrific crime. Yet, once you saw what we had and who I was, you have done nothing but help us survive this crazy situation with love and the support we needed to continue to grow and build our relationship. Thank you for supporting us even when you might not have felt like it. You put Chelsea first and gave her the support only a truly loving mother could. We really needed that to make it where we are today. I love you very much and am proud for so many reasons to call you my family.

Thank you to my loving family who has always remained by my side, through all my many incarcerations, mishaps in life, and beyond. Missi and Ken Clyde, Katrina, Robert, Bailee and Aaron Dunavant, Michael and Cassie Hennings, Nancy Fiedler, and Aryanna Branch (you are like a daughter to me and I will always love you as such).

Special thanks is also due to all the people incarcerated and formerly incarcerated who were brave enough to share your stories with me and Debbie throughout this project. There were so many of you it's impossible to name you all. Some of you I've known forever, while others I've never even met. But you had faith to allow Debbie and me to share your story with the world. Thank you for trusting us, I hope we did you proud. You are the bravest journalists I know! This project would not be possible without each and every one of you. The work you do, risk you take, and the trauma you relive to share your stories is the very reason we will one day see the reform we seek from these torture chambers. This is, and will always be, a collective movement. So I greatly thank all of you for trusting us with your story.

Kwaneta Harris, you are one of the main people leading this. Our bond of friendship and willingness to fight these injustices on a united front are so important to me. Standing by your side in this is a real privilege. You are a warrior sis! I truly look forward to all the good we'll accomplish together as we move forward on our path together.

I have to thank my co-author Professor Deborah Zalesne. I bet you never thought this is where your life was heading when you met me all those years back. You are an incredible human and partner in this work. I am so grateful for you and I love you dearly! You have become a family member to me. I'm so happy Ella, your incredibly brilliant daughter, connected us. Ella, Thanks for being open minded in your classes in high school – look at the domino effect of you getting involved and connecting all of us. You're one rad kid, and I cannot wait to see the mark you leave on this world!

Dr. Terry Kupers, what an honor to know I have the privilege to fight with you in these spaces. When you told me you've been fighting side by side with folks like Angela Y. Davis and the Black Panthers since the 1960s in Los Angeles, I felt a deep honor to be mentored in these spaces by such an incredible warrior. I have the utmost respect for you and the path you, along with many others, have laid for people like me to continue to educate and organize in these spaces.

Jeffrey Erwin Ellis, my long time attorney who has fought tirelessly to bring me home to my loved ones. You are not just my attorney, you are family. You are one of the most incredible humans I know. Your devotion to bring people home and commitment to righting the mishaps of the law are second to none. It is a true blessing to have you by my side, my dear friend! I love and respect you so much and I cannot wait 'til the day when you can renew my vows with Chelsea.

I'm also so very blessed to have so many talented journalists around me since I started my writing career. I would have NEVER made it this far without all of your mentorship and guidance. You guys are hugely responsible for the writer I am today. Thank you Emily Nonko (my partner in all this), Jamie Beth Cohen (my Donna and mentor), Jessica Schulberg (my little sister), Mari Cohen (my dear friend), Rachel Zarrow (my teacher), Ethan Corey, Sarah Sax, the entire Jewish Currents family, The Appeal, Jean Casella, Valerie Kiebala, Juan Moreno Haines and the Solitary Watch family, Aviva Shen, Nina Zweig and Kristine Bruch at Type Media Center, Glyn Fox at the New York Times, Jack Mirkinson at The Nation, George Zornick and Noah Michelson at HuffPost, Jessica Sposato at Narratively, Laura Bennett and Hannah Riley at The Center for Just Journalism, the folks at the Humans of San Quentin, and so many more. I am honored to be in commUNITY with all of you. Many of you have become like family to me.

Christian Farias, thank you so much for introducing me to Jessica Sandoval. I bet you had no clue what you would start by connecting us. Jessica, I am so grateful for you and the dope folks at the Unlock the Box Campaign: Anisah Sabur, Della Maggio, Jane Bloom, Sarah Kissel! WOW! Connecting with all of you to create a national bus tour centered on the book and ending solitary confinement has been one of the most powerful projects of my life. Being in community with all of you means the world to me. Thank you for taking a leap with me Jessica, I will never forget it.

I also want to thank my entire Look2Justice team. All of you stepped up so much to support this project as it developed into a national tour – a legitimate movement! Kyle Jones, YQ Jiang, Eugene Youngblood, Sherri Caldellis, Antoine E. Davis, Connie Palmersheim, and Katherin Hervey. Working with all of you every day is a true blessing. I am also extremely grateful for our Board of Directors at Look2Justice. It is through all of you that we continue to make this work possible. Thank you Cassandra Butler, Devon Adams, Atif Rafay, Martina Kartman, Michael (Mike D) Daniels, Sandra Hebert, Udi Ofer, and Dan Berger.

Much of the work centered on solitary confinement in Washington State wouldn't even be possible without my guy Anthony Blankenship, Rachael Seevers and our Survivors Opposing Solitary Coalition (SOS). Thank you for stepping up and leading the way!

Many people have been strong mentors to me over the years and I am just so blessed to have learned and to continue to learn from all of you as I grow into myself more and more. Without the key role you all played in my life, I would have never made it this far. Each one of you is a cornerstone in my development. Thank you for all your energy, time, love and support: Steve Fleishman, Glenn Martin, Dr. Michael Kimmel, Dan Berger, Garrett Felber, Udi Ofer, Jason Flom and Alex Duran and Aliyah Salim at Galaxy Gives.

Thank you Tom and Julie Palmersheim for your support in helping me edit my personal story early on in this project. I am so grateful for the time you took to help make this a powerful story. I love and care for both of you very much.

Many of my very close friends who have supported me in the work around this project and the work we've participated in for decades deserve a ton of love. You all ride with me day in and day out. I got BIG love for you guys. All of you are the brothers and sisters I never had. I will always be here to have your back, as you have had mine time and time again. Many of you mentored me in some form or fashion. All of you have done the most when it comes to keeping me whole, thank you. Having these real types of friendships means more to me than anything: Devon Adams, Jeremiah Bourgeois, Cassandra Butler, Noel Caldellis, Jamie Beth Cohen, Mari Cohen, David Hackney, David Heppard, Burnis Herring Jr., Daniel Landsman, Matthew J. Murphy, Emily Nonko, Tim Pauley, Atif Rafay, Jessica Schulberg, Anthony Wright, and many more.

Gabe Galanda, brother you are a true warrior for our Indigenous community! Thank you for always being willing to fight injustice. Many forget about us when we come to prison. You never have! Thank you!

The following people are real leaders in the commUNITY! You all fight to make this world a better place day in and day out. I look up to all of you. You are real transformers and there will never be enough folks like you: Martina Kartman and the rest of the HEAL family, Gail Brashear, Marriam Oliver, Johnny Perez, Dolores Canales, Jack Morris, and Troy Williams.

Judy Pigott, Laney Ellisor, Aileen Balahadia, Ashely McCready, Shannon Small, and Deb Carstens, thank you for always supporting me and the work I do. All of you are always there to lend a hand anyway you can. I have so much respect and love for all of you and the way you move in the world.

Thank you to all my college professors who pushed me to become the writer I am today. I know I was such a cry baby as I made my way through many of your classes, but you continued to nurture me and helped me develop into a decent writer: Carrie Matthews, Dr. Gilda Sheppard, Dr. Megan Ming Francis, Dr. Katherine Beckett, Dr. Steve Herbert, and so many more!

I want to thank the following people for always working to expand the reach of my work. You all have been true friends in offering so much of your time and energy into our upcoming documentary and podcast. Thank you to Katherin Hervey, Chris Panizzon, Katie Sedgwick, Laura Pellicer, and Colby Davis for devoting so much of yourselves to this work with me.

I must also thank my good friend Glenn Ruga at Social Documentary Network. You have continued to build and partner with me on so much. It is always such an honor to work with you, my friend. Thank you for helping me educate society on the issues related to incarceration in America.

I have to thank all my brothers in our Indigenous community on the inside. Having a community of brothers to lean on, hold ceremony with, and continue learning about this journey called life has meant so much. Many who come to prison feel isolated and alone. I have never felt this because of our Indigenous community. Thank you for all your love and support throughout the years.

Lastly, I want to acknowledge three people who meant the world to me, but have since gone home to the Creator during my incarceration. Patrick Gosney, my uncle – but in reality, you were more like a father to me. I learned so much from you throughout my life. And I am so thankful for each one of those memories. Teresa Hennings, regardless of the fact you were my little cousin, you were more like a sister to me. I will always feel a bit of guilt for how your life turned out. I am so sorry life was so cruel and hard on you. You never deserved that. I just wish I could have taken the pain away. And last is my dearest grandma, Opal Reeder. You are my FAVORITE person, grandma! You always made me feel so special – only you could do that the way you did. I'm so grateful for each and every moment I was able to share with you. I'm just sorry there were not more. I owe you a big hug and I promise to give it to you one day. I think of you three often. Losing you guys while in here was hard. I never really got to say goodbye. One day, you were just gone and it still does not seem real. Maybe it never will. I love you guys so very much and I just wish I could have shared this incredible accomplishment with you three the most.

Notes

PROLOGUE

1. Rideau, Wilbert. *In the Place of Justice: A Story of Punishment and Deliverance*. Alfred A. Knopf, 2010.

CHAPTER 1: INTRODUCTION

1. Parts of this introduction were originally published in Christopher Blackwell, "Just a Kid," *Compassion Prison Project*, February 27, 2021, https://compassionprisonproject.org/just-a-kid/
2. Charles Dickens, *American Notes for General Circulation* (London: Bradbury & Evans, 1842), p. 103.

CHAPTER 2: BURIED ALIVE

1. Lacino Hamilton, "I Am Buried Alive in a Michigan Prison," *Truthout*, April 1 2018; See also Ruth Chan, "Buried Alive: The Need to Establish Clear Durational Standards for Solitary Confinement," *UIC John Marshall Law Review* 53 (2020): 235; Nathaniel Penn, "Buried Alive: Stories from Inside Solitary Confinement," *GQ*, March 2, 2017; Michael Stern, "Like Being 'Buried Alive': Charles Dickens on Solitary Confinement in America's Prisons," *The American Prospect*, October 8, 2015.
2. Unlock the Box Campaign, "Calculating Torture," May 23, 2023, https://unlocktheboxcampaign.org/2023/05/23/calculating-torture/
3. Washington State House Democrats, "Bill Limiting the Use of Solitary Confinement Passes House Community Safety, Justice & Reentry Committee," January 24, 2023, https://housedemocrats.wa.gov/peterson/2023/01/24/bill-limiting-the-use-of-solitary-confinement-passes-house-community-safety-justice-reentry-committee/#:~:text=The%20Department%20of%20Corrections%20has%20worked%20to%20reform%20the%20use%20of%20solitary%20confinement%20for%20years%2C%20yet%20over%20six%20hundred%20individuals%20remain%20in%20restrictive%20housing%20within%20the%20Department%20of%20Corrections%20prison%20system

4. According to the United Nations' Standard Minimum Rules for the Treatment of Prisoners (the "Mandela Rules"): "For the purpose of these rules, solitary confinement shall refer to the confinement of prisoners for 22 hours or more a day without meaningful human contact." United Nations, *Standard Minimum Rules for the Treatment of Prisoners* (the "Mandela Rules"), UN Office on Drugs & Crime, December 2015.
5. Blackwell and Light-Roth, "The Unceasing Noise of Solitary Confinement," *The Progressive Magazine*, July 28, 2023.
6. In many states, Death Row is either a separate solitary confinement unit or is enclosed in a larger solitary confinement/supermax facility. Separate from the question of whether the death sentence should be abolished is the question whether there is any reasonable penological objective, or humanity, in condemning death-sentenced individuals to solitary confinement while they wait to die. See Terry Kupers, "Waiting Alone to Die," in *Living on Death Row*, Eds. Hans Toch, James Austin, and B.M. Bonventre (Washington, DC: American Psychological Association Press, 2018), pp. 47–69.
7. Originally published in Aaron Olson, "In the Hole," *Jewish Currents*, April 20, 2023, https://jewishcurrents.org/in-the-hole
8. Originally published in Kevin Light-Roth, "When You've Been in the Hole Long Enough, Even Your Dreams Take Place in a Cell," *The Small Bow*, January 28, 2025, https://thesmallbow.substack.com/p/recovery-from-solitary-is-an-illusion
9. "Solitary Confinement in the United States: The Facts," *Solitary Watch*, https://solitarywatch.org/facts/faq/
10. Frontline, "Solitary by the Numbers," *PBS Frontline*, http://apps.frontline.org/solitary-by-the-numbers/
11. "Albert Woodfox, Survivor of 42 Years in Solitary Confinement, Dies at 75," *The New York Times*, August 5, 2022, www.nytimes.com/2022/08/05/us/albert-woodfox-dead.html
12. Supreme Court of the United States. *Petition for a Writ of Certiorari*, No. 21-1065, January 28, 2022, https://tinyurl.com/5n8k5ms2

CHAPTER 3: A BRIEF HISTORY OF SOLITARY CONFINEMENT IN AMERICA

1. Peter Scharff Smith, "The Effects of Solitary Confinement on Prison Inmates: A Brief History and Review of the Literature," *Crime and Justice* 34 (2006): 441–457.
2. Elizabeth Bennion, "Banning the Bing: Why Extreme Solitary Confinement Is Cruel and Far Too Usual Punishment," *Indiana Law Journal* 90 (2015): 741–746.

3. Thomas L. Hafemeister and Jeff George, "The Ninth Circle of Hell: An Eighth Amendment Analysis of Imposing Prolonged Supermax Solitary Confinement on Inmates with a Mental Illness," *Denver University Law Review* 90 (2012): 1–54.
4. Torsten Eriksson, *The Reformers: An Historical Survey of Pioneer Experiments in the Treatment of Criminals* (1976), p. 49, quoting Gustave de Beaumont and Alexis de Tocqueville; Alexander A. Reinert, "Solitary Troubles," *Notre Dame Law Review* 93 (2018): 927–938.
5. Ibid.
6. *In Re Medley*, 134 U.S. 160, 167 (1890).
7. Ibid.
8. There were exceptions to the trend away from solitary confinement in the first half of the twentieth century. For example, in 1934 Alcatraz Prison, as we know it, began operating. Alcatraz featured what was known as "The Hole" – the prison's solitary confinement hallway. Ruth Chan explains that one room along this hallway, nicknamed "The Oriental," "confined inmates in a cell with no light and no toilet except for a hole in the ground." Incarcerated individuals in this room "were kept naked and were provided food and water through a small hole in the door."
9. The Sentencing Project. "Mass Incarceration: Trends in the United States." Accessed January 9, 2025, www.sentencingproject.org/reports/mass-incarceration-trends/
10. Elizabeth Bennion, "A Right to Remain Psychotic? A New Standard for Involuntary Treatment in Light of Current Science," *Loyola of Los Angeles Law Review* 47 (2013): 251–260.
11. Currently "95% of those public psychiatric hospital beds have disappeared, but community psychiatric care exists for fewer than half the patients who need it" (ibid., p. 260, quoting E. Fuller Torrey et al., *Treatment Advocacy Center, No Room at the Inn: Trends and Consequences of Closing Public Psychiatric Hospitals* [2012], 7).
12. Craig Haney, "The Psychological Effects of Solitary Confinement: A Systematic Critique," *Crime and Justice* 47(2018): 365–416. https://doi.org/10.1086/696041
13. David Garland, *The Culture of Control: Crime and Social Order in Contemporary Society* (Chicago: University of Chicago Press, 2001).
14. Craig Haney and Mona Lynch, "Regulating Prisons of the Future: A Psychosocial Analysis of Supermax and Solitary Confinement," *NYU Review of Law & Social Change* 23 (1997): 478–491.
15. Alexander A. Reinert, "Solitary Troubles," *Notre Dame Law Review* 93 (2018): 927–940.

16. Jules Lobel, "Mass Solitary and Mass Incarceration: Explaining the Dramatic Rise in Prolonged Solitary in America's Prisons," *Northwestern University Law Review* 115 (2020): 159–164.
17. Ibid., p. 177; Unlock the Box, "Resources, A Solitary Timeline." Accessed August 18, 2024, https://unlocktheboxcampaign.org/resources/
18. Ruth Chan, "Buried Alive: The Need to Establish Clear Durational Standards for Solitary Confinement," *UIC John Marshall Law Review* 53 (2020) 235–243; Peter Scharff Smith, "The Effects of Solitary Confinement on Prison Inmates: A Brief History and Review of the Literature," *Crime and Justice* 34 (2006): 441–442.
19. Supermax facilities grew in popularity: by 1997, there were 55 supermax facilities in the US. Since then, however, the number has decreased due to the cost of running them as well as criticism over treatment of those inside. In 2012, the annual cost to run one facility in Illinois was $26 million (*NPR*, June 19, 2012, www.npr.org/2012/06/19/155359553/the-high-costs-of-high-security-at-supermax-prisons). As of 2021, there were still over 30 supermax state facilities (*National Review*, August 23, 2021, www.nationalreview.com/2021/08/the-problem-with-supermax-prisons/).
20. Chan, "Buried Alive," pp. 243–244.
21. Daniel Mears, "Evaluating the Effectiveness of Supermax Prisons, Urban Institute Justice Policy Center," 2005, www.ojp.gov/pdffiles1/nij/grants/211971.pdf
22. Chan, "Buried Alive," pp. 235, 243–244.
23. Mikel-Meredith Weidman, "The Culture of Judicial Deference and the Problem of Supermax Prisons." *UCLA Law Review* 51 (2004): 1505–1527.
24. *Ashker v. Governor of the State of California*, no. C09-05796 CW (N.D. Cal. Sep. 6, 2016).
25. Lobel, "Mass Solitary," pp. 178–182.
26. Ibid., pp. 194–195.
27. Ibid., p. 177.
28. *Hutto v. Finney*, 437 U.S. 678 (1978).
29. *Rhodes v. Chapman*, 452 U.S. 337, 347 (1981).
30. Ibid.
31. *Hewitt v. Helms*, 459 U.S. 460 (1983).
32. *Sandin v. Conner* 515 U.S. 472 (1995).
33. Ibid., p. 474.
34. See, e.g., *Ruiz v. Texas*, 139 S. Ct. 2183 (2019) (Breyer, J., dissenting); *Apodaca v. Raemish*, 500 U.S. 1319 (1991) (Sotomayor, J., concurring).

CHAPTER 4: WHO GETS SENT TO THE HOLE

1. A version of this story was first published in Christopher Blackwell, "Chaos and Noise: One Man's Harrowing Stint in Solitary Confinement," *Narratively*, March 27, 2024. www.narratively.com/p/chaos-noise-one-mans-harrowing-stint-in-the-hole?utm_campaign=post&utm_medium=web
2. Terry A. Kupers, "Who's in SHU? A Survey of Solitary Confinement," *Prison Legal News*, July 1, 2020, www.prisonlegalnews.org/news/2020/jul/1/whos-shu-survey-solitary-confinement/
3. Originally Published in Aaron Olson, "In the Hole," *Jewish Currents*, April 20, 2023, https://jewishcurrents.org/in-the-hole
4. Emily Parker, "Due Process in Prison Disciplinary Hearings: How the 'Some Evidence' Standard of Proof Violates the Constitution," *Washington Law Review* 96 (2021): 1613.
5. James E. Robertson, "One of the Dirty Secrets of American Corrections: Retaliation, Surplus Power, and Whistleblowing Inmates," *Michigan Journal of Law Reform* 42 (2009).
6. Vera Institute of Justice. "Solitary Confinement: Misconceptions and Safe Alternatives," *Vera Institute of Justice*, 2015, https://vera-institute.files.svdcdn.com/production/downloads/publications/solitary-confinement-misconceptions-safe-alternatives-report_1.pdf
7. Ibid.
8. Christopher Blackwell and Jessica Sandoval, "Seeing the Light," *Inquest*, December 2, 2021, https://inquest.org/seeing-the-light/
9. Piper Kerman, "Testimony Before the U.S. Senate Judiciary Committee," *U.S. Senate Judiciary Committee*, February 25, 2014, www.judiciary.senate.gov/download/02-25-14-kerman-testimony; see also Blackwell and Sandoval, "Seeing the Light."
10. Originally published in Kwaneta Harris, "The Hell Inside Hell: Solitary Confinement in Texas Hides the Sexual Abuse of Women and Girls," *Scalawag*, May 30, 2024, https://scalawagmagazine.org/2024/05/hell-inside-hell-texas-solitary-confinement-sexual-abuse/
11. Note that policies and the use of solitary vary from state to state and not all of the things on this list would lead to solitary in every state.
12. "Solitary Confinement in the United States: The Facts," *Solitary Watch*. Accessed January 10, 2025, https://solitarywatch.org/facts/faq/.
13. Francisco Rodriguez, "Solitary Confinement in Immigrant Detention," *Solitary Watch*, February 6, 2025, https://solitarywatch.org/wp-content/uploads/2025/02/SW-Fact-Sheet-9-Immigration-Detention-v20250204.pdf

14. "Solitary Confinement is Never the Answer," *Unlock the Box*, June 2020, https://unlocktheboxcampaign.org/wp-content/uploads/2021/02/UTB-Covid-19-June2020Report.pdf
15. Originally published in Christopher Blackwell, "Quarantined in Solitary is Still Solitary," *The Prison Journalism Project*, May 4, 2021, https://prisonjournalismproject.org/2021/05/04/quarantined-in-solitary-is-still-solitary/
16. Keramet Reiter, *32/7: Pelican Bay Prison and the Rise of Long-Term Solitary Confinement* (New Haven: Yale University Press, 2016).
17. Ibid.

CHAPTER 5: CRUEL AND UNUSUAL PUNISHMENT: STORIES OF TORTURE

1. See "Performance-Based Standards and Expected Practices for Adult Correctional Institutions," *American Correctional Association*, March 2021, pp. 78–79, www.aca.org/ACA_Member/ACA/ACA_Member/Marketplace/Item_Detail.aspx?iProductCode=651E&Category=PUBS-STAND; "Standards for Health Services in Prisons," *National Commission on Correctional Health Care*, 2018, https://www.ojp.gov/ncjrs/virtual-library/abstracts/standards-health-services-prisons-1#:~:text=These%20standards%20represent%20recommended%20minimum,and%20NCCHC%20health%20services%20accreditation
2. From Jarvis Jay Masters, Finding Freedom: How Death Row Broke and Opened My Heart, © (2020). Reprinted by arrangement with Shambhala Publications, Inc., Boulder, CO. pp. 32–33, www.shambhala.com
3. See "Performance-Based Standards and Expected Practices for Adult Correctional Institutions," *American Correctional Association*, March 2021, pp. 78–79, www.aca.org/ACA_Member/ACA/ACA_Member/Marketplace/Item_Detail.aspx?iProductCode=651E&Category=PUBS-STAND; "Standards for Health Services in Prisons," *National Commission on Correctional Health Care*, 2018, https://www.ojp.gov/ncjrs/virtual-library/abstracts/standards-health-services-prisons-1#:~:text=These%20standards%20represent%20recommended%20minimum,and%20NCCHC%20health%20services%20accreditation
4. David Cloud et al., "'We Just Needed to Open the Door': A Case Study of the Quest to End Solitary Confinement in North Dakota," *Health and Justice* 9, no. 28 (2021), https://doi.org/10.1186/s40352-021-00155-5
5. Terry A. Kupers, "Testimony in *Willie Russell v. Christopher Epps/Mississippi Department of Corrections*, 670 So.2d 816" (E.D. Miss. 1995).

CHAPTER 6: THE PHYSICAL AND PSYCHOLOGICAL HARMS OF SOLITARY

1. While solitary confinement is extreme isolation to begin with, there are ways to make it even more inhumane. Powers was housed in ADX Control Unit Prison in Florence, Colorado – ADX is the only federal supermax prison in the United States, and the Control Unit is the most secure and restrictive isolation unit within ADX, housing the most violent and high-risk incarcerated persons.
2. Andrew Cohen, "An American Gulag: Descending into Madness at Supermax," *The Atlantic*, June 8, 2012, www.theatlantic.com/national/archive/2012/06/an-american-gulag-descending-into-madness-at-supermax/258323/
3. Brittany Hailer, "Were the 2015 Reforms on Solitary Confinement in PA Enough to Protect Vulnerable Inmates?" *PublicSource*, February 17, 2021, www.publicsource.org/were-the-2015-reforms-on-solitary-confinement-in-pa-enough-to-protect-vulnerable-inmates/
4. Dana G. Smith, "Neuroscientists Make a Case Against Solitary Confinement." *Scientific American*, January 17, 2018, www.scientificamerican.com/article/neuroscientists-make-a-case-against-solitary-confinement/
5. Lauren Brinkley-Rubinstein et al., "Association of Restrictive Housing During Incarceration With Mortality After Release," *JAMA Network Open*, October 4, 2019, https://jamanetwork.com/journals/jamanetworkopen/fullarticle/2752350
6. Stuart Grassian, "Psychiatric Effects of Solitary Confinement," *Washington University Journal of Law & Policy* 22 (2006): 325–383. https://openscholarship.wustl.edu/law_journal_law_policy/vol22/iss1/24
7. Ibid., p. 354.
8. Kayla James and Elena Vanko, *The Impacts of Solitary Confinement* (New York: Vera Institute of Justice, April 2021), www.vera.org/publications/the-impacts-of-solitary-confinement
9. Originally published in Frank De Palma with Mary Buser, *Never to Surrender! 22 Years in Solitary: The Battle for My Soul in a U.S. Prison* (Brooklyn: Homelawn Publishing, 2024), pp. 166–167.
10. Originally published in Christopher Blackwell, Aaron Edward Olson, Antoine Davis, Raymond Williams, and Jonathan Kirkpatrick, "In the Hole," *Jewish Currents*, April 20, 2023, https://jewishcurrents.org/in-the-hole
11. Daniel Mears et al., "Work in Long-Term Restrictive Housing and Prison Personnel Perceptions of the Humanity of People Who Are

Incarcerated," *Criminal Justice and Behavior*, June 2024, https://doi.org/10.1177/00938548221104980; E.M. Higgins, J. Smith, and K. Swartz, "'We Keep the Nightmares in Their Cages': Correctional Culture, Identity, and the Warped Badge of Honor," *Criminology*, Advance online publication, 2022, https://doi.org/10.1111/1745-9125.12306

12. U.S. Department of Health and Human Services, "Our Epidemic of Loneliness and Isolation: The U.S. Surgeon General's Advisory on the Healing Effects of Social Connection and Community" 2023, www.hhs.gov/sites/default/files/surgeon-general-social-connection-advisory.pdf
13. Originally published in Christopher Blackwell, Aaron Edward Olson, Antoine Davis, Raymond Williams, and Jonathan Kirkpatrick, "In the Hole," *Jewish Currents*, April 20, 2023, https://jewishcurrents.org/in-the-hole
14. Nancy G. La Vigne, "The Cost of Keeping Prisoners Hundreds of Miles from Home," *Urban Institute*, February 3, 2013, www.urban.org/urban-wire/cost-keeping-prisoners-hundreds-miles-home
15. Carol Schaeffer, "'Isolation Devastates the Brain': The Neuroscience of Solitary Confinement," *Solitary Watch*, May 11, 2016, https://solitarywatch.org/2016/05/11/isolation-devastates-the-brain-the-neuroscience-ofsolitary-confinement/
16. Brian O. Hagan et al., "History of Solitary Confinement is Associated with Post-Traumatic Stress Disorder Symptoms Among Individuals Recently Released from Prison," *Journal of Urban Health* 95, no. 2 (2018): 141–148, https://pubmed.ncbi.nlm.nih.gov/28281161/
17. The qualifier "complex" is not included in the *DSM-5* description of PTSD, but is widely accepted and prominently discussed in the clinical literature.
18. Jennifer J. Freyd, "Betrayal Trauma: Traumatic Amnesia as an Adaptive Response to Childhood Abuse," *Ethics & Behavior* 4, no. 4 (1994): 307–329.
19. See, e.g., Lamya Khoury et al., "Substance Use, Childhood Traumatic Experience, and Posttraumatic Stress Disorder in an Urban Civilian Population," *Depression and Anxiety* 27, no. 12 (2010): 1077–1086, https://www.ncbi.nlm.nih.gov/pmc/articles/PMC3051362/; International Society for Traumatic Stress Studies. "Traumatic Stress and Substance Abuse Problems." Accessed January 10, 2025, https://istss.org/public-resources/friday-fast-facts/substance-use-and-traumatic-stress; M.T. Fullilove et al., "Crack Hos and Skeezers: Traumatic Experiences of Women Crack Users," *Journal of Sex Research* 29 (May 1992); C.J. Boyd et al., "Putting Drug Use in Context: Life-Lines of

African American Women Who Smoke Crack," *Journal of Substance Abuse Treatment*, 15, no. 3 (1998): 235–249.

20. D.P. Mears and J. Watson. "Towards a Fair and Balanced Assessment of Supermax Prisons." *Justice Quarterly* 23, no. 2 (2006): 232–270; B. Way et al., "Factors Related to Suicide in New York State Prisons," *International Journal of Law and Psychiatry* 28, no. 3 (2005): 207–221; R.F. Patterson and K. Hughes. "Review of Completed Suicides in the California Department of Corrections and Rehabilitation, 1999 to 2004," *Psychiatric Services* 59, no. 6 (2008): 676–682.
21. Gisli H. Gudjonsson, *The Psychology of Interrogations and Confessions: A Handbook* (Chichester, UK: Wiley-Blackwell, 2003).
22. Lacino Hamilton, "I Am Buried Alive in a Michigan Prison," *Truthout*, 2018, https://truthout.org/articles/i-am-buried-alive-in-a-michigan-prison/
23. "The Box: 27 Years in Solitary Confinement." *Fault Lines*, June 27, 2023, www.aljazeera.com/program/fault-lines/2023/6/27/the-box-27-years-in-solitary-confinement
24. Terry Kupers, "Repetitive Self-Harm in Solitary Confinement," *Correctional Health Care Report* 24, no. 3 (2023).
25. Ibid.
26. Iatrogenic means "harm induced unintentionally by a physician or surgeon or by medical treatment or diagnostic procedures" (*Merriam-Webster Dictionary*. Accessed January 10, 2025, www.merriam-webster.com/dictionary/iatrogenic).
27. A version of this story was previously published in Lanae Tipton, "Voices From Solitary: The Toll Isolation Takes," *Solitary Watch*, February 21, 2025, https://solitarywatch.org/2025/02/21/voices-from-solitary-the-toll-isolation-takes/
28. Originally published in Christopher Blackwell, Aaron Edward Olson, Antoine Davis, Raymond Williams, and Jonathan Kirkpatrick, "In the Hole," *Jewish Currents*, April 20, 2023, https://jewishcurrents.org/in-the-hole. For more about the long-term physical and psychological effects of solitary confinement, see T. Kupers, The SHU Post-Release Syndrome, Correctional Mental Health Report, 17, 6, March/April 2016.
29. Originally published in Kwaneta Harris, "In Solitary Confinement, Banned Books Are a Lifeline," *The Emancipator*, October 2, 2023, www.theemancipator.org/articles/in-solitary-confinement-banned-books-are-a-lifeline
30. Joseph Shapiro, "Coming Home Straight from Solitary Damages Inmates and Their Families," *NPR*, June 12, 2015, www.npr.org/

2015/06/12/413730912/coming-home-straight-from-solitary-damages-inmates-and-their-families

31. Peter Scharff Smith, *When the Innocent are Punished: The Children of Imprisoned Parents* (New York: Palgrave Publishers, 2014).
32. Katja Ridderbusch, "Rising Amid COVID, Solitary Confinement Inflicts Lasting Harm to Prisoner Health," *NPR*, October 4, 2021, www.npr.org/sections/health-shots/2021/10/04/1043058599/rising-amid-covid-solitary-confinement-inflicts-lasting-harm-to-prisoner-health
33. "Solitary Confinement Effects," *Medical News Today*. Accessed January 10, 2025, www.medicalnewstoday.com/articles/solitary-confinement-effects?c=751186234847
34. Jeffrey L. Metzner and Jamie Fellner, "Solitary Confinement and Mental Illness in U.S. Prisons: A Challenge for Medical Ethics," *Journal of the American Academy of Psychiatry and the Law* 38, no. 1 (March 19, 2010): 104, https://jaapl.org/content/38/1/104

CHAPTER 7: MENTAL ILLNESS AND SOLITARY CONFINEMENT

1. Treatment Advocacy Center and National Sheriff's Association, "The Treatment of Persons with Mental Illness in Prisons and Jails: A State Survey," April 8, 2014, www.researchgate.net/publication/296333518_The_Treatment_of_Persons_with_Mental_Illness_in_Prisons_and_Jails_A_State_Survey
2. Mischa H. Karplus, "Forgotten in Solitary: Mentally Ill Inmates in Solitary Confinement and How the Law Can Protect Them," *Stanford Journal of Civil Rights & Civil Liberties* 19 (August 31, 2023), https://law.stanford.edu/publications/forgotten-in-solitary-mentally-ill-inmates-in-solitary-confinement-and-how-the-law-can-protect-them/
3. Elizabeth Bennion, "Banning the Bing: Why Extreme Solitary Confinement Is Cruel and Far Too Usual Punishment," *Indiana Law Journal* 90 (2015): 741, 749; Corey Weinstein, "Even Dogs Confined to Cages for Long Periods of Time Go Berserk," in *Building Violence: How America's Rush to Incarcerate Creates More Violence*, Ed. John P. May and Khalid R. Pitts (Mishawaka: Better World Books, 2000), pp. 118–123; Human Rights Watch, *Cold Storage: Super-Maximum Security Confinement in Indiana* (New York: Human Rights Watch, 1997), pp. 18–20.
4. Gurtej Gill et al., "Solitary Confinement in Prison Systems and Future Psychopathological Effects," *Primary Care Companion for CNS Disorders* 25, no. 6 (2023), www.psychiatrist.com/pcc/solitary-confinement-prison-systems-future-psychopathological-effects.

5. Katja Ridderbusch, "Solitary Confinement's Effects on Prisoner Mental Health," *KFF Health News*, October 5, 2021, https://kffhealthnews.org/news/article/solitary-confinement-effects-on-prisoner-mental-health/
6. Jessica Schulberg, "He Needed Medical Help. He Ended Up in Jail and Died Weeks Later," *HuffPost*, April 17, 2023, www.huffpost.com/entry/joshua-mclemore-death-preventable-lawsuit_n_64358cbde4b06e56d695aa4a?uu4
7. Equal Justice Initiative. "Solitary Confinement Leads to Social Death," *Equal Justice Initiative*, https://eji.org/news/solitary-confinement-leads-to-social-death/; Christopher Blackwell and Deborah Zalesne, "Eric Adams' Thoughts on Solitary Confinement are Dangerous and Cruel," *The Appeal*, February 7, 2024, https://theappeal.org/eric-adams-new-york-solitary-confinement/
8. *Policy Number ADM.019.003*, State of New Jersey Department of Corrections (2021), www.documentcloud.org/documents/23822055-adm019003-close-custody-units
9. *Criteria for Assigning Inmates to The Restorative Housing Unit (R.H.U.)*, N.J. Admin. Code § 10A:5-9.1 (2021).
10. From Jarvis Jay Masters, Finding Freedom: How Death Row Broke and Opened My Heart, © (2020). Reprinted by arrangement with Shambhala Publications, Inc., Boulder, CO. p. 31, www.shambhala.com
11. Chad S. Briggs et al., "The Effect of Supermaximum Security Prisons on Aggregate Levels of Institutional Violence," *Criminology* 41 (2003): 1341–1376.
12. Terry Allen Kupers et al., "Beyond Supermax Administrative Segregation: Mississippi's Experience Rethinking Prison Classification and Creating Alternative Mental Health Programs," *Criminal Justice and Behavior* 36 (2009): 1037–1050; David H. Cloud et al., "'We Just Needed To Open The Door': A Case Study of the Quest to End Solitary Confinement in North Dakota," *Health and Justice*, October 18, 2021, https://doi.org/10.1186/s40352-021-00155-5

CHAPTER 8: JUVENILES IN SOLITARY

1. Richard Hofstader applied the term Age of Reform to the period between the 1890s in the USA through the New Deal (R. Hofstander, *The Age of Reform* [London: Vintage Books, 1955]); David Garland terms that period, continuing until the mid-1970s, the period of "penal welfarism," when the rehabilatative model prevailed in corrections, to be followed since the 1970s by a "Culture of Control" (D. Garland, *The Culture of Control* [Chicago: University of Chicago Press, 2001]).

2. Harris, "The Hell Inside Hell," *Scalawag*, May 2024, https://scalawagmagazine.org/2024/05/hell-inside-hell-texas-solitary-confinement-sexual-abuse/
3. Michele Deitch et al., *Conditions for Certified Juveniles in Texas County Jails*, Special Project Report (Texas: Lyndon B. Johnson School of Public Affairs, The University of Texas at Austin, May 2012), https://lbj.utexas.edu/sites/default/files/file/news/Conditions%20for%20Certified%20Juveniles%20in%20Texas%20County%20Jails-FINAL-3.pdf.
4. Judith Herman, *Trauma and Recovery: The Aftermath of Violence—From Domestic Abuse to Political Terror* (New York: Basic Books, 2015).
5. In quite a few states, including Michigan and New York, youth aged 16 or 17 are automatically tried as adults and, if convicted, incarcerated in adult prisons. There they are typically housed in solitary confinement until they reach the age of 18 and can be released into general population.
6. A version of this story was previously published in Christopher Blackwell, Aaron Edward Olson, Antoine Davis, Raymond Williams, and Jonathan Kirkpatrick, "In the Hole," *Jewish Currents*, April 20, 2023, https://jewishcurrents.org/in-the-hole

CHAPTER 9: RACISM

1. Robert Hilary King and Terry Kupers, "Slavery in US Prisons – Interview with Robert King & Terry Kupers," video, posted January 25, 2010, *YouTube*, 10:59, www.youtube.com/watch?v=8crPbPH428c
2. Matthew J. Mancini, *One Dies, Get Another: Convict Leasing in the American South, 1866–1928* (South Carolina: University of South Carolina Press, 1996); David M. Oshinsky, *Worse Than Slavery: Parchman Farm and the Ordeal of Jim Crow Justice* (New York: Free Press, 1997).
3. See Solomon Northrup, *Twelve Years a Slave*, Ed. David Wilson (David Wilson, 1853). The Memoir was the basis of the 2013 film directed by Steve McQueen from a screenplay by John Ridley.
4. Jill Lepore, "The Invention of the Police: Why Did American Policing Get So Big, So Fast, The Answer is Mostly Slavery," *New Yorker*, July 13, 2020, www.newyorker.com/magazine/2020/07/20/the-invention-of-the-police
5. See ACLU & University of Chicago Global Human Rights Clinic, "Captive Labor: Exploitation of Incarcerated Workers," *ACLU*, June

15, 2022, https://assets.aclu.org/live/uploads/publications/2022-06-15-captivelaborresearchreport.pdf

6. The Angola Three were Black incarcerated persons at Angola State Prison in the early 1980s when a guard was murdered. The warden immediately concluded that the three had killed the guard. The three prisoners had organized a Black Panther chapter at the prison, and the warden wanted to hang something on them so he could be done with them as they rotted in solitary. Everyone at the prison knew another incarcerated person who was serving a life sentence had murdered the guard, but the warden insisted the Angola Three were the murderers and kept them in solitary confinement for those many decades. See "The Angola 3 Case: What You Need to Know," *The Angola Three*. Accessed January 9, 2025, https://angola3.org/the-case/; Holly Genovese, "'The Only Panthers Left': An Intellectual History of the Angola Three," *Rapoport Center for Human Rights and Justice, University of Texas at Austin*, June 2019, https://law.utexas.edu/humanrights/projects/the-only-panthers-left-an-intellectual-history-of-the-angola-3/
7. Robert Hillary King, *From the Bottom of the Heap: The Autobiography of Black Panther Robert Hillary King* (New York: PM Press, 2009), pp. 154–156.
8. Albert Woodfox, *Solitary: My Story of Transformation and Hope* (New York Grove Press, 2019).
9. Ibid., p. 407.
10. Nazgol Ghandnoosh, Celeste Barry, and Luke Trinka, "One In Five: Racial Disparity in Imprisonment: Causes and Remedies," *The Sentencing Project*, December 7, 2023, www.sentencingproject.org/publications/one-in-five-racial-disparity-in-imprisonment-causes-and-remedies/; Ashley Nellis, "The Color of Justice: Racial and Ethnic Disparity in State Prisons," *The Sentencing Project*, October 13, 2021, www.sentencingproject.org/wp-content/uploads/2016/06/The-Color-of-Justice-Racial-and-Ethnic-Disparity-in-State-Prisons.pdf
11. Andreea Matei, "Solitary Confinement in U.S. Prisons," *Urban Institute Justice Policy Center*, August 2022, www.urban.org/sites/default/files/2022-08/Solitary%20Confinement%20in%20the%20US.pdf
12. Juleyka Lantigua-Williams, "The Link Between Race and Solitary Confinement," *The Atlantic*, December 5, 2016, www.theatlantic.com/politics/archive/2016/12/race-solitary-confinement/509456/
13. Brandy F. Henry, "Disparities in Use of Disciplinary Solitary Confinement by Mental Health Diagnosis, Race, Sexual Orientation, and Sex: Results from a National Survey in the United States of America," *HHS Public Access*, April 2022, https://pmc.ncbi.nlm.nih.gov/articles/PMC9373232/pdf/nihms-1827640.pdf

14. Ryan T. Sakoda and Jessica T. Simes, "Solitary Confinement and the U.S. Prison Boom," *Criminal Justice Policy Review* 32, no. 1 (2021): 66–102, https://doi.org/10.1177/0887403419895315
15. "Time in Cell: A 2021 Snapshot of Restrictive Housing: Based on a Nationwide Survey of Prison Systems," *Correctional Leaders Association and the Arthur Liman Center for Public Interest Law at Yale Law School*, August 2022, https://law.yale.edu/sites/default/files/area/center/liman/document/time_in_cell_2021.pdf
16. Juleyka Lantigua-Williams, "The Link Between Race and Solitary Confinement," *The Atlantic*, December 5, 2016, www.theatlantic.com/politics/archive/2016/12/race-solitary-confinement/509456/
17. Ibid.
18. Matei, "Solitary Confinement in U.S. Prisons."
19. Michael Schwirtz et al., "The Scourge of Racial Bias in New York State's Prisons," *The New York Times*, December 3, 2016, www.nytimes.com/2016/12/03/nyregion/new-york-state-prisons-inmates-racial-bias.html.
20. Ibid.

CHAPTER 10: SEXUAL ASSAULT AND GENDER-BASED INJUSTICES IN THE HOLE

1. Julie Kunselman et al., "Nonconsensual Sexual Behavior," in *Prison Sex: Practice and Policy*, Ed. Christopher Hensley (Boulder: Lynne Reiner Publishers 2002); see generally Cindy Struckman-Johnson and David Struckman-Johnson, "Sexual Coercion Rates in Seven Midwestern Prison Facilities for Men," *The Prison Journal* 80, no.4 (1964): 379, https://doi.org/10.1177/00328855000800040; see also "What We Do," *Just Detention International*. Accessed January 10, 2025, https://justdetention.org/what-we-do/
2. Terry A. Kupers, "The Role of Misogyny and Homophobia in Prison Sexual Abuse," *UCLA Women's Law Journal* 18, no. 1 (2010): 107, 109–112, https://escholarship.org/uc/item/6p54x5qm
3. Dorothy Q. Thomas et al., "Sexual Abuse of Women in U.S. State Prisons," *Human Rights Watch*, December 1996, www.hrw.org/legacy/reports/1996/Us1.htm; "Not Part of My Sentence: Violations of the Human Rights of Women in Custody," *Amnesty International*, May 1999, www.amnesty.org/en/wp-content/uploads/2021/06/amr510011999en.pdf
4. See, e.g., *Everson v. Mich. Department of Corrections*, 222 F. Supp. 2d 864 (E.D. Mich. 2002) (No. 00-73133); *Neal v. Department of Correc-*

tions, No. 285232, 2009 Mich. App. LEXIS 182, *1 (Mich. Ct. App. January 27, 2009).

5. "Prisons and Jail Standards," *Implementation, National PREA Resource Center.* Accessed January 10, 2025, www.prearesourcecenter.org/implementation/prea-standards/prisons-and-jail-standards
6. See "Powerless in Prison: Surviving Sex Abuse," *KTVU Fox2*, posted September 23, 2022, 25:56, www.youtube.com/watch?v=GtgtEOLig84
7. A version of this story was originally published in the Marshall Project at www.themarshallproject.org/2025/03/10/solitary-confinement-guards-sexual-abuse-texas
8. Ibid.
9. "Powerless in Prison: Surviving Sex Abuse," *KTVU Fox2*, posted September 23, 2022, 25:56, www.youtube.com/watch?v=GtgtEOLig84
10. See Daniel W. Penny and Terry Kupers, Season 3, Episode 1, "What Does Prison Reveal About Toxic Masculinity? With Dr. Terry Kupers," *Non-Toxic*, podcast, October 1, 2024, 32 min, transcript at www.researchgate.net/publication/387460968_First_Episode_Third_Season_of_Non-toxic_a_Podcast_with_Daniel_Penny_Terry_Kupers
11. Terry A. Kupers, "Rape and the Prison Code," in *Prison Masculinities*, Eds. Don Sabo, Terry A. Kupers, and Willie London (Philadelphia: Temple University Press, 2001), pp. 111, 116.
12. Valerie Jenness et al., "Violence in California Correctional Facilities: An Empirical Examination of Sexual Assault," *UC Irvine: Center for Evidence Based Corrections*, May 16, 2007, p. 30, https://bpb-us-e2.wpmucdn.com/sites.uci.edu/dist/0/1149/files/2013/06/PREA_Presentation_PREA_Report_UCI_Jenness_et_al.pdf
13. *Giraldo v. California Department of Corrections & Rehabilitation*, 168 Cal. App. 4th 231, 238 (Cal. Ct. App. 2008).

CHAPTER 11: ENVIRONMENTAL INJUSTICE AND ITS EFFECT ON SOLITARY

1. Parts of this chapter were originally published in Christopher Blackwell and Sarah Sax, "Decarceration is the Best Way Prisons Can Adapt to Climate Change," *Prism*, July 25, 2024.
2. "New Orleans: Prisoners Abandoned to Floodwaters," *Human Rights Watch*, September 21, 2005, www.hrw.org/news/2005/09/21/new-orleans-prisoners-abandoned-floodwaters
3. Tamar Sarai, "Climate Change puts the Health and Lives of Incarcerated People at Risk," *Prism Reports*, November 18, 2020, https://prismreports.org/2020/11/18/climate-change-puts-the-health-and-lives-of-incarcerated-people-at-risk/

4. Alleen Brown, "Trapped in the Floods," *The Intercept*, February 12, 2022, https://theintercept.com/2022/02/12/prison-climate-crisis-flood/
5. Alleen Brown, "Dark, Smoky Cells," *The Intercept*, February 12, 2022, https://theintercept.com/2022/02/12/wildfires-prisons-climate-california/
6. Alleen Brown, "Boiling Behind Bars," *The Intercept*, February 12, 2022, https://theintercept.com/2022/02/12/prisons-texas-heat-air-conditioning-climate-crisis/
7. Brown, "Trapped in the Floods."
8. Brown, "Dark, Smoky Cells."
9. Kwaneta Harris, "'I wasn't Sentenced to be Cooked': Heat Desperation in a Texas Prison," *Prism Reports*, July 12, 2023, https://prismreports.org/2023/07/12/heat-desperation-texas-prison/
10. Jolie McCullough, "As the Death Toll in Stifling Texas Prisons Climbs, Congressional Democrats Ask for Investigation," *The Texas Tribune*, August 21, 2023, www.texastribune.org/2023/08/21/texas-prison-heat-deaths/
11. Originally published in Kwaneta Harris and Leigh Goodmark, "Summer Heat is Killing Incarcerated People – It's Cruel and Unusual Punishment," *Truthout*, September 12, 2023.
12. Originally published in Lanae Tipton, "Cooked in Custody." *Prism Reports*, September 11, 2024, https://prismreports.org/2024/09/11/cooked-in-custody/
13. There was over $4 billion budgeted for 2024. See Texas Department of Criminal Justice, "Agency Operating Budget 2024," *Texas Board of Criminal Justice*, August 25, 2023, www.tdcj.texas.gov/documents/bfd/FY24_Agency_Operating_Budget.pdf
14. Originally published in Xandan Gulley, "Cooked in Custody," *Prism Reports*, September 11, 2024, https://prismreports.org/2024/09/11/cooked-in-custody/
15. A version of this story was previously published in Kwaneta Harris, "It Never Warms Up': Surviving Extreme Cold in Texas Prisons," *Prism Reports*, April 1, 2024, https://prismreports.org/2024/04/01/it-never-warms-up-extreme-cold-texas-prisons/
16. In *Jones-El v. Berge*, a class action barring incarcerated persons with serious mental illness from solitary, a post-settlement ruling by the federal judge required the Wisconsin Department of Corrections to install air conditioning at the Supermax in Boscobel for that reason (*Jones-El v. Berge* 374 F.3d 541, 545 [7th Cir. 2004]).
17. John Yang et al., "People in Prison Struggle to Survive Unrelenting Heat Without Air Conditioning," *PBS News*, July 15, 2023, 8:54, www.pbs.org/newshour/show/prison-inmates-struggle-to-survive-unrelenting-heat-without-air-conditioning

18. "Deferred Maintenance Crisis: Predicting Negative Effects," *CGL Companies*. Accessed January 10, 2024, https://cglcompanies.com/wp-content/uploads/2020/07/CGL-White-Paper-Deferred-Maintenance-Crisis.pdf
19. Luke Barr, "All 123 US Federal Prisons Need 'Maintenance': Inspector General," *ABC News*, May 25, 2023, https://tinyurl.com/55b8n4kb
20. Linda Poon, "How Mass Incarceration Takes a Toll on the Environment," *Bloomberg*, July 30, 2015, www.bloomberg.com/news/articles/2015-07-30/how-mass-incarceration-takes-a-toll-on-the-environment-nearby-communities-and-prisoners
21. Ray Levy Uyeda, "Prison Abolition is Environmental Justice," *Prism Reports*, March 22, 2023, https://prismreports.org/2023/03/22/prison-abolition-is-environmental-justice/
22. "Locked into Emissions," www.researchgate.net/publication/346498889_Locked_into_Emissions_How_Mass_Incarceration_Contributes_to_Climate_Change
23. "Climate Change Adaptation," *California Department of Corrections and Rehabilitation*. Accessed January 10, 2025, www.cdcr.ca.gov/green/cdcr-green/climate-change-adaptation/
24. Ray Levy Uyeda, "California's Plan to Rebrand Prisons Doesn't Consider Climate Change," *Prism Reports*, December 14, 2023, https://prismreports.org/2023/12/14/california-plan-rebrand-prison-climate-change/
25. Aishah Abdalah et al., "Hidden Hazards. The Impacts of Climate Change on Incarcerated People in California State Prisons," *Ella Baker Center*, June 2023 (Los Angeles: University of California, 2023) https://ellabakercenter.org/wp-content/uploads/2023/06/Hidden-Hazards-Report-FINAL.pdf
26. Ibid.
27. Brentin Mock, "How New Orleans Stopped Making Jailing a Business," *Bloomberg*, June 18, 2015, www.bloomberg.com/news/articles/2015-06-18/new-orleans-has-reduced-its-jail-population-by-67-percent-since-hurricane-katrina
28. Michelle Russell, "5 Years In, 5 Things to Know About Louisiana's Justice System," *Pew Trusts*, November 1, 2022, www.pewtrusts.org/en/research-and-analysis/articles/2022/11/01/5-years-in-5-things-to-know-about-louisianas-justice-system

CHAPTER 12: AFTER SOLITARY

1. A version of this story was previously published at Christopher Blackwell, Aaron Edward Olson, Antoine Davis, Raymond Williams, and

Jonathan Kirkpatrick, "In the Hole," *Jewish Currents*, April 20, 2023, https://jewishcurrents.org/in-the-hole

2. Lauren Brinkley-Rubenstein et al., "Association of Restrictive Housing During Incarceration with Mortality After Release," *Jama Network Open* 2, no.10 (2019), https://jamanetwork.com/journals/jamanetworkopen/fullarticle/2752350
3. "The Box: 27 Years in Solitary Confinement." *Fault Lines*, June 27, 2023, www.aljazeera.com/program/fault-lines/2023/6/27/the-box-27-years-in-solitary-confinement
4. Originally published in Kevin Light-Roth, "When You've Been in the Hole Long Enough, Even Your Dreams Take Place in a Cell," *The Small Bow*, January 28, 2025, https://thesmallbow.substack.com/p/recovery-from-solitary-is-an-illusion
5. Originally published at Christopher Blackwell, Aaron Edward Olson, Antoine Davis, Raymond Williams, and Jonathan Kirkpatrick, "In the Hole," *Jewish Currents*, April 20, 2023, https://jewishcurrents.org/in-the-hole
6. Terry Kupers, "The SHU Post-Release Syndrome," *Correctional Mental Health Report* 17, no. 6 (2016): 81–96, https://tinyurl.com/rykk8zc5

CHAPTER 13: THE LEGAL BOUNDARIES OF SOLITUDE

1. *Rhodes v. Chapman*, 452 U.S. 337 (1981) (Brennan, J., dissenting).
2. Jack T. Donson and Keramet Reiter, "Understanding Federal 'Restrictive Housing Unit' Environments," *Federal Sentencing Reporter* 31, no. 2 (2018): 126, 127, https://myfederalprisonconsultant.com/wp-content/uploads/2020/06/fsr_2018_31_2_126.pdf
3. Ibid.
4. Ibid.
5. US Government Accountability Office, *Bureau of Prisons: Additional Actions Needed to Improve Restrictive Housing Practices*, GAO-24-105737 (Washington, DC, 2024), p. 48. Accessed January 10, 2025, www.gao.gov/assets/gao-24-105737.pdf
6. Ibid. While governing statutes for federal solitary confinement originally fell under 28 C.F.R. § 541 subparts (A) through (E) (28 C.F.R. § 541), the policy was split into (1) Program Statement 5270.09 "Inmate Discipline;" and (2) Program Statement 5270.10, "Special Housing Units," issued respectively on July 8, 2011 and August 1, 2011. Donson and Reiter, "Understanding Federal 'Restrictive Housing Unit' Environments." These were joined by Program Statement 5217.02, "Special Management Units" in 2016 which updated an earlier 2008 policy, and Program Statement 5212.07, "Control Unit Programs" (other-

wise known as the Administrative Maximum Facility or ADMAX) which has existed for "decades." See U.S. Department of Justice Federal Bureau of Prisons, "Inmate Discipline Program," 5270.09, July 8, 2011, www.bop.gov/policy/progstat/5270_009.pdf; Donson and Reiter, "Understanding Federal 'Restrictive Housing Unit' Environments."

7. Donson and Reiter, "Understanding Federal 'Restrictive Housing Unit' Environments."
8. Ibid.
9. Ibid.
10. *Weems v. United States*, 217 U.S. 349, 378 (1910); see also *Trop v. Dulles*, 356 U.S. 86, 101 (1958).
11. While the Court found Weems's punishment cruel and unusual, it is worth noting this decision protected an American officer in a Philippines court (the Philippines were a U.S. colony at the time) (*Weems*, 217 U.S., p. 357).
12. Ibid., p. 371.
13. *Trop v. Dulles*, 356 U.S. 86, 101 (1958).
14. *Holt v. Sarver II*, 309 F. Supp. 362 373 (E.D. Ark 1970).
15. Thirty-five Supreme Court cases subsequent to *Weems*, and a plethora of state cases, have consistently failed to view solitary confinement as cruel and unusual punishment. Maria A. Luise, "Solitary Confinement: Legal and Psychological Considerations," *New England Journal on Criminal & Civil Confinement* 15, no. 2 (1989): 301, 311.
16. Ruth Chan, "Buried Alive: The Need to Establish Clear Durational Standards for Solitary Confinement," *UIC J. Marshall Law Review* 53, no. 2 (2020): 243, https://repository.law.uic.edu/cgi/viewcontent.cgi?article=2815&context=lawreview.
17. *Colon v. Howard*, 215 F.3d 227 (2d cir. 2000).
18. *Siverstein v. Fed. Bureau of Prisons*, 559 F. App'x 739 (10th cir. 2014).
19. "Prisoner's Constitutional Rights: Segregated Confinement as Cruel and Unusual Punishment, *Sostre v. McGinnis*, 442 F.2d 178 (2d Cir. 1971)," *Washington University Law Quarterly* 1972, no. 2 (1972): 350–351, https://openscholarship.wustl.edu/cgi/viewcontent.cgi?referer=&httpsredir=1&article=2730&context=law_lawreview
20. *Novak v. Beto*, 453 F.2d 661, 665 (5th cir. 1971).
21. *Hawkins v. Hall*, 644 F.2d 914, 918 (1st cir. 1981).
22. Ibid.
23. See, e.g., *Sostre v. McGinnis*, 442 F.2d 178 (2d cir. 1971).
24. *Newman v. State of Alabama*, 559 F.2d 283 (5th cir. 1977).
25. Ibid.
26. Ibid.
27. *Farmer v. Brennan*, 511 U.S. 825, 834 (1994).

28. Ibid.
29. Ibid.
30. *Hudson v. McMillan*, 503 U.S. 1, 6 (1992).
31. *Johnson v. Prentice*, 144 S. Ct. 11 (2023).
32. Ibid., p. 12 (Jackson, J., dissenting).
33. Ibid.
34. *Ruiz v. Johnson*, 37 F. Supp. 2d 855, 915 (S.D. Tex. 1999), holding that conditions in the prison's administrative segregation unit violated constitutional standards when imposed on mentally-ill prisoners), rev'd and remanded on other grounds, 243 F.3d 941 (5th Cir. 2001), adhered to on remand, 154 F.Supp.2d 975 (S.D.Tex.2001); see also *Madrid v. Gomez*, 889 F. Supp. 1146, 1267 (N.D. Cal. 1995).
35. *Johnson v. Prentice*, 144 S. Ct. 11, 12 (2023); see Austin Sarat, "Supreme Cruelty: SCOTUS Refuses to Limit the Tortures of Solitary Confinement," *The Hill*, December 1, 2023, https://thehill.com/opinion/judiciary/4335472-supreme-cruelty-scotus-refuses-to-limit-the-tortures-of-solitary-confinement/
36. Ariane de Vogue, "Supreme Court Rejects Appeal of Illinois Prisoner Kept in Solitary for Three Years," *CNN*, November 13, 2023, https://tinyurl.com/ybykhx9f
37. Barack Obama, "Why We Must Rethink Solitary Confinement," *Washington Post*, January 25, 2016, https://tinyurl.com/33c6zzz2
38. *Juvenile Solitary Confinement*, 18 U.S.C. § 5043 (2018).
39. *Juvenile Justice and Delinquency Prevention Act*, 42 U.S.C. § 5601 (2000); "Juvenile Justice and Delinquency Prevention Act (JJDPA) Fact Sheet Series," National Youth Justice Network, last modified February 21, 2019, https://tinyurl.com/a2ptcf9n
40. *Juvenile Justice Reform Act of 2018*, Public Law 115-385, *U.S. Statutes at Large* 132 (2018): 5123–5160; "Summary of the Juvenile Justice Reform Act of 2018," *Resources, Coalition for Juvenile Justice.* Accessed January 10, 2025, www.juvjustice.org/sites/default/files/resource-files/Summary%20of%20the%20Juvenile%20Justice%20Reform%20Act%20of%202018.pdf
41. "Juvenile Justice and Delinquency Prevention Act (JJDPA) Fact Sheet Series," *National Youth Justice Network.* Accessed February 21, 2019, https://tinyurl.com/a2ptcf9n
42. "Federal Bipartisan Laws that Limit Youth Solitary Confinement," *Stop Solitary for Kids.* Accessed January 10, 2025, https://stopsolitaryforkids.org/wp-content/uploads/2019/01/CCLP-Summary_-JJDPA-FSA_Federal-Laws-Affecting-Youth-Solitary_1-14-19.pdf; "Juvenile Justice and Delinquency Prevention Act (JJDPA) Fact Sheet Series," *National Youth Justice Network.* Accessed February 21,

2019, https://tinyurl.com/a2ptcf9n; "Summary of the Juvenile Justice Reform Act of 2018," *Resources, Coalition for Juvenile Justice*. Accessed January 10, 2025, www.juvjustice.org/sites/default/files/resource-files/Summary%20of%20the%20Juvenile%20Justice%20Reform%20Act%20of%202018.pdf

43. Anne Teigen, "States that Limit or Prohibit Juvenile Shackline and Solitary Confinement," *National Conference of State Legislatures*, February 1, 2024, www.ncsl.org/civil-and-criminal-justice/states-that-limit-or-prohibit-juvenile-shackling-and-solitary-confinement
44. Patrick Riley, "Against Changing Tide, 11 States Haven't Limited Solitary Confinement of Juveniles," *Juvenile Justice Information Exchange*, April 28, 2023, https://tinyurl.com/4wnr56nx
45. *Wolff v. McDonnell*, 418 U.S. 539, 560 (1974).
46. *Bell v. Wolfish*, 441 U.S. 520, 546 (1979).
47. *Sandin v. Conner*, 515 U.S. 472 (1995).
48. *Wilkinson v. Austin*, 545 U.S. 209, 223 (2005).
49. See, e.g., *Skinner v. Cunningham*, 430 F.3d 483, 487 (1st Cir. 2005) (holding that a six-week period of total isolation, imposed while the petitioner was a suspect in an ongoing murder investigation, did not meet the *Wilkerson* standard for a due process violation).
50. See, e.g., *Incumaa v. Stirling*, 791 F.3d 517, 526 (4th Cir. 2015) (holding that the petitioner's conditions of confinement, including extreme isolation and severe deprivation, were atypical and significant compared to those faced by the general prison population).
51. See, e.g., *Perry v. Spencer*, 94 F.4th 136 (1st Cir. 2024) (holding that two years of solitary, due to involvement in a violent altercation, constituted an atypical and significant hardship when contrasted with the conditions experienced by the general prison population).
52. *Ramirez v. Galaza*, 334 F.3d 850 (9th Cir. 2003).
53. See discussion of this issue in *Perry*, 94 F.4th, 159–160.
54. *Wolff v. McDonnell*, 418 U.S. 539 (1974).
55. *Wolff*, 418 U.S. p. 568.
56. Nkechi N. Erondu, "Doubling Down on Due Process: Toward A Guaranteed Right to Legal Counsel in Jail Disciplinary Proceedings," *Columbia Law Review* 123, no. 1 (2023): 105.
57. *Hewitt v. Helms*, 459 U.S. 460 (1983).
58. Ibid., p. 497 (Stevens, J., dissenting).
59. See, e.g., *Williams v. Secretary*, 848 F.3d 549 (3d Cir. 2017); *Westefer v. Snyder*, 422 F.3d 570 (7th Cir. 2005).

CHAPTER 14: REFORM, ADVOCACY, AND ACTIVISM BY IMPACTED PEOPLE AND THE COMMUNITY

1. Unlock the Box, "Banning Torture: Legislative Trends and Policy Solutions for Constricting and Ending Solitary Confinement Throughout the United States," January 2023, https://unlocktheboxcampaign.org/wp-content/uploads/2023/01/UTB-BanningTorture-Trend Report-January2023.pdf
2. https://solitarywatch.org/wp-content/uploads/2023/05/Calculating-Torture-Report-May-2023-R2.pdf
3. Lew Blank, "A Bipartisan Majority of Voters Support Strongly Restricting Solitary Confinement, Including Placing a Four-Hour Limit on the Practice," *Data for Progress*, November 16, 2022, https://www.dataforprogress.org/blog/2022/11/16/a-bipartisan-majority-of-voters-support-strongly-restricting-solitary-confinement-including-placing-a-four-hour-limit-on-the-practice
4. Erik Ortiz, "Bill to 'End Solitary Confinement' in Federal Institutions Introduced in Senate," *NBC News*, December 5, 2023, https://www.nbcnews.com/politics/politics-news/bill-end-solitary-confinement-federal-government-introduced-senate-rcna128148
5. "A Teen Vogue Guide to Solitary Confinement," *Teen Vogue*, https://www.teenvogue.com/collection/end-solitary-confinement
6. "Solitary Confinement," *Last Week Tonight with John Oliver*, April 3, 2023, www.youtube.com/watch?v=_uSZwErdH3I
7. The Agreement to End Hostilities was a written document, signed by incarcerated persons of all the different races, to halt hatred and violence across racial lines. Rather, incarcerated persons need to stand together and speak up for their shared rights. To this day, there is much less interracial violence in the CDCR because of the Agreement.
8. RICO, Racketeer Influenced and Corrupt Organizations Act, is a federal law designed to combat organized crime.
9. United Nations Office on Drugs and Crime, *The Nelson Mandela Rules: United Nations Standard Minimum Rules for the Treatment of Prisoners* (Vienna: United Nations, 2015), www.unodc.org/documents/justice-and-prison-reform/Nelson_Mandela_Rules-E-ebook.pdf
10. United Nations Human Rights Office, "United Nations Rules for the Protection of Juveniles Deprived of Their Liberty," *United Nations*. Accessed January 18, 2025, www.ohchr.org/en/instruments-mechanisms/instruments/united-nations-rules-protection-juveniles-deprived-their-liberty
11. United Nations Office on Drugs and Crime, *The Bangkok Rules: United Nations Rules for the Treatment of Women Prisoners and Non-Custodial*

Measures for Women Offenders (Vienna: United Nations, 2015), www.unodc.org/documents/justice-and-prison-reform/Bangkok_Rules_ENG_22032015.pdf

12. United Nations, *Basic Principles for the Treatment of Prisoners* (Vienna: United Nations). Accessed January 18, 2025, www.un.org/ruleoflaw/blog/document/basic-principles-for-the-treatment-of-prisoners/
13. Peter Scharff-Smith, "Solitary Confinement—Effects and Practices from the Nineteenth Century until Today," in "Solitary Confinement: Effects, Practices, and Pathways toward Reform" (Jules Lobel and Peter Scharff Smith, eds, Oxford University Press, 2020) pp. 21–42.
14. Unlock the Box, "Banning Torture: Legislative Trends and Policy Solutions for Constricting and Ending Solitary Confinement Throughout the United States," January 2023, https://unlocktheboxcampaign.org/wp-content/uploads/2023/01/UTB-BanningTorture-TrendReport-January2023.pdf
15. First Step Act of 2018, Pub. L. No. 115–391, § 613, 132 Stat. 5194, 5230 (codified at 18 U.S.C. § 5043), www.congress.gov/bill/115th-congress/senate-bill/3747/text#toc-iddf565a43-5d49-48a4-9f05-011eb4e57668
16. Unlock the Box, "Banning Torture: Legislative Trends and Policy Solutions for Constricting and Ending Solitary Confinement Throughout the United States," January 2023, https://unlocktheboxcampaign.org/wp-content/uploads/2023/01/UTB-BanningTorture-TrendReport-January2023.pdf
17. David H. Cloud, "One State's Push to End Solitary Confinement," *Public Health Post*, February 17, 2022, https://publichealthpost.org/health-equity/solitary-confinement/
18. Ibid.
19. Rick Raemisch, "My Night in Solitary," *New York Times*, Op-Ed, February 20, 2014, www.nytimes.com/2014/02/21/opinion/my-night-in-solitary.html.
20. www.nysfocus.com/2022/09/26/prisons-are-illegally-throwing-people-with-disabilities-into-solitary-confinement/
21. Nazgol Ghandnoosh, "Ending 50 Years of Mass Incarceration: Urgent Reform Needed to Protect Future Generations," *The Sentencing Project*, February 8, 2023, www.sentencingproject.org/policy-brief/ending-50-years-of-mass-incarceration-urgent-reform-needed-to-protect-future-generations/
22. "Reducing Jail and Prison Populations During the COVID-19 Pandemic," *Brennan Center for Justice*, January 7, 2022, www.brennancenter.org/our-work/research-reports/reducing-jail-and-prison-populations-during-covid-19-pandemic?utm_medium=PANTHEON_STRIPPED&utm_source=PANTHEON_STRIPPED

23. "Connecticut Cuts Prison Population, Keeps Crime Rate Low," *Connecticut House Democrats*, July 28, 2023, www.housedems.ct.gov/node/26144#:~:text=Connecticut%20has%20significantly%20reduced%20its,29%25%20during%20the%20same%20period
24. "A/HRC/54/CRP.7: International Independent Expert Mechanism to Advance Racial Justice and Equality in the Context of Law Enforcement – Visit to the United States of America," *OHCHR*, September 26, 2023, www.ohchr.org/en/documents/country-reports/ahrc54crp7-international-independent-expert-mechanism-advance-racial
25. "What to Know About the El Salvador Mega-Prison Where Trump Sent Deported Venezuelans," *The Guardian*, March, 2025, www.theguardian.com/world/2025/mar/20/cecot-el-salvador-venezuela-prison-trump-deportations
26. "Human Rights Watch Declaration on Prison Conditions in El Salvador for the J.G.G. v. Trump Case, Juanita Goebertus," *Human Rights Watch*, March 20, 2025, ww.hrw.org/news/2025/03/20/human-rights-watch-declaration-prison-conditions-el-salvador-jgg-v-trump-case

CHAPTER 15: SOLITARY BY ANY OTHER NAME

1. Washington State Department of Corrections, "PRESS RELEASE: DOC Pledges to Drastically Reduce Use of Solitary Confinement and Announces Closure of Minimum-Security Prison," Press Release, June 26, 2023, www.doc.wa.gov/news/2023/06262023.htm
2. A previous version of this section was published in Christopher Blackwell, "End Solitary in All its Forms," *The Progressive Magazine*, December 28, 2021, https://progressive.org/op-eds/end-solitary-all-forms-blackwell-211228/
3. Mike Carter, "Washington DOC Ends Use of Solitary Confinement as Punishment Study Shows It Doesn't Work," *Seattle Times*, September 30, 2021, www.seattletimes.com/seattle-news/washington-doc-ends-use-of-solitary-confinement-as-punishment-after-study-shows-it-doesnt-work/
4. Vera Institute of Justice and Washington State Department of Corrections, "Safe Prisons, Safe Communities: From Isolation to Dignity and Wellness Behind Bars," Memorandum, December 2020, www.doc.wa.gov/corrections/incarceration/docs/restrictive-housing-vera-institute-of-justice-closing-memo.pdf
5. Office of the Corrections Ombuds Washington State Department of Corrections, "Investigative Report," May 6, 2021, https://oco.wa.gov/sites/default/files/Admin%20Seg%20at%20MCC%20Report%20with%20DOC%20Response.pdf

6. A previous version of this section was published in Christopher Blackwell and Rachael Seevers, "Abolish All Forms of Solitary Confinement in Washington State," *Seattle Times*, October 6, 2021, www.seattletimes.com/opinion/abolish-all-forms-of-solitary-confinement-in-washington-state/
7. Christopher Blackwell, "End Solitary in All Its Forms," *The Progressive Magazine*, December 28, 2021, https://progressive.org/op-eds/end-solitary-all-forms-blackwell-211228/
8. Bill no. 5413, Washington State Legislature (2021), https://app.leg.wa.gov/billsummary?BillNumber=5413&Initiative=false&Year=2021; see Christopher Blackwell and Rachael Seevers, "Abolish All Forms of Solitary Confinement in Washington State."
9. A previous version of this was published in Christopher Blackwell and Nina Zweig, "Prisoners Say New Jersey's Alternative to Solitary Confinement is Pretty Much the Same," *HuffPost*, October 7, 2023, www.huffpost.com/entry/new-jersey-solitary-confinement-investigation_n_651578bee4b09c7605f9527d
10. New Jersey Assembly Bill 314, New Jersey Assembly (2018), https://legiscan.com/NJ/text/A314/2018
11. Dustin Racioppi, "NJ to Limit Use of Solitary Confinement under New Law Signed by Phil Murphy," *NorthJersey.com*, July 11, 2019, www.northjersey.com/story/news/new-jersey/2019/07/11/nj-limit-use-solitary-confinement-new-law-signed-phil-murphy/1708427001/
12. New Jersey Administrative Code, "Title 10A, Corrections, Chapter 5: Close Custody Units, Subchapter 9: Restorative Housing Unit (RHU), Section 10A:5-92: Structure of the Restorative Housing Unit (RHU)," https://casetext.com/regulation/new-jersey-administrative-code/title-10a-corrections/chapter-5-close-custody-units/subchapter-9-restorative-housing-unit-rhu/section-10a5-92-structure-of-the-restorative-housing-unit-rhu
13. Liman Center for Public Interest Law, *Time in Cell: The Liman 2021 Report on Solitary Confinement in the United States* (New Haven: Yale Law School, 2021), https://law.yale.edu/sites/default/files/area/center/liman/document/time_in_cell_2021.pdf
14. Chris Blackwell and Rachael Seevers, "Abolish All Forms of Solitary Confinement in Washington State."
15. Stephanie Wykstra, "Solitary by Another Name," *Progressive Magazine*, October 7, 2021, https://progressive.org/magazine/solitary-by-another-name-wykstra/
16. Victoria Law, "Massachusetts Is Still Using Solitary Confinement," *Bolts Magazine*, March 29, 2024, https://boltsmag.org/massachusetts-solitary-confinement/

17. Rafaela Jinich, "'Trapped in Hell': Battle Over Solitary Confinement Brews as Michigan Reduces Use," *Medill on the Hill*, May 30, 2024, https://medillonthehill.medill.northwestern.edu/2024/05/solitary/
18. "Open MI Door Campaign Urges Lawmakers to End Solitary Confinement in Michigan Prisons," *Fox 47 News*, www.fox47news.com/neighborhoods/state-capitol/open-mi-door-campaign-urges-lawmakers-to-end-solitary-confinement-in-michigan-prisons
19. "Virginia Finally Curbs Solitary Confinement – But Not Enough," *Washington Post*, March 10, 2023, www.washingtonpost.com/opinions/2023/03/10/virginia-solitary-confinement-prisons-bill/
20. Senate Bill No. 719, Virginia Senate (2024), https://legacylis.virginia.gov/cgi-bin/legp604.exe?241+ful+SB719#:~:text=No%20incarcerated%20person%20in%20a,placement%20in%20restorative%20housing%20or
21. *Solitary by Many Other Names: A Report on the Persistent and Pervasive Use of Solitary Confinement in New York City Jails* (New York: Center for Justice at Columbia University, December 2023). https://centerforjustice.columbia.edu/sites/default/files/content/Solitary%20By%20Many%20Other%20Names%20Report%20Final.pdf
22. www.nbcnewyork.com/investigations/rikers-island-dismantled-one-shower-cage-why-is-the-jail-is-keeping-8-others-intact/3918451/
23. https://queenseagle.com/all/solitary-by-another-name-ny-lawmakers-slam-citys-new-isolation-plan

CHAPTER 16: THE CASE AGAINST SOLITARY CONFINEMENT

1. Originally published in Blackwell, Christopher. "In the Hole." *Jewish Currents*, September 6, 2022, https://jewishcurrents.org/in-the-hole
2. Craig Haney. "Mental Health Issues in Long-Term Solitary and "Supermax" Confinement," *Crime & Delinquency* 49, no. 1 (2003): 124–156.
3. National Institute of Corrections. "Supermax Prisons: Overview and Issues for Congress," https://s3.amazonaws.com/static.nicic.gov/Library/019835.pdf
4. Bureau of Justice Statistics, *Reentry Trends in the United States* (Washington, DC: US Department of Justice, 2008), https://bjs.ojp.gov/content/pub/pdf/reentry.pdf
5. Laura Rafner, "The Impact of Solitary Confinement on Reentry Skills," *New Life K9s*, July 28, 2022, www.newlifek9s.org/post/the-impact-of-solitary-confinement-on-reentry-skills#:~:text=REENTRY%20

AFTER%20SOLITARY%20CONFINEMENT&text=Two%20ways%20living%20in%20solitary,lack%20of%20normal%20everyday%20interactions

6. Bennion notes that "prisoners who reenter society directly from solitary confinement have a higher recidivism rate than those who spend time in the general population after solitary confinement and before release. The differential in a national study was 64% versus 41%." In one study, the recidivism rates after three years for incarcerated persons who were released directly from solitary were 26 percent higher than rates for incarcerated persons released from the general population of that prison in that same year. Another study that matched the incarcerated persons from general population to the incarcerated persons in solitary based on age, criminal history, and propensity for violence, found that, among incarcerated persons who committed new crimes after release, those released directly from solitary committed new crimes within 12 months, compared to 27 months for incarcerated persons from the general population.
7. Keramet Reiter, "The Root of America's Over-Use of Solitary Confinement in Prison and How Reform Can Happen," *Scholars Strategy Network*, November 2, 2018, https://scholars.org/brief/root-americas-over-use-solitary-confinements-prison-and-how-reform-can-happen#:~:text=Solitary%20confinement%20is%20not%20only,cost%20of%20public%20university%20tuition
8. Vera Institute of Justice, *The Impacts of Solitary Confinement* (New York: Vera Institute of Justice, 2012), www.vera.org/downloads/publications/the-impacts-of-solitary-confinement.pdf#:~:text=Numerous%20studies%20have%20also%20found%20that%20solitary%20has,safer%2C%20and%20may%20actually%20make%20them%20less%20safe
9. Ibid.
10. James Dean, "Short Stays in Solitary Can Increase Recidivism, Unemployment," *Cornell University News*, June 16, 2020, https://news.cornell.edu/stories/2020/06/short-stays-solitary-can-increase-recidivism-unemployment
11. Rideau, Wilbert. *In the Place of Justice: A Story of Punishment and Deliverance*. Alfred A. Knopf, 2010.

Index

The Pluto Press Newsletter

Hello friend of Pluto!

Want to stay on top of the best radical books we publish?

Then sign up to be the first to hear about our new books, as well as special events, podcasts and videos.

You'll also get 50% off your first order with us when you sign up.

Come and join us!

Go to bit.ly/PlutoNewsletter